The Role of Constructs in Psychological and Educational Measurement

Pictured are conference participants Gail Baxter, Henry Braun, John Carroll, Henry Chauncey, Robert Glaser, Edmund Gordon, Anthony Greenwald, Robert Guion, Jan-Eric Gustaffson, Willem Hofstee, Wayne Holtzman, Eleanor Horne, Sidney Irvine, Phil Jackson, Ann Jungeblut, Nathan Kogan, Robert Linn, David Lohman, Samuel Messick, Delroy Paulhus, Larry Pervin, Michael Scriven, Irv Sigel, David Wiley, and Warren Willingham, among others.

The Role of Constructs in Psychological and Educational Measurement

Edited by

Henry I. Braun
Educational Testing Service

Douglas N. Jackson
Sigma Assessment Systems, Inc.

David E. Wiley
Northwestern University

LAWRENCE ERLBAUM ASSOCIATES, PUBLISHERS
2002   Mahwah, New Jersey   London

Lawrence Erlbaum Associates, Inc., Publishers
10 Industrial Avenue
Mahwah, New Jersey 07430

Cover design by Kathryn Houghtaling Lacey

Library of Congress Cataloging-in-Publication Data

The role of constructs in psychological and educational measurement / edited by
Henry I. Braun, Douglas N. Jackson, David Wiley.
    p. cm.
  "In honor of Sam Messick"--Pref.
  Includes indexes.
  ISBN 0-8058-3798-1 (alk. paper)
    1. Psychological tests--Congresses. 2. Educational tests and
measurements--Congresses. I. Braun, Henry I., 1949- II. Jackson, Douglas Northrop,
1929- III. Wiley, David E. IV. Messick, Samuel.

  BF176 .U64 2001
  150'.28'7--dc21

                                    2001042311

Books published by Lawrence Erlbaum Associates are printed on acid-free paper,
and their bindings are chosen for strength and durability.

Printed in the United States of America
10 9 8 7 6 5 4 3 2 1

CONTRIBUTORS

Gail P. Baxter
Educational Testing Service

Anton Bosma
University of Iowa

John B. Carroll
University of North Carolina
at Chapel Hill

Donald W. Fiske
University of Chicago

Robert Glaser
University of Pittsburgh

Anthony G. Greenwald
University of Washington

Jan-Eric Gustafsson
Göteborg University

Willem K. B. Hofstee
University of Groningen,
Netherlands

Wayne H. Holtzman
University of Texas at Austin

Douglas N. Jackson
Sigma Assessment Systems, Inc.

Philip W. Jackson
University of Chicago

Nathan Kogan
New School University

Robert L. Linn
University of Colorado at Boulder

David F. Lohman
University of Iowa

Delroy L. Paulhus
University of British Columbia

Michael Scriven
Clarement Graduate University

David E. Wiley
Northwestern University

Warren W. Willingham
Educational Testing Service

CONTENTS

PREFACE

In September 1997, the Educational Testing Service hosted a conference in honor of Sam Messick on the occasion of his retirement as an officer of ETS, a position he held for some 30 years. It was a wonderful event, not only because the invited speakers and guests included many leading researchers in psychology and educational measurement but also because each brought strong personal and professional connections to Sam. Held at the Chauncey Conference Center on the ETS campus, the conference gave Sam's many friends and colleagues at ETS an opportunity to participate in a milestone event and add their good wishes to those of the participants.

This volume has much to offer the reader. It comprises a set of chapters based on papers presented at the conference. As befits a scientist of Sam's wide-ranging interests, the chapters cover a broad spectrum of topics in the areas of personality and intellect, with particular focus on constructs, validity, and values. A number of authors seized the occasion to provide a review of work in a particular area and to suggest directions for further research. Some took a more critical stance and focused on the more troubling issues in the field and indicated how they might be resolved. Others presented their own leading edge work. All acknowledged their debts to Sam and his seminal work that spanned more than 40 years.

One sad note at the conference was the fact that Dick Snow, Sam's dear friend, was not able to attend due to his increasingly fragile health. Dick died in December 1997, followed in August 1998 by the death of Ann Jungblut. Ann, of course, was Sam's longtime collaborator and inseparable companion. Her death was a shock to us all, but most of all to Sam, and Betty, his wife. But there was more sadness to come. Sam fell ill in September and, despite a valiant struggle, died on October 6, 1998. In 13 short months we had gone from the "high" of the conference to the loss of three very special people. As I write almost exactly 2 years later, it is still difficult to come to terms with that sense of loss and the realization that these three might have accomplished even more had they been accorded a little more time.

Along with Sam and his assistant Kathy Howell, Ann and Dick were deeply involved in organizing the conference. Indeed, they were planning to edit the present volume as part of their tribute to Sam. Sadly that was not to be. I agreed to take on the task and recruited Doug Jackson and David Wiley, both conference participants, to serve as coeditors with me. They readily agreed and I am grateful for their contributions in making this volume available to the scientific community. I also want especially to thank Kathy Howell who has played an instrumental role throughout the process. The staff at Lawrence Erlbaum Associates has been both accommodating and professional and it has been a pleasure to work with them.

Henry I. Braun
Princeton, New Jersey

I

PERSONALITY—
THEORY AND ASSESSMENT

1

The Constructs in People's Heads

Douglas N. Jackson
Sigma Assessment Systems, Inc.

In this chapter I describe how one can employ the conceptions of personality that exist in ordinary people to further the process of construct validation in personality. I illustrate how Sam Messick strongly influenced me in the development of my thinking about constructs and construct validation by introducing me to the quantitative analysis of judgments of psychological similarity. Messick convinced me that multidimensional scaling, regarded by some as an arcane method for evaluating psychophysical judgments, had the potential to permit the representation of the constructs of ordinary people as projections on dimensions in a geometric space. This in turn provided an orderly, rigorous way of measuring and thinking about people's constructions of important entities in their psychological world.

Because these important entities are often other people, multi-dimensional scaling methods have provided a foundation for research into the organization of the constructs of ordinary people about personality because these methods do not require prior specification of a dimensional structure. And the evidence supports the view that psychologists can learn a great deal about their own constructs from studying the consructs of ordinary people. But before discussing some of this evidence, I would like to say something about my early association with Sam Messick, particularly about the first year of our collaboration that began in 1955 shortly after each of us had completed our graduate work.

When I first met the Sam Messick we both were National Institute of Mental Health Postdoctoral Fellows at the Menninger Foundation. Gardner Murphy, one of the leading personality theorists of the mid-century era, was our sponsor. I was immediately struck by Messick's skill as a communicator, whether in explaining the intricacies of multidimensional scaling, of test theory, or of modern literary criticism. I was also fascinated with Sam as a person, one who was full of complexity. In many ways he was a reconciliation of contradictions: a person who arose from a modest background—his father, a police officer, died when Sam was young—but who possessed champagne tastes and high aspirations; liberal intellectually and politically, but with strong traditional and family values; a psychometrician, but with wide-ranging interests; a bon vivant and, connoisseur of the arts, but a loyal fan of the Philadelphia baseball club; and one who held the position of vice president for research at the Educational Testing Service with decorum and propriety, but who could entertain as a raconteur, which he accomplished, as with all things, with creativity and zest.

Although Sam and I had different educational backgrounds—I graduated with a PhD in clinical psychology and he completed the ETS-sponsored PhD psychometric fellowship program at Princeton University—we immediately became intellectual allies and personal friends, beginning a collaborative venture that extended over decades and resulted in more than 25 jointly-authored papers. One of the first of these was a multidimensional scaling study of the perception of personality (Jackson, Messick, & Solley, 1957), which I, after reading Sam's doctoral dissertation, proposed to him and to Charles Solley, who shared with us the position of postdoctoral research fellow. We must have been dedicated to this research project, as each of us spent many hours at a mechanical calculator extracting dimensions by hand. In this chapter I discuss some of the many studies that followed in the wake of that initial study.

AN EVOLUTIONARY PERSPECTIVE ON THE PERSPECTION OF PERSONALITY

Jane Loevinger (1957/1967), in seeking to elucidate the term, construct, argued that "traits exist in people; constructs (here usually about traits) exist in the minds and magazines of psychologists. People have constructs too, but that is outside of the present scope (p. 83)." People's constructs are not out of the scope of this chapter, nor should they be, in my view, outside of the scope of any consideration of construct validity and personality. I set out to provide evidence in support of three points: (a) one of the most fruitful avenues for identifying and confirming constructs is through the systematic study of human judgment as it applies to personality; (b) the study of people's constructs can be undertaken with the same rigor as one normally associates with psychophysical judgment; and (c) the study of people's knowledge of constructs and of construct interrelationships provides a solid basis for investigating and understanding a key facet of social intelligence, an important but neglected aspect of human intelligence.

I begin with the latter point. Imagine a point in prehistory, say 50,000 years ago, when one of our ancestors was rounding a mountain pass on a foraging expedition when suddenly and without warning he or she encountered three sturdily-built Neanderthal strangers. A quick calculation was required to estimate and predict their probable behavior. Should one exchange pleasantries, if necessary with sign language or grunts, ignore them, or run away? The fact that you and I are here, while other potential ancestors in countless past generations perished, gives us some confidence that our ancestors made the correct calculation. And capacity for such calculations might be conveyed in a cumulative fashion in the transmission of culture and in the gene pool. The point that I make is that social intelligence is not a trivial set of cognitive abilities, but central to the survival and success of individuals and of humankind.

But we need not limit our consideration of the development of social intelligence to human prehistory. Humans are higher primates, and if there's a single description that characterizes higher primates, it is their social ability. N. Humphrey (as reported by Shreeve, 1996), in reporting on his observations of mountain gorillas remarked:

> I cannot help being struck by the fact that all of the animals in the forest, the guerrillas seemed to live the simplest existence. Gorillas live in areas with a benign climate, abundant food, no natural animal enemies, and little to do but eat, sleep, and play. How have guerrillas and other great apes evolved the remarkable intelligence that has been observed? (p. 292)

Humphreys believed that this source of gorilla social intelligence was other gorillas. The great apes are characterized by long periods of socialization of young and a great deal of direct tuition. Infants and juveniles are indirectly taught survival skills, and how to get along in a hierarchical extended family group—of siblings, parents, grandparents, cousins, uncles, and aunts—each blessed with superior intelligence. They learned individually how to compete for mates, food, the best sleeping places, and to avoid being hurt by the larger animals. Humphrey characterizes a game of "plot and counter plot." "Social primates," Humphrey stated,

> are required by the very nature of the system they create and maintain to be calculating beings. . . . They must be able to calculate the consequences of their own behavior, to calculate the likely behavior of others, to calculate the balance of the advantage and loss—and all this in a context where the evidence on which the calculations are based is ephemeral, ambiguous and liable to change, not least as a consequence of their own actions . . . It asks for levels of intelligence which is, I submit, unparalleled in any other sphere of living. (p. 293)

And the social pressures on evolving human populations were even greater. This was particularly true after the advent of agriculture well over ten thousand years ago, when it became more necessary to form alliances with nonkin. The growth of consciousness about the personalities of others arose in part out of an outgrowth and adaptation to processing the bewildering complexity of information from the social sphere, the "collegiate community" of more-or-less like-minded individuals. Social intelligence is honed in a variety of ways—by providing a social context for learning, by surrounding the individual with other clever individuals who are simultaneously looking after the group but also, probably with greater motivation, themselves, by providing challenges involving communication, deceit, threat, bluff, promise, and counter-threat. After the invention of agriculture and the opportunity for sedentary individuals to live in larger communal groups, sophisticated solutions were required for the social problems of living and working together in limited groups and for sharing limited resources. According to Shreeve, in such a complex world, ordinary intelligence might not suffice:

> The advantage would go to the player who was not only a keen observer of others' behavior, but who could also peek inside their minds and anticipate their next moves. No one has yet evolved a nervous system capable of directly reading the minds of others. But we have evolved the means to read our own. By providing awareness of the motivations and consequences our own actions, consciousness grants us the insight into the actions of others as well.

Obviously we were not born with our social identity nor with insight into the personality of ourselves and others. But our brain has evolved in such a way that acquisition of the knowledge and skill necessary to acquire social intelligence is present.

Although making enormous advances in the measurement and understanding of cognitive ability, psychologists and educators have been hard-pressed to demonstrate empirically the kind of social intelligence about which I describe, although, as Sechrest and I (Sechrest & Jackson, 1961) demonstrated many years ago, ordinary people had no trouble in reliably judging the degree of social intelligence in others. They also convincingly differentiated social intelligence from academic intelligence. I believe that the approach that I and my collaborators have employed might offer a foundation for understanding one important facet of social intelligence, namely, the manner in which we infer the likelihood of a certain type of behavior given limited information about the person being judged.

My approach to understanding the inferential relationships among personality-motivated behavior stems from at least three sources. The first derives from the process of creating and evaluating a personality item. The second—and I have Sam Messick to thank for this—is drawn from experience with powerful judgment methods in psychology, particularly multidimensional scaling. The third springs from two of the branches of applied psychology with which I've had some experience, namely, clinical psychology, where clinical judgment is regarded as having a central place, and industrial psychology, where an understanding of the decision-making processes of the employment interviewer has been an important focus of research—my own and that of others.

PERSONALITY ASSESSMENT

I have probably reviewed and evaluated more than 15,000 personality, vocational interest, and attitude items in various assessment ventures. Even when I had reviewed only a fraction of that number, I recognized that it was possible to judge quite accurately how the item would correlate with its targeted scale, and what its relationship would be with irrelevant scales, as well as with sources of evaluative bias. But given the Meehl (1945) manifesto on empirical strategies for personality scale construction and his argument for the method of contrasted groups, I was at first reluctant to make claims for the role of human judgment. Instead, I and my colleagues, including Sam Messick, devised ever more complicated multivariate techniques to show what we already knew that the great majority of items prepared for given personality scale performed as expected (Jackson, 1971). When I tried to make the point privately with colleagues, that I can judge with considerable accuracy the degree of relevance of an item to a scale, they were often surprisingly willing to agree that I had superior insight into personality. However flattering this was, I doubted it and not only because many people granting me this insight were my present and former graduate students.

The question arose as to how one could demonstrate the critical importance of "the constructs in people's heads" in formulating the mini-hypotheses that comprise the creation of a personality item? One of my first ventures in such a demonstration (Jackson, 1971) was a simple multidimensional scaling analysis of judgments of hypothetical people and of items. Consider the following person designed to represent the positive pole of the personality dimension of Autonomy.

> *Edward Archer* is a free-lance writer. At one time he worked for a newspaper, but quit because he felt restricted by the company's regulations. He now enjoys his work because he is his own boss. Edward spent the last year traveling alone through several European countries. He has currently taken up temporary residence in a large city's Bohemian district. Edward strongly advocated the view that today's young people are mere imitations of each other. He frequently tells other people that the world needs more "individuals." His friends describe him as independent, headstrong, and freedom-loving.

Similar personality capsules were written for the negative pole of Autonomy and of two other Personality Research Form scales, Impulsivity and Dominance. Also included were positively and negatively keyed personality items from each of the scales. Two sets of judges of hardly greater than average sophistication regarding personality rated the joint probabilities of occurrence of the behavior described by the people and by the items. Each set yielded three dimensions each defined only by the exemplars relevant to a particular scale. The average correlation between the corresponding projections on the three dimensions between the two separate sets of judges was .99, indicating that when given the appropriate opportunity, ordinary people can make informed judgments about the relevance of the personality constructs reflected in persons and items.

It might be argued that the above demonstration was based on items that had already undergone empirical scrutiny, which was true. Accordingly, I directed my attention to the entire initial pool of items for the first set of seven scales constructed for the PRF, which comprised before screening, from 100 to 140 items per scale. I evaluated the frequency with which each item was miskeyed, that is, should have been included in the selected items of an alternative scale based on that item's pattern of correlations with targeted and irrelevant scales. In no case did the number of miskeyed items exceed a percentage of one tenth of 1%. Again, this illustration of human judgment in the item creation process supports the idea that the "constructs in people's heads" show a correspondence with how other people respond consistently to construct-oriented personality items and scales.

Results such as these gave me the confidence to issue a challenge (Jackson, 1971). I suggested that the fruits of a couple of hours of work in preparing items by ordinary people be pitted against the most elaborate empirical item analyses using external criteria available, to determine which method yielded higher validities. Ashton and Goldberg (1973) accepted the challenge. They reported that journeyman item writers produced validities more than comparable with those obtained from California Psychological Inventory (CPI) scales, which are considered by many to be the finest example of the empirical method of personality scale construction. In a replication of Ashton and Goldberg, I (Jackson, 1975) found that when given a clear scale definition of the construct underlying a scale, individual undergraduate students produced scales yielding three times the validity of CPI scales of comparable length. Human judgment regarding constructs of personality indeed warrant greater respect than accorded it by the radical empiricists among past generations of psychologists.

HOW ACCURATE ARE PERSONALITY-BASED JUDGMENTS OF BEHAVIOR?

This is a contentious issue in personality research. Historically many researchers found little evidence supporting accuracy in person perception. I and my collaborators have approached this issue with a construct approach, one that requires that the information provided judges, and the behavioral outcomes that they are predicting, have some clear, demonstrable relationship with a personality construct, and in addition, that traits and behaviors be linked in both inferential and empirical networks. We have often found it convenient and illuminating to study the accuracy of inferential judgments of personality by employing personality items (i.e., the statements of that comprise personality scales). The advantage of using personality items is that we know great deal about their psychometric properties, particularly their correlation with the personality factor that they were designed to measure, as well as their correlations with irrelevant factors arising from other traits and from the evaluative bias.

One such study dealt with the focal issue of person perception, the validity of implicit personality theory (Bruner & Tagiuri, 1954). A number of prominent authors, including Bandura (1969), Mischel (1968), Schneider (1973), and Shweder (1975) argued that inferential trait relationships were based on semantic similarity, and, accordingly, were "illusory" with little or no validity. Our research was a response to findings reported by Mirels (1976), which offered empirical findings that seemed to call into question the validity of implicit personality theory and support the view that it was illusory. Mirels employed 21 items from the Personality Research Form (PRF), one from each content scale, and asked judges to rate the conditional probability of pairs of these items, by asking a question like "If a man answers True to Item A, what is a probability that he will Answer True to Item B?" Mirels found that conditional probabilities correlated only .17 with the actual empirical co-endorsements between the items based on the self-descriptive responses of persons to the PRF items. Mirels referred to "dramatic inferential illusions" in his conclusion. We took the position that humans do not think in terms of conditional probabilities about single items of behavior, but, rather, in terms of constructs. Accordingly, Jackson, Chan, and Stricker (1979) employed correlation coefficients rather than conditional probabilities because we believed that people think about implicative relationships in terms of distances, not conditional probabilities. Furthermore, we viewed the empirical relationships between endorsements of individual items as exemplars of underlying constructs. This encouraged us to consider not only the judged and empirical relationships between individual items, but relationships between underlying scales, and between items and scales as well. Thus, we analyzed the correlation between the scales underlying the pairs of items for which Mirels obtained co-endorsements, as well as the correlations between an item and the scale represented by the item with which it was paired. These various comparisons yielded an average correlation of .81 between judgments of co-endorsement and indices of actual trait relationships. Given that none of the items were from the same scale (thus requiring judges to have accurate knowledge of the implicative distances between scales) and given the acknowledged construct underrepresentation of a single item, I regard these findings as strong evidence that the "constructs in people's heads" mirror more than mere illusion.

NONVERBAL TRAIT INFERENCE

There is a widespread view, held particularly by social psychologists, that the observed consistencies in judging other people are attributable to similarity in the meanings of trait names, rather than to lawful process derived from the actual perception of personality. Paunonen (Paunonen & Jackson, 1979) addressed this question by developing a nonverbal representation of 17 scales of the PRF. Figure 1.1 contains two samples, the first (A) was designed to reflect Thrillseeking (negative Harmavoidance) in the central character and the second (B), Nurturance. We had previously identified, using multivariate procedures, profiles of two recurring types of respondents in a set of 796 profiles. The first was marked by high scores on Affiliation, Exhibition, Play, Impulsivity, and Nurturance, and the second by high scores on Aggression, Autonomy, Dominance, and Thrillseeking. Having both verbal and nonverbal materials made it possible to vary systematically how information about the person to be judged was described, as well as the means by which ratings were collected. Thus, a target person could be described verbally, or described in terms of the characteristic behavior depicted in a line drawings. Similarly, in rating predicted behavior, judges could either estimate the likelihood that a target person would engage in certain behaviors described by verbal items or by nonverbal items. Paunonen systematically varied, in a randomized design, verbal and nonverbal descriptions of target persons. He also had judges predict behavior using either a verbal or a nonverbal format. Paunonen found strikingly high reliabilities in ratings of implicative relationships, ranging from .93 to .99 with a median of .97 for various combinations of verbal and nonverbal informational and rating conditions, indicating substantial consensuality regarding perceived trait and behavior relationships. But at the individual level not everyone was equally reliable or sensitive to the implicative link between behaviors. Paunonen also determined how well judges could generate in their predictions the empirically-based PRF profiles from the limited verbal or nonverbal information they were given. He did this is by correlating the profile arising from the judgments with the actual PRF profiles generated for that personality type from the multivariate analysis of 796 PRF respondents. These correlations ranged from .58 to .95 (median = .83), with only minor

FIG. 1.1. Sample nonverbal items depicting thrillseeking behavior and nurturant behavior.

differences between the results from verbal or nonverbal informational or rating conditions. The import of these findings is that judges could quite accurately infer the patterning of the entire set of 17 PRF scales with limited information, and that this accuracy did not depend crucially on the use of verbal trait names or descriptors. Finally, Paunonen conducted a principal components factor analysis that showed that more than 88% of the variance in the judgments was attributable to personality content, about 8% to the use of verbal versus nonverbal rating scales, and less than 3% to the verbal or nonverbal medium for providing the personality information.

Clearly, the hypothesis that the structure of implicative personality relationships reflect "nothing but" the structure of semantic relationships is not supported in the Paunonen data. Neither is the view that semantic overlap accounts for the major portion of the variance. Rather, the most plausible interpretation is that the "constructs in people's heads" and their perceived interrelationships are responsible for what has proven to be a surprisingly accurate representation of the organization of traits in other people, which translates into accurate predictions regarding their behavior.

Subsequently, MacLennan (MacLennan & Jackson, 1985), using similar nonverbal materials, demonstrated consistent developmental trends in accuracy in the perception of personality in four groups of judges ranging in age from 5 years to 22 years.

CONSTRUCT RELATIONSHIPS IN CLINICAL JUDGMENTS OF PSYCHOPATHOLOGY

Reed and Jackson (1975) employed a construct approach in the study of clinical judgments of psychopathology. We provided the judges with a brief description of three persons, each representing a different form of psychopathology: *clinical depression, psychopathy,* and *paranoid personality.* We did not to pull these descriptions out of thin air, nor did we base them on impressionistic clinical experience. Rather, each description was based on a replicated syndrome of psychopathology that was derived from multivariate classification analyses of several hundred psychiatric patients. The following is a description of the psychopathy target:

> Jack Cole has been arrested several times for theft. Usually his crimes have been poorly planned and rather reckless. He says that he does not feel guilty about his behavior and often explains his stealing something by simply saying he wanted it. In interviews Jack frequently mentions his strong dislike for rules and discipline, and he seldom speaks of friends.

Consistent with our multivariate findings, the Jack Cole psychopathology description was based on construct-oriented psychopathology scales for Desocialization, Impulsivity, Rebelliousness, and Socially Deviant Attitudes.

Judges were assigned the task of rating the probability that the given target person would endorse each of a set of 52 heterogeneous psychopathology items. When judges were assigned randomly to two groups and the correlation computed between their aggregated judgments, inter-judge reliabilities were high: .97, .99, .99, and .99, respectively, for the three clinical targets and for a fourth nonclinical control target. Reed also correlated the judgments of each individual rater with the group consensus judgment. These covered a range of values; in the case of the Jack Cole target the values ranged from slightly negative to .89, with a median value of .74, indicating wide individual differences in this type of judgmental accuracy. Furthermore, there was strong evidence that clinical accuracy was generalizable across different targets. Our results suggested that this type of task could serve as a measure of clinical judgmental skill regarding psychopathology, although, of course, an ideal measure would sample psychopathological types much more broadly than the three that we employed. In a follow-up unpublished study Reed (1976) demonstrated that judgments of the responses of designated psychopathological targets corresponded strongly with the actual responses of psychiatric patients belonging to the same syndrome as the targets described in the brief passages. For example, in the case of the Jack Cole target, Reed found that when content judgments were combined with information from judgments of base rates and of desirability responding, a multiple correlation of .95 was obtained.

It is interesting to speculate as to why the model employed by Reed yielded a high degree of judgmental consensus in contrast to much previous research that found little or no consensus in clinical judgment. I submit that what distinguishes Reed's research from that of others is that he employed an explicit set of constructs, as well as exemplars in the form of personality items that have been linked empirically and substantively to the constructs. Furthermore, the judged targets represented empirically identified types that showed a lawful, replicated organization. When provided relevant information, ordinary people do have insight into the organization, not only of normal personality types, but also of rarer psychopathological syndromes. The problem is not with the judges, but with the construct-poor materials that they have been asked to judge in many studies. When given information bearing on constructs, they can and do show high levels of judgmental accuracy, even to the point that professionals might benefit from studying the structure that emerges from the judgments of ordinary people, particularly when they are aggregated as in the Reed study or in systematic multidimensional scaling analyses of the structure of implicit theories of psychopathology (Chan & Jackson, 1979).

IMPLICIT CONSTRUCTS OF PERSONALITY AND WORK BEHAVIOR

If one considers the kinds of information that can be gleaned from the employment interview, one is likely to recognize that information about personality is salient and is usually the most sought after. However, the great majority of the studies examining the employment interview sidestep the issue of personality and its relation to job performance, whether this relation is examined empirically or in terms of the constructs employed by interviewers. My collaborators and I have undertaken a number of experimental studies examining in some detail the links between personality and perceived job demands. These studies have focused on the degree of congruence between the personality of the applicant and the personality associated with a particular occupation. We have undertaken studies with a wide variety of occupations examining the relative influence on judgments of candidate suitability of personality congruence and other variables, for example, work experience, education, the desirability of self-referent statements made during the interview, and letters of recommendation. We have presented interview information in a variety of formats to judges, including printed transcripts, tape recordings, and videotapes of simulated interviews. We were aided considerably in these ventures by knowing of the results of a study (Siess & Jackson, 1970) that permitted us to identify personality profiles for different clusters of occupations, and by having hundreds of personality items that had known relationships with different personality constructs, items that could be inserted smoothly into simulated interview transcripts as self-referent statements made by job applicants.

An example of such a study would be useful. In Experiment 1 from the Jackson, Peacock, and Smith (1980) study, judges evaluated candidates for one of four jobs: *accountant, advertiser, industrial supervisor,* and *orchestral librarian.* Each job had a distinctive personality profile based on the Siess and Jackson findings. For example, the accountant occupation was marked by high Order and Cognitive Structure, and Low Impulsivity, Change, and Autonomy. The advertiser occupation was defined by an opposite pattern. Similarly, the job of industrial supervisor was marked by high Aggression and Dominance scores, whereas the mirror opposite orchestral librarian job was marked by high scores on Harmavoidance and Abasement. When personality information was embedded into interview transcripts by inserting statements reflecting congruent and incongruent personality information, suitability and predicted job performance ratings of candidates were powerfully influenced by personality congruence, so much so that they washed out the effects of prior work experience. When personality information was congruent, judges were very much more likely to find the applicant suitable and to expect superior job performance.

In another of the studies reported by Jackson et al., (1980) the desirability of self-reference statements was varied systematically independent of personality congruence for several different occupations. In general, personality congruence had a considerably stronger effect than did the desirability of the statements made by job candidates. But there was a notable exception. Siess and Jackson had found that the job of guidance counselor was defined by desirability responding, as well as by personality traits such as Dominance, Exhibition, and Nurturance. For the guidance counselor job an interaction emerged, indicating that if the self-presentation skills were seen as deficient by judges, high personality congruence was insufficient to elicit high suitability and job performance ratings.

The import of these findings concerning personality in the employment interview is that ordinary people are sensitive to the nuances of personality requirements of different jobs, possessing "constructs in their heads" that not only permit inferences about the relationships between personality characteristics, but, accurate knowledge of the network of relationships between personality and work behavior, as well, even differentiating jobs that require a high-order self-presentations skills, and affording such skills greater weight when appropriate.

OVERVIEW

I have attempted to show in brief outlines of a few illustrative studies how Sam Messick's introducing me to powerful judgmental methods and affording me the opportunity to work with him on construct validation problems had ramifications that neither one of us fully realized at the outset. By thinking in terms of personality constructs rather than isolated facts or simple empirical findings, one can hope for progress. My message is thus consistent with T. H. Huxley's famous dictum that those who do not go beyond fact rarely get as far as fact. The use of a construct approach, even in some quite applied areas of psychology, like personality assessment, person perception, clinical judgment, and the employment interview, will contribute to an understanding of certain of the processes underlying these endeavors, and will, perhaps, contribute to the betterment of the human condition.

REFERENCES

Ashton, S. G., & Goldberg, L. R. (1973). In response to Jackson's challenge: The comparative validity of personality scales constructed by the external (empirical) strategy and scales developed intuitively by experts, novices, and laymen. *Journal of Research in Personality, 7*, 1–20.

Bandura, A. (1969). Principles of behavior modification. New York: Holt, Rinehart & Winston.

Bruner, J. S., & Tagiuri, R. (1954). The perception of people. In G. Lindzey (Ed.), *Handbook of social psychology* (Vol. 2). Cambridge, MA: Addison-Wesley.

Chan, D. W., & Jackson, D. N. (1979). Implicit theory of psychopathology, *Multivariate Behavioral Research, 14,* 3–19.

Jackson, D. N. (1971). The dynamics of structural personality tests. *Psychological Review, 78,* 229–248.

Jackson, D. N. (1975). The relative validity of scales prepared by naive item writers and those based on empirical methods of personality scale construction. *Educational and Psychological Measurement, 35,* 361–370.

Jackson, D. N., Chan, D. W., Stricker, L. J. (1979). Implicit personality theory: Is it illusory? *Journal of Personality, 47,* 1–10.

Jackson, D. N., Messick, S. J., & Solley, C. M. (1957). A multidimensional scaling approach to the perception of personality. *The Journal of Psychology, 44,* 311–318.

Jackson, D. N., Peacock, A. C., & Smith, J. P. (1980). Impressions of personality in the employment interview, *Journal of Personality and Social Psychology, 39,* 294–307.

Loevinger, J. (1957). Objective tests as instruments of psychological theory. *Psychological Reports, 3,* 635-694. Reprinted in D. N. Jackson & S. Messick (Eds.) (1967). *Problems in human assessment,* New York, McGraw-Hill.

MacLennan, R. N., & Jackson, D. N. (1985). Accuracy and consistency in the development of social perception. *Developmental Psychology, 21,* 30–36.

Meehl, P. E. (1945). The dynamics of "structured" personality tests. *Journal of Clinical Psychology, 1,* 296–303.

Mirels, H. L. (1976). Implicit personality theory and inferential illusions. *Journal of Personality, 44,* 467–487.

Mischel, W. (1968). *Personality and assessment.* New York: Wiley.

Paunonen, S. V., & Jackson, D. N. (1979). Nonverbal trait inference. *Journal of Personality and Social Psychology, 37,* 1645–1659.

Reed, P. L., & Jackson, D. N. (1975). Clinical judgment of psychopathology: A model for inferential accuracy. *Journal of Abnormal Psychology, 84,* 475–482.

Reed, P. L. (1976). *Assessing inferential accuracy in clinical judgement and person perception.* (Doctoral dissertation, University of Western Ontario, London, Canada). Dissertation Abstracts International, 1977, 37, 5333B.

Schneider, D. J. (1973). Implicit personality theory: A review. *Psychological Bulletin, 79,* 294–309.

Sechrest, L., & Jackson, D. N. (1961). Social intelligence and accuracy of interpersonal predictions. *Journal of Personality, 29,* 167–182.

Shreeve, J. (1996). *The Neandertal enigma: Solving the mystery of modern human origins.* New York: Avon Books.

Shweder, R. A. (1975). How relevant is an individual difference theory of personality? *Journal of Personality, 43,* 455–484.

Siess, T. F., & Jackson, D. N. (1970). Vocational interests and personality: An empirical integration. *Journal of Counseling Psychology, 17,* 27–35.

2

The Questionnaire Construction of Personality: Pragmatics of Personality Assessment

Willem K. B. Hofstee
University of Groningen, Netherlands

OVERVIEW

I view personality questionnaires as a means to communicate about personality. From this perspective, a number of recommendations are listed for state-of-the art personality assessment. Item formulations should avoid denials, conditionals (specifically, counterfactuals), adjectival phrasings (especially if they result in paradoxes), and conspirational language. The questionnaire should not contain repetitive items, stylistic variation, and flippant instructions to the assessor. Averaging over multiple raters is a condition for proper assessments. With respect to the scoring and reporting of results, the use of principal component analysis, correction for acquiescence, anchored scores, and natural confidence intervals are recommended. In discussing applications, I argue that the use of personality questionnaires in institutional settings is problematic, but in individual settings self-management is served by designs attending to personality–environment fit.

QUESTIONNAIRES IN PERSONALITY ASSESSMENT

In most research and applications, personality comes from answers to questions of what a person is like. The basic script involves three roles—an investigator, who asks the questions; an assessor, who gives the answers; and the principal character or target person, whom the questions are about.

In the compact version of the script, where people are asked to assess themselves, the latter two roles are played by one and the same person; in other words, the questions are asked in the second person singular ("What are you like") rather than the third ("What is he or she like"), although the actual grammatical phrasing may vary. In the full-size version, the investigator would command a sufficient number of independent assessors per target to attain an elementary level of normal-scientific precision (Hofstee, 1994). Conversely, in a subcompact version, an individual would ask questions about himself or herself, therefore, in the first person singular ("What am I like" or even "Who am I"); this philosophical rather than psychological script is not considered here.

Two developments have extended a beginning of scientific respectability to the questionnaire construction of personality. First, research in behavior genetics has established heritability coefficients in the order of .4 for traits assessed by questionnaire (Loehlin, 1992). This figure is in the same order of magnitude as the generalizability of a questionnaire score over time, item samplings, and assessors (Hofstee, 1994). Thus the modest generalizability raises an argument a fortiori: As one increases the generalizability of questionnaire scores, the heredity coefficients would approach unity. Confirmation of this argument is found in a study by Riemann, Angleitner, and Strelau (1997) using two assessors per target. The heredity coefficients rose to the upper .60's, which is what would have been expected under the hypothesis of perfect heritability of the true score.

Second, questionnaire investigators are taking steps toward getting their conceptual book-keeping in order. I feel less and less inclined (see also Hofstee, 1997; Hofstee, Ten Berge, & Hendriks, 1998) to take sides in arguments on numbers like the big 5, the giant 3, or other numerological entities. But I do find progress in the exploitation of the lexical hypothesis—which holds that novel trait concepts can generally be represented in ordinary language—and, especially, of the well-tried Eckart-Young Theorem, which provides us with a sequence of principal components of personality that follow the law of diminishing returns.

Still, questionnaire research has a reputation of being quick and dirty. There is the story of the young psychologist who followed his wife to a distant post and mailed a question to his Rabbi "What can I do by way of research in the middle of nowhere"; he received an immediate reply: "Good question, my son; all you need is to keep asking them". More seriously however, there is nothing unscientific about asking questions to others.

Investigators may mostly prefer to find out by themselves, through experimentation and objective measurement. At some point, one may thus be able to predict individual differences in extraversion, agreeableness, conscientiousness, emotional stability, and the like by genetic diagnosis. But in the meantime—which may last longer than some would expect—there is a contribution to be made to accurate assessment; even the progress of molecular-genetic research of personality depends on it.

However, complacency about the questionnaire construction of personality is not in order. I summarize some recommended further improvements in the interest of an optimal performance of the questionnaire script. Certain of these are quite technical, but the general point of view is discourse-analytic: I present questionnaires as a way of communicating with people, about people. Finally, I discuss questionnaire applications in various contexts.

COMMUNICATION WITH THE ASSESSOR

Administering questionnaires had better not be viewed as a form of objective measurement; rather, it is a way of communicating with the assessor (not with the target person). The investigator depends on the assessor for his or her information—for better or for worse, if one wishes. Once this simple point is accepted, it serves as a powerful organizer of do's and don'ts in questionnaire construction and administration. Generally speaking, the investigator's questions had better make sense to the assessor. Note that this recommendation is specific, obvious though it may be: If one measures a subject's brain mass as an indicator of his or her intelligence, the measurement does not depend on whether it makes sense to the person. Preoccupation with measurement (as distinct from assessment) may well be the reason why elementary rules of sensible communication are frequently violated.

Illustrations of item formulation that will hinder the process of communication between the investigator and the assessor are the following:

Denials

The technical problem with negatively formulated items like "Is not easily frustrated" is that a denial may logically have two quite different meanings, namely, the absence of a trait or its opposite. The communicative problem is that the question may drive people mad. In the event that the target person happens to be quite Stable and Agreeable, the assessor may be able to muster sufficient intellectual sophistication to read "not easily frustrated" as a litotes (Oxford: expressing of an affirmative by the negative of its contrary). The answer would go like "Yes, you might say that he/she is [I am] not easily frustrated, if you insist on using an understatement." If, however, the person happens to be Easily Frustrated, the expected response from the assessor is "No, it is not at all so that this person is not easily frustrated," thus, a reversal of a litotes, or a quadratic understatement. In our experience, even thorough-bred intellectuals may find this too much of a good thing, and wonder why the question could not be posed in a normal way.

Note that even affirmative items carry the problem to some extent. If the item is phrased as "Is easily frustrated," and the target person is quite Stable and Agreeable, the assessor is still supposed to respond with an understatement. The problem may be met by defining the other pole of the trait in an affirmative manner, for example, "Keeps his/her cool"; the assessor would be asked which of the two expressions would apply more. In many cases, however, the expressions would both have partly a specific meaning, so that the assessor would have difficulty seeing them as opposites.

Conditionals

Example: "Helps doing the dishes"; in general: "trait conditional upon situation." Conditionals may follow from an interactionistic paradigm, where traits like helpfulness are indeed supposed to be tied to specific situations. (One may wonder, of course, where interactionism ends: Should we distinguish a separate helpfulness with respect to dish-washing in the morning versus evening, toward males *versus* females, on using a detergent or not?). More often, however, conditionals seem to come from an investigator's lack of trust in the ability of the assessor to perform an aggregation operation ("does the target show helping behavior in general, more or less than others?"). The idea is to use the respondent as a vicarious observer rather than an assessor; Buss and Craik's (1983) act frequency approach embodied that idea in the purest form. However, people assess and generalize all the time, and hardly ever observe in a detached scientific manner. So the investigator might as well try to capitalize on that expertise.

A special problem with conditionals is that they may be counterfactual, as can be illustrated by the above example: If the household contains a dishwasher, the item would read like "Would he/she help doing the dishes, if not for the fact that there is a dishwasher?". The case arises when a work attitude scale is tested (counterfactually) on a student sample. The most notorious example is the opinion pollster's question: "If elections were held today, for whom would you vote?" (for a discussion, see Hofstee & Schaapman, 1990). Assessors may find it fun to engage in speculation, but that is hardly what the investigator intended them to do.

Adjectivals

Many questionnaire items revolve around a trait-descriptive adjective. This is not the way talking about people happens in everyday life. De Raad (1985) found that personalities are discussed in terms of behaviors denoted by verbs; trait adjectives are seldom used. In word counts of ordinary language their frequencies are among the lowest. Trait adjectives may be found in ceremonial and official discourse like eulogies, letters of reference and, most notably, psychological reports. In such communications, they may serve the purpose of diplomatic vagueness. However, that is hardly what an investigator wants from assessors. In past years, we have spent much time and effort in developing a large pool of brief concrete sentences for personality assessment. Whereas they appear to fit in the same multidimensional space as trait adjectives, both their communalities and their self-peer validities run higher than those of adjectives (Hendriks, 1997).

A special problem with many adjectives arises when they are used in self-report (Hofstee, 1990). One may describe a third person as Modest or Superficial, but self-description in such terms is paradoxical. Any claim that I would be a Modest person would only testify to my immodesty; if I declare myself to be a superficial character, my audience must presuppose a measure of profoundness on my part without which I would be incapable of finding myself Superficial—and that would be precisely the intention of my disclaimer. Thus to administer such items for self-report is to place the assessor in a classical double bind. Some might react like the bridge-player who cannot be misled because he or she lacks fantasy. However, they would hardly rate as ideal assessors.

Conspirationals

To assess is to be in office; assessors of personality are not asked about their likes or dislikes, any more than peer reviewers are supposed to exercise their predilections. The investigator should thus avoid giving off the impression of inviting a conspiracy at the expense of the target person. Colloquialisms including fashionable barbarisms and other idiomatic language, invectives and positive emotional expressions, and sexisms, ethnocentrisms, and the like, interfere with the descriptive scenario. Questionnaires have to be impeccable.

Turning now from item formulation to the level of the questionnaire, illustrations of improper pragmatics at that level are:

Repetitiveness

A frequent complaint voiced by respondents to personality questionnaires is that their consistency is being checked. In a sense, that apprehension is correct: To attain reliability and construct validity, the investigator has to represent a construct in several guises. However, that psychometric principle is no excuse for repetitiveness. First, high redundancy indicates a "bloated-specific" (Cattell, 1964) construct; any trait that is worth assessing is broad enough to have many diverse manifestations. Second and most important in the present context, redundancy is a form of rudeness. In ordinary life, one would get slapped in the face when posing essentially the same question twice, let alone 10 or 20 times.

An elegant technical solution for the dilemma is available that is rarely applied. It consists of principal-component scoring, so that every item obtains a nonzero weight for every construct scale. We (Hofstee et al., 1998) have shown that principal-component scoring is the logical consequence of selecting items on the basis of their item-scale correlation. (More generally, I cannot think of any excuse to use unit weights in any scoring key). With this flexible and efficient procedure, items can be used that are blends of underlying constructs; for example, Cordiality is between Extraversion and Agreeableness, Determination blends Emotional Stability and Conscientiousness. That approach enhances the diversity of item content without introducing specific item variance, which would otherwise be needed to achieve content variety but that is psychometrically improductive.

A practical heuristic that is easily implemented through word-search routines in text processing programs is the following: In each item, mark the item's core lemma—for the sake of clarity, the item should revolve around just one core word—and prevent it from occurring more than once in the questionnaire.

Stylistic variation

Angleitner, John, and Löhr (1986) provide a classification of questionnaire items. Prototypical are overt ("I often go to parties") and covert ("I think a lot about myself") behaviors that together make up over 50% of the items. But other categories are symptoms ("I sweat a lot"), trait attributions ("I am a talkative person"), wishes and interests ("Sometimes I would really like to curse"), biographical facts ("I had some trouble with the law when I was younger"), attitudes ("I think the law should be strictly enforced"), social effects ("at parties, I am the center of attention"), and bizarre items ("Someone is trying to poison me"). On the assumption that an investigator is trying to obtain an assessment of a target's personality by an assessor, such items hardly belong in the questionnaire. They deflect the assessor from the task of giving an accurate description of the target.

Flippant Instructions

Just about the foremost example of poor manners of questionnaire designers is the standard instruction to the assessor: "Don't think too long about a question; there are no right or wrong answers." Compare the bridge player who says to his spouse: "Let me do the no-trumps, dear" (no-trump play being the difficult part of the game). The implication is that the thinking is going to be done by the investigator, that assessors cannot expect to fathom the meaning of their own responses, and that the best they can do is behave like a jar of liquid into which a litmus paper is stuck.

In any serious conception of personality, there are more and less correct answers, and if anything, the questionnaire instruction should stress accuracy, while acknowledging inevitable uncertainty on the part of the assessor. In fact, this shift toward stressing accuracy involves a reclaiming of personality questionnaires by trait psychologists, at the expense of two other paradigms: the social-perception paradigm, in which personality only exists in the eye of the beholder; and the clinical paradigm in which assessors cannot know what they are talking about. These paradigms are losing ground in view of the behavior-genetic evidence as discussed previously; here, the emphasis is on their aversive contribution to the public relations of personality psychology.

MULTIPLE ASSESSORS

Among the most misleading expressions in the psychological jargon is personality *test* (for a questionnaire), carrying a suggestion of objectiveness that is largely unwarranted. Administering a self-report questionnaire to a number of persons, for example, is quite different from administering an intelligence test. Each person gets the same intelligence test and scoring key, but each responder to a questionnaire is scored by a different assessor, namely, that person himself or herself. Even if one would opt for a test sampling design and administer a different intelligence test to each person, the comparability among persons would still be higher: total scores on IQ batteries may be expected to correlate above .8, whereas the ceiling for different assessors is about .6. So the usual questionnaire administration is akin to having each applicant select a different IQ-test to his or her liking, whose generalizabilities would be far below standard. Needless to say, internal consistency coefficients of questionnaire scales, which may be quite high, have nothing to do with this argument (to the extent that a questionnaire's alpha is less than unity, it only detracts further from its generalizability).

A minimal condition to bring personality assessment up to elementary standards is aggregation: averaging over a number of independent judges. The assessment will not thereby be objective, but a sufficient degree of intersubjectivity can be attained. The argument is not specifically directed against self-assessment: The person himself or herself, as an assessor, has certain strengths and weaknesses (Hofstee, 1994), and it is an empirical question whether self-assessments are more or less representative and valid than other-assessments. The cardinal point is that self-reports have the unsurmountable handicap of being single by definition. So at the very least, they would have to be supplemented by other-assessments.

The aggregation argument is primarily technical; its formalization follows the law of large numbers and the function derived independently by Spearman (1910) and Brown (1910). However, it has profound discursive implications. The assessor is approached as an exchangeable element of a set of experts. That position of exchangeability shows resemblance to being a subject of research. So on the one hand, assessors are coworkers of the investigator, who depends on them for their privileged information; however on the other, they are not approached for their personal point of view; they should realize that any unique variance in their assessments is part of the error term. (The same holds for other forms of assessment and evaluation, most notably, peer review). In our Five-Factor Personality Inventory (FFPI; Hendriks, 1997) we drive home the point by maintaining a third-person formulation even in the case of self-report. Another implementation is to instruct assessors to predict the average assessment, and to reward them to the extent that they succeed (Hofstee, 1995).

COMMUNICATION OF RESULTS

Communication of questionnaire results is an integral part of personality assessment. Recently, we (Hofstee et al., 1998; Hofstee, Ten Berge, & Snijders, 1997) have applied ourselves at aspects of it. This section contains a restatement of some results.

The Inadequacy of Relative Scales

Almost all personality constructs, when scored in socially desirable direction, have a negatively skewed raw-score distribution; mean scores are above the neutral midpoint (e.g, 3 on a scale from 1 to 5) of the scale. Customary procedures of relative scaling therefore involve moving the midpoint. That would be inconsequential with unipolar scales where any midpoint would not have a natural meaning. With the bipolar scales of personality, however, the midpoint is where a trait shifts into reverse gear. Moving the midpoint is thus a manoeuvre that can pretty well ruin the construct.

Less metaphorically: A person whose Conscientiousness or Emotional Stability would be assessed as somewhat above the scale midpoint, would obtain a somewhat negative score on the relative scale. That is not what the assessor had in mind. Other cases suffer from the rough treatment as well, though less dramatically: A somewhat Sloppy person, for example, would be reported to be clearly Sloppy.

A radical solution to this problem is to resort to absolute scores. Hofstee and others (1998) present the appropriate procedures for the use of absolute scores, in particular, a version of raw-score principal component analysis producing optimally weighted average scores on the same scale as the items. Care must be taken to express the item scores as deviations from the scale midpoint (e.g., -2, -1, 0, 1, 2 in case of a five-point scale); failure to do so would be inconsistent and invariably results in a huge first principal component and little else. Even so, the factor structure is mathematically different from the one that would be obtained by standard principal component analysis. We have not yet investigated empirically what the extent of the difference would be in representative cases.

A less radical solution is anchored scoring retaining the midpoint but not the spread of the raw scores. We present a procedure resulting in a factor structure that is identical with the outcome of standard principal component analysis. It amounts to carrying out standard PCA, calculating the factor scores of a person who would endorse the midpoint of the scale for each item, and subtracting these factor scores from all others. Thus the factor scores become centered around the midpoint instead of the mean. As the midpoint-person's factor scores will generally be negative, the subtraction results in an over-all increase of the empirical factor scores. We argue that the spread of the raw scores (on a scale consisting of a fairly arbitrary number of points) does not have the same untouchable status as the midpoint, so that the anchored-scores solution is defensible.

The above reasoning presupposes that questionnaire items adequately represent the construct, particularly, that the items are not on average on the wrong side of the midpoint of the social desirability scale. However, this requirement holds in all cases; it is dubious practice to label an Assertiveness scale as Dominance, or a Conscientiousness scale as Compulsivity or Rigidity, as often happens. The requirement would amount to choosing a scale label on the appropriate side of the scale midpoint.

Correction for Differential Acquiescence

Intra-individual distributions of responses to questionnaire items differ. In particular, some assessors find more items applicable to targets than others. If a scale were to be balanced-for example, if it consisted of pairs of logical opposites like Friendly—Unfriendly, the so-called acquiescent response set would automatically be corrected in taking a total score. However, the only logical opposites are negations, which should not be used as they are confusing and repetitive (see previous discussion). So pairs of opposite items have to be spotted in an empirical way.

The investigator, however, is now confronted with a chicken-and-egg problem. For, differential acquiescent responding makes the correlations between items more positive; in other words, high negative correlations are unlikely to be found. Hofstee, Ten Berge, and Hendriks (1998) present iterative partial solutions to this problem, starting from pairs of semantic opposites. For a complete solution, however, one would have to prove or at least demonstrate that all admissible starting configurations lead to the same end result.

Two misunderstandings should be briefly discussed. One is the confusion between socially desirable responding and acquiescent response set, which we have encountered even at the level of our reviewers. With unidirectional scales consisting of positive items only or negative items only, the two cannot be distinguished, which is probably the reason for the confusion. However with bidirectional scales, acquiescence is the tendency to endorse both positive and negative items, whereas social desirability would involve endorsing positive items and rejecting undesirable items. Another misunderstanding is that acquiescence is a minor artifact (e.g., Nunnally, 1967, p. 611–612). We found acquiescence variance to be comparable in size to the third principal component in heterogeneous sets of questionnaire items (Hofstee et al., 1998).

At the level of pragmatics, I subscribe to the reservation that correcting for response artifacts like acquiescence is a form of deception of the assessor. However, the objection could be met by informing the assessor. Part of the communication between the investigator and the assessors is an unsentimental discussion of their weaknesses as well as their strengths.

Natural Confidence Intervals

The reporting of statistics—including questionnaire scores—in the form of point estimates is crude and potentially misleading (as the receiver is likely to underestimate the margin of error). Using classical or Bayesian confidence or credibility intervals would be a step forward. Hofstee and others (1997) have developed natural confidence intervals that do not require an arbitrary decision with respect to the probability mass that is covered (80%, 90%, and so on). In our proposition, the posterior distribution of a target person's true score is pitted against an appropriate background distribution, for example, the prior distribution of true scores in a relevant population or subpopulation. The natural confidence interval is located between the intersection points of the target and background distributions. Thus, the reporting of a score interval is constructed as a bet between the investigator and an opponent who would, in the example, find the individual assessment uninformative: The natural interval is where the investigator's probability is higher, therefore, it is the interval on which the investigator places his or her stakes. A spectacular property of this natural confidence interval is that its midpoint is the target's observed score rather than the true score as in classical test theory.

APPLICATIONS

With respect to questionnaire application, a sharp distinction should be made between individual and institutional decision contexts. Generally speaking, assessments of personality have their place in individual rather than institutional contexts.

Institutional Contexts

Institutional application contexts like personnel selection and student admission are basically contexts of maximum performance, whereas personality summarizes typical behavior. Thus the pragmatics of selection and admission situations constitute a formidable obstacle against personality description. Consequently, answers to the question of what a person is like can only be ambiguous in that setting.

According to a widespread but primitive notion, the answer to an item like "Do you tend to keep your appointments" would come about as follows: The self-assessor makes up his or her mind on the basis of past behavior, and subsequently engages in self-enhancement in socially desirable direction; thus the answer confounds individual differences in punctuality and faking good. This notion has given lead to attempts to control for social desirability. The failure of that approach was documented in the early 1960's by Dicken (1963) and, most recently, by Ones, Viswesvaran, and Reiss (1996).

In a more subtle conception, the answers are programmatic. After all, from the point of view of the applicant, the institution cannot legitimately be interested in his or her past behavior; the task is to preview applicants' future comportment. First, applicants will correctly realize that behavior is subject to situational effects: For example, employees tend to behave in a more socially desirable manner than students. Second, selection settings carry an element of bargaining. A notoriously lazy person may sincerely promise to be punctual, through his or her answers to a questionnaire; the weaker the bargaining position of the applicant, the more likely it is that such promises are made. Tragically, the less self-insight the applicant has, and the more his or her ideas are influenced by voluntaristic theories on the changeability of personality, the easier promises are submitted. But there need not be any question of lying or faking.

Can instructions to the (self-)assessor be devised that would remove response ambiguity? The standard instruction to respond naively and spontaneously is so far removed from the pragmatics of the selection situation that it can only function as an insult to the applicant's intelligence. A realistic instruction would be the following: "For each item, it will be quite evident what the most socially desirable response option is. The more socially desirable your answers, the higher are your chances. Also, there is no way of checking them. Only, in the longer run you may have done yourself and others a disservice if you misrepresent yourself. Also, don't fool yourself into thinking that you could actually change your personality to become entirely socially desirable." That would also not help much: Cynical and short-sighted applicants would still be at an advantage. However, the instruction would comply with requirements of informed consent, and would be beneficial to the public relations of applied psychology.

A coherent solution would consist of turning the personality questionnaire into a cognitive test. The instruction to the applicant would consist of an explicit challenge to find the most desirable response option. The criterion providing the scoring key might be found by asking key persons in the organisation what the most desirable option is, and averaging their answers. The test would measure empirical intelligence-ability to predict a state of affairs—or more specifically, psychological intelligence. The reader may wonder if such a thing exists, that is, if the test would be reliable and valid. However, quite comparable (Hofstee, 1997) procedures called tests of practical intelligence (Sternberg, Wagner, Williams, & Horvath, 1995) appear to do well in organizational settings. Also, the prediction task is not trivial in the sense that the most socially desirable option would appear to be the same in all cases.

Using personality questionnaires as a test of psychological intelligence may be found throwing out the baby with the bathwater. With increasing societal emphasis on the autonomy of the individual, however, I can see no bright future for personality assessment as such, by questionnaire or otherwise, in institutional settings.

Individual Contexts

To end on a brighter note, much more use can be made of state-of-the-art personality assessment in individual decision contexts. Briefly but quite generally put, personality assessment might help people to avoid environments that do not fit their personality. I do not pretend to exhaust that issue, but present a few central considerations.

First, people do have personality traits. They can try to deny them, and the importance of traits is not to be overemphasized. Within the normal range of personality, there are wide margins with respect to fittingness; it is unrealistic to suppose deterministic, one-to-one personality environment fits. But if the bounds are exceeded, people may become quite miserable. Undoubtedly also, traits can be controlled to some extent for some time. But it may be more efficient to invest in changing the situation than in self-control.

Second, personality traits along with abilities are more central to self-management than are interests, motivation, values, attitudes, and even skills, all of which are changeable by definition (to the extent they are not, they should be called traits). Still, most of the research on person environment fit has dealt with these more ephemeral phenomena (for an overview, see Kristof, 1996). Another limitation of that research tradition is its focus on work environments. Personality environment fit pertains also to, for example, educational, leisure-time, and partner environments.

In preparation to operationalizing personality environment fit, the idea that environments have personalities that may or may not be fitting should probably be avoided. Such notions violate the principle of methodological individualism and divert the attention from the genotypic foundation of personality. (One can attribute personality to animals and plants, but not meaningfully to objects or aggregates). Mainly, however, they invite a methodology whereby intra-individual comparisons are made between someone's perceptions, of his or her own personality and the environment's. Such comparisons are seriously contaminated as the assessor is one and the same.

An appropriate definition of environment in this context consists of the expectations by relevant others regarding an incumbent's personality. Accordingly, the environment is assessed by using a standard personality questionnaire, phrased in the third person singular. A representative sample of relevant judges could be asked how desirable or undesirable it would be in that environment for someone if he or she Takes time out to chat, Gets angry easily, Acts without planning, and so on. Interestingly, there may be more or less agreement on the desired personality. Its confidence intervals are an integral part of the definition of environment.

Since the 1990's, I have experimented with this technique, especially in settings of professional education, using a variant of the Five-Factor Personality Inventory (FFPI; Hendriks, 1997). The instrument is sensitive enough to register differences in desired personality profiles, although all five factors are judged desirable for almost all environments (the exception being Agreeableness for higher-level management of a fast-growing fashion chain). Extraversion peaks in commercial training programs, Agreeableness in social service and health care, Conscientiousness in clerical environments and in lower rather than higher level jobs, Emotional Stability does not differentiate much, and Intellectual Autonomy is especially desirable for higher professional levels. Technical schools so far seem to have relatively little use for personality traits.

In a complete vocational-guidance script, an atlas of desired personality profiles would be available, and a state-of-the-art assessment would be undertaken of the client's own personality. It would lead to propositions like the following: "You find yourself to be pretty extraverted, but that may be because you have set your mind on becoming a salesperson; however, the people who know you well agree that you are more of an introvert". Many more applications could of course be imagined.

To conclude with a note of caution: I do not wish to contribute to an unrestricted maximizing of personality environment fits. As a student of individual differences, I enjoy them primarily for their own sake. The variety of personality is a main determinant of the quality of human life. Even on taking an instrumental perspective, one should realize that personality is of marginal utility, in the literal sense of the word: Only if margins are exceeded, can psychologists hope to make a positive contribution to personality management.

REFERENCES

Angleitner, A., John, O. P., & Löhr, F-J. (1986). It's *what* you ask and *how* you ask it: An itemmetric analysis of questionnaires. In A. Angleitner & J. S. Wiggins (Eds.), *Personality assessment via questionnaires* (pp. 61–108). Berlin: Springer.

Brown, W. (1910). Some experimental results in the correlation of mental abilities. *British Journal of Psychology, 3,* 296–322.

Buss, D. M., & Craik, K. H. (1983). The act frequency approach to personality. *Psychological Review, 90,* 105–126.

Cattell, R. B. (1964). The importance of factor-trueness and validity, versus homogeneity and orthogonality, in test scales. *Educational and Psychological Measurement, 24,* 3–30.

De Raad, B. (1985). *Person-talk in everyday life: Pragmatics of utterances about personality.* Unpublished doctoral dissertation, University of Groningen, Netherlands.

Dicken, C. (1963). Good impression, social desirability, and acquiescence as suppressor variables. *Educational and Psychological Measurement, 23,* 699–720.

Hendriks, A. A. J. (1997). *The construction of the Five-Factor Personality Inventory (FFPI).* Unpublished doctoral dissertation, University of Groningen, Netherlands.

Hofstee, W. K. B. (1990). The use of everyday personality language for scientific purposes. *European Journal of Personality, 4,* 77–88.

Hofstee, W. K. B. (1994). Who should own the definition of personality? *European Journal of Personality, 8,* 149–162.

Hofstee, W. K. B. (1995). *Beoordelen: Wetenschap of kunst? [Assessment and evaluation: Science or art?].* Amsterdam: Royal Netherlands Academy of Sciences.

Hofstee, W. K. B. (1997, July 14-16). *Personality and intelligence: Do they mix?* Paper presented at The Second Spearman Seminar, Plymouth (UK).

Hofstee, W. K. B., & Schaapman, H. (1990). Bets beat polls: Averaged predictions of election outcomes. *Acta Politica, 25,* 257–270.

Hofstee, W. K. B., Ten Berge, J. M. F., & Hendriks, A. A. J. (1998). How to score questionnaires. *Personality and Individual Differences, 25,* 897–909.

Hofstee, W. K. B., Ten Berge, J. M. F., & Snijders, T. A. B. (1997). *Natural relative confidence intervals for test scores and other quantities.* Unpublished manuscript, University of Groningen, Netherlands.

Kristof, A. L. (1996). Person-organisation fit: An integrative review of its conceptualizations, measurement, and implications. *Personnel Psychology, 49,* 1–49.

Loehlin, J. C. (1992). *Genes and environment in personality development.* Newbury Park, CA: Sage.

Nunnally, J. C. (1967). *Psychometric theory.* New York: Mc. Graw Hill.

Ones, D. S., Viswesvaran, C., & Reiss, A. D. (1996). The role of social desirability in personality testing for personnel selection: The red herring. *Journal of Applied Psychology, 81,* 660–679.

Riemann, R., Angleitner, A., & Strelau, J. (1997). Genetic and environmental influences on personality: A study of twins reared together using self- and peer report NEO-FFI scales. *Journal of Personality, 65,* 449–475.

Spearman, C. (1910). Correlation calculated from faulty data. *British Journal of Psychology, 3,* 271–295.

Sternberg, R. J., Wagner, R. K., Williams, W. M., & Horvath, J. A. (1995). Testing common sense. *American Psychologist, 50,* 912–927.

3

Personality Theory and Assessment: Current and Timeless Issues

Wayne H. Holtzman
University of Texas at Austin

The 1961 volume of the Annual Review of Psychology was the first to have a chapter devoted entirely to recent research on personality structure. It is interesting to note that the psychologist commissioned to write this review was Samuel Messick (1961) whom we are honoring at this symposium. Four years later, I wrote the third review on personality structure (Holtzman, 1965), a task made much simpler by Messick's outstanding scholarship and definitive work. My acquaintance with Messick goes back to his arrival with Douglas Jackson in 1956 on the campus of the Menninger Foundation in Topeka, Kansas, where both of them were post-doctoral research fellows under Gardner Murphy in the field of personality assessment. This meeting was the beginning of a close friendship and professional collaboration that has continued to this day. I was privileged at that time to be a research consultant who periodically visited the Foundation where a vigorous, exciting research program had been developed under Murphy's leadership. It was a distinct honor and pleasure to be called back to ETS on the happy occasion of this conference.

At an APA symposium in 1963 commemorating the 25th anniversary of the classical publication, Explorations in Personality, by Henry Murray and his associates, I presented six major unresolved issues related to recurring dilemmas in personality assessment as follows: (1) the meaning of personality assessment, (2) how many things must be known about an individual to understand his personality, (3) how personality variance can be separated from method variance, (4) whether we are building a culture-bound theory and technique of assessment, (5) whether we can ever develop a systemic, comprehensive personality theory closely linked with empirical data, and (6) the moral dilemmas created by personality assessment (Holtzman, 1964). Today most of these issues continue to persist although in somewhat different form, one has faded from the scene, and new ones have taken its place.

IDIOGRAPHIC VERSUS NOMOTHETIC PERSONALITY ASSESSMENT

The meaning of personality assessment continues to be an important, unresolved issue, depending on one's point of view. Personologists and many clinical psychologists continue to insist that one must know a great deal about an individual to truly understand his personality. Specific scale or factor scores are viewed as either irrelevant or too superficial to prove useful without a thorough analysis of an individual's motivations, aspirations, history, and life circumstances. Although some personality measures may have a limited use to confirm personal impressions or to provide supplementary information, they are generally dismissed as incidental to a deep understanding of personality.

Psychometrically oriented personality psychologists differ strongly with this idiographic point of view, insisting that a true science of personality must focus on measurement if any progress is to be made. The primary focus of scientific study should be the development of more reliable, valid measures of important aspects of personality that can then provide a stable framework within which to gain a deeper understanding of the individual.

Many personality psychologists believe a stable framework is now at hand with the convergence of psychometric thinking on a hierarchical system dominated by the general Big Five factors. But such enthusiastic optimism is probably premature. There are good reasons why the idiographic-versus-nomothetic debate that raged vigorously in the 1960s has apparently faded away. Psychology has become more fragmented and compartmentalized with the growth in numbers, the diversity of research, and the proliferation of specialized societies and scholarly journals. Consequently, the many thousands of psychologists in applied settings who engage daily in personality appraisals for practical reasons have little discourse with the academic, psychometrically oriented psychologists engaged in personality research. Each group has a different mission and set of priorities that rarely meet. The fact that the issue has faded from the radar screen only means that the two groups have little more to say to each other at present.

IS THE GAP BETWEEN CLINICAL ASSESSMENT AND PERSONALITY ASSESSMENT FINALLY NARROWING?

The different worlds of clinical assessment and psychometrically based personality assessment are once again beginning to collide and even show signs of a healthy collaboration. The most notable example is the long-term success of the MMPI in clinical assessment as well as in personality research. Because the purposes of the two worlds are quite different— assessing psychopathology versus assessing normal personality and empirical, clinical, criterion-based methods versus rational construct-validity-based methods—collaboration has been uneasy, difficult, and often doomed to failure. Several trends since the 1980s point to a more optimistic future for resolution of these issues.

First, the rapid rise of computer-based clinical assessment methods in psychodiagnosis has forced clinicians to think differently about their methods. At the same time, these new computer methods have greatly increased the efficiency and power of those clinicians who have learned to use them wisely. Second, a growing number of younger, highly competent clinician-researchers and personality psychologists have a shared background in both camps, challenging each other to develop hybrid instruments and systems of assessment. And third, academic leaders in both camps are actively debating their points of view, encouraging graduate students and colleagues to reorganize their ideas and to undertake new kinds of studies.

But perhaps the most important new trend accelerating a change of thinking among clinicians is the external marketplace that is demanding more accountability and value for the money from the thousands of practitioners whose livelihood depends on it. The old ways, of sprinkling a lot of projective-technique jargon into a standard case history and summing up with a diagnosis that justifies the proposed treatment or satisfies the referring psychiatrist, are no longer acceptable to many managed-care payers. And in many situations, the clinical or counseling psychologist's uniquely valued contribution to the improvement of a client is being challenged in that same marketplace by social workers and other therapists whose services are available for a lower price. Therefore it is incumbent on those leading the way in clinical assessment to develop stronger, efficient, more valid methods that capitalize on the psychologist's special training and role as a mental health service provider.

A good example of these emerging new developments is the special diagnostic area known as personality disorders. As clinicians increasingly embrace the widely accepted diagnostic standards that are periodically refined under leadership of the American Psychiatric Association, known as the Diagnostic and Statistical Manual of Mental Disorders or DSM IV (APA, 1994), there is a compelling new opportunity for collaboration between clinicians and personality psychologists. One serious shortcoming of the revised DSM IV has become apparent in the lack of widely accepted diagnostic categories and efficient techniques for the assessment of personality disorders. Realization of this problem has already stimulated a flurry of new research and development that will undoubtedly be expanded. Unlike any other area of psychodiagnosis, personality disorders are an obvious target for fruitful collaboration between clinicians and personality psychologists.

EMPIRICALA, CRITERION-REFERENCED SCALES VERSUS RATIONAL SCALE CONSTRUCTS

One old issue that heats up occasionally concerns the relative value of the empirical method of developing scales by selecting items that correlate with an external criterion of special interest as contrasted with the rational method of starting out with a theoretical construct and then developing items that are chosen or discarded according to the degree of homogeneity produced in the final scale. One side of this controversy argues that if you have a known criterion to be predicted, such as the accurate diagnosis of paranoid schizophrenia, the best approach is a strictly empirical one. The MMPI is an excellent example of a successfully developed personality inventory based on criterion-referenced items. The other side insists just as strongly that a science of personality has to be built upon theoretical constructs where construct validity is the stern taskmaster that should dictate the method of scale construction. Then once the scales are appropriately constructed, a sound theoretical framework can be developed for mapping the relationships between the known personality factors and other independently recognized characteristics or specific behavior of interest.

Unlike unresolved issues between clinicians and academic personality psychologists, the empirically oriented advocates and the rational scale supporters share certain beliefs in common that make it far easier for them to interact productively. First of all, they are dedicated to improving personality measurement through research based on sound psychometric methods. Second, they generally begin with objective, time-honored, linguistically based items in questionnaires, peer ratings, or expert observations of actual behavior. And third, they both come from strong research-based academic settings where similar-minded colleagues judge their productivity. Currently this debate is best represented by two leading groups, the empirically-minded Minnesota group, led by James Butcher (Butcher & Rouse, 1996) and Yossef Ben-Porath (1994), which rallies around the MMPI, and the Big Five group, led by Jerry Wiggins (Wiggins & Pincus, 1992), Lewis Goldberg (1990), Robert McCrea and Paul Costa (1997), which believes they have finally converged on a small set of general personality dimensions having universal significance.

A small group of investigators in the 1990s has been developing clinical assessment instruments that begin with a rationally conceptualized, personality scale approach that is then empirically refined by the use of clinically accepted criterion groups. Among these are Jackson's (1989) Basic Personality Inventory and Morey's (1991) Personality Assessment Inventory. Still a third hybrid approach is the Millon Clinical Multiaxial Inventory (Millon, 1994) which was developed as a set of personality scales to aid in the classification of personality disorders as defined within Axis II of the Diagnostic and Statisical Manual. No doubt these hybrid approaches will become more useful as the nature of personality disorders becomes clearer in subsequent clinical research that will eventually work its way into diagnostic practice.

GENERAL VERSUS SPECIFIC TRAITS

Broad, general personality traits or typologies have alluring features of parsimony, elegance, and pervasiveness that have attracted theorists for centuries. Today among personality psychologists they take the form of general or second-order factors that can be repeatedly found in different settings and cultures, leading to a lofty status that commands reverence from their most dedicated advocates. On the other hand, specific, narrowly defined traits have the advantage of more direct linkage to observed behavior and to the common language of personality description that has evolved over thousands of years of human interaction. The modern version of this debate began in the nineteenth century, later flourishing with the differing points of view of Guilford, Cattell, Vernon, and Eysenck. Today the focus of many personality psychologists on the so-called Big Five of Extraversion, Emotional Stability, Conscientiousness, Nurturance, and Inquiring Intellect can be contrasted with such specific scales as Spielberger's (1983) State-Trait Anxiety Inventory, the Beck Depression Inventory (Beck, Steer, & Garbin, 1988), or the Buss and Perry (1992) scales for measuring four aspects of aggression.

Nearly everyone now agrees that both general and specific traits have a rightful place in any comprehensive personality system. But what that place should be is still a continuing issue. A hierarchical system with three or four levels varying from highly specific to general traits is widely accepted even though individual preferences may focus on only one or two components or levels. Whether a personality system and its components should be conceptualized entirely on the basis of a somewhat arbitrary, although widely accepted, method of factor analysis, however, remains to be seen. As Loevinger (1994, p. 6) has pointed out, "There is no reason to believe that the bedrock of personality is a set of orthogonal...factors, unless you think that nature is constrained to present us a world in rows and columns."

DIRECT VERSUS INDIRECT APPROACHES

The direct methods of asking someone questions dealing specifically with traits or asking others to rate an individual on such traits are the most popular approaches to personality assessment for obvious reasons. They have an appealing face validity, they are usually simple, straightforward methods, they are based on commonly understood language used to describe personality, and they are economical to employ, especially for large numbers of individuals. But they also suffer from ease of faking, various response sets, variance due to the situation, and other extraneous factors that lower their validity in all too many situations. Considerable attention has been given to embedding disguised validity scales in the more sophisticated personality inventories such as the MMPI, but they still frequently fall short. And even more important, any comprehensive approach to personality must delve into enduring personal dispositions and stylistic behavior that reflect levels of organization and functioning beneath the surface of verbal expression or interpersonal behavior.

Indirect methods, by contrast, involve assessments where the meaning of the measurements is disguised so that the individual hasn't the slightest idea how his responses will be interpreted. Such methods often involve asking an individual to perform a specific, standardized task such as using his imagination in viewing meaningless colored inkblots and reporting what he sees. The Thematic Apperception Test, the Rorschach or its more psychometrically based offspring, the Holtzman Inkblot Technique, are favored by many clinicians as projective techniques for personality assessment because it is very difficult to fake one's responses or malinger when reacting to such ambiguous stimuli.

The most comprehensive studies of indirect approaches to personality assessment are still those of Raymond Cattell and his associates that were done over forty years ago. Cattell (1963) stated that over a thousand different behavioral measures were developed and studied in a number of factor-analytic, multivariate matrices during the 1940s and 1950s. Many of these measures were performance scores on ingenious tasks that survived as part of his revised Objective-Analytic Personality Factor Batteries designed to measure what he called 21 primary personality dimensions (Hundleby, Pawlik, & Cattell, 1964). A basic difficulty with most of them, however, was the very low order of intercorrelation between these indirect, objective test scores and either behavior ratings or personality questionnaire scores.

The possibility of indirect, performance tests of personality were so appealing in the 1950s, largely because of Cattell's work and the studies of field dependency by Witkin, that a national conference was held in 1959 that I chaired under sponsorship of the National Institute of Mental Health to review this rapidly growing, new field to summarize the work to date, and to point the way to future promising areas of research. A wide range of interesting performance tests, many of them derived from experimental studies of perception, learning, or cognition, were discussed. Many proved to be highly reliable measures of individual differences that were interesting in their own right but failed to correlate appreciably with any other measures of personality.

As a result of these disappointing results, the focus upon performance tests of personality faded away and greater efforts were devoted to a better understanding of how the objective measurement of personality could be improved by a deeper understanding of how personality variance could be separated from method variance. Moreover, some perceptual and cognitive measures proved sufficiently interesting to stimulate more attention to the possibility that at least some them might well be useful as moderator variables or as valid indicators of coping strategies in problem solving.

CAN PERSONALITY VARIANCE BE SEPARATED FROM METHOD VARIANCE?

A particularly frustrating and persistent problem in personality assessment is the confounding of personality traits with the particular method for assessing them. One special kind of such confounding that is characteristic of some personality inventories is the presence of such response styles as social desirability, a tendency to agree with items that cast the individual in a favorable social image whether true or not, and acquiescence, the tendency to agree with an item regardless of content. Social desirability and acquiescence were topics of great debate 30 years ago that have been fairly well resolved. Most contemporary personality inventories have dealt fairly well with this kind of method variance by incorporating additional scales designed specifically to measure and isolate these response styles and other test-taking attitudes.

The more difficult, unresolved issue is the extent to which variation in the method of measuring a purported personality dimension produces method variance that swamps the underlying, generally low order, relationship. All too often, personality studies are conducted with insufficient variation in method and in surface personality traits to detect or adjust for the overriding methods variance characteristic of constructs in this field, leading to premature and erroneous conclusions. The widely quoted multitrait, multimethod matrix design for isolating method variance, as proposed years ago by Campbell and Fiske (1959), is a sobering, wise constraint. In many cases the design has properly dampened the misplaced enthusiasm of investigators who have used it. Would that it were possible to employ this demanding approach more often in studies of convergent and discriminant validity!

TO WHAT EXTENT ARE PERCEPTUAL AND COGNITIVE STYLE VARIABLES REALLY PERSONALITY DEMENSIONS?

The flurry of research in the 1950s and 1960s on perceptual and cognitive style variables resulted from the widespread belief that these stylistic measures would have theoretical and practical use as indirect approaches to personality. Herman Witkin's important experimental studies of the rotating chair in a conflicting visual field, the Rod-and-Frame Test, the Embedded Figure Test, and other perceptual tasks with conflicting visual and kinesthetic cues led to the important concept of field dependency that he later broadened to the less precise, vague concept of psychological differentiation (Witkin, Dyk, Faterson, Goodenough, & Karp, 1962). A second main stream of activity, shortly after Witkin, focused on cognitive style variables growing out of early work by Riley Gardner and his colleagues (Gardner, Holzman, Klein, Linton, & Spence, 1959) at the Menninger Foundation and by Samuel Messick, Douglas Jackson and their colleagues, first at the Menninger Foundation and then at Educational Testing Service. Messick's review in 1961 of personality structure included research to date on stylistic variables in perception, judgment, and memory, and such cognitive control variables as leveling-sharpening, focusing or scanning, constricted-flexible control, equivalence range, and tolerance for unrealistic experiences, in addition to field dependency.

As with hundreds of other indirect approaches to personality, failure of these perceptual and cognitive variables to correlate appreciably with well-known personality trait measures from self-report inventories, peer ratings, and independent behavioral observations proved disappointing to many investigators though not to such leaders in the field as Messick and Witkin who always conceived of reliable individual differences in cognition and perception as valid domains within a broadly conceived field of personality assessment. It is interesting to note that personality psychologists who now advocate the Big Five as the basic dimensions of personality include imagination, inquiring intellect or openness to experience as the fifth dimension in their Big Five personality model, thereby making room for Messick's view after all these years.

IS CURRENT THEORY AND ASSESSMENT ADVOCATED BY LEADING PERSONALITY PSYCHOLOGISTS CULTURE-BOUND?

One frequently hears the criticism that personality theories and assessment, especially trait-based inventories, are cultural-bound because of their derivation from the languages of Western Europe. Expansion of cross-cultural studies of personality throughout the world in the late 20th century has produced convincing evidence that the main dimensions of personality found in America and Europe are more universal than earlier critics have believed. Recent reviews by Butcher and Rouse (1996) of clinical assessment and by McCrae and Costa (1997) of personality trait structure reveal a large number of major studies in just the past several years that demonstrate the wide applicability of personality assessment across many different cultures and languages.

The issue that now seems to be emerging is not whether personality assessment is culture-bound, but rather, how are the basic dimensions of personality expressed in different cultures and do cultural values and customs influence this expression. Most likely there will be continuing expansion of cross-cultural research on these important questions in the near future, spurred on by the growing agreement concerning the nature of personality-trait structure and facilitated by high-speed, inexpensive, international communication.

ARE THERE CONINUING MORAL DILEMMAS CREATED BY PERSONALITY ASSESSMENT?

Thirty-five years ago there was considerable concern about public indignation over possible misuses of personality assessment. Although public mistrust still exists in some quarters, psychologists and others have properly addressed the legitimate ethical and social issues. Adequate safeguards for the protection of human subjects have been built into the entire process from reviewing research grant applications to monitoring the collection and analysis of data while protecting the confidentiality of participants. Many of us find these restrictions and procedures frustrating and time-consuming. Nevertheless, such safeguards are necessary. At least the educated public in highly developed countries is much better informed than in the past. And yet, the fears that psychologists have powerful, secret techniques for uncovering private information about an individual or controlling his personality still lurk in the background as a potential threat to the conduct of scientific research.

Moral dilemmas created by personality assessment in other, more autocratic, less openly democratic countries are more likely to become a serious problem that will bear watching carefully in the coming years. The protection of human subjects, the education of the general public, and establishment of high standards of ethical conduct are important regardless of where the personality assessment is done.

The last fifty years of the 20th century have seen a great deal of progress in the development of personality theory and measurement. In spite of these important scientific advances, current issues in the field have a remarkable similarity to the issues and controversies debated many years ago. Of course they are usually expressed in a different form today. Whether these same issues will still be of major concern 10 or 20 years from now is difficult to say. But one thing is virtually certain. The complex and changing nature of personality will continue to be a major challenge to those who seek a truly comprehensive understanding of the individual and social interaction. The field has more promising leads for young investigators to pursue than ever before, assuring that reinvigorated personality and clinical measurement will advance more significantly than in the past.

REFERENCES

American Psychiatric Association (1994). *Diagnostic and Statistical Manual of Mental Disorders (DSM-IV)*. Washington, DC: American Psychiatric Association, 4th ed.

Beck, A. T., Steer, R. A., & Garbin, M. G. (1988). Psychometric properties of the Beck Depression Inventory: twenty-five years of evaluation. *Clininical Psycholy Review, 8*, 77–100.

Ben-Porath. Y. S. (1994). The MMPI and MMPI-2: Fifty years of differentiating normal and abnormal personality. In S. Strack & M. Lorr (Eds). *Differentiating Normal and Abnormal Personality*. New York: Springer.

Buss, D. M., & Perry, M. (1992). The aggression questionnaire. *Journal of. Personality and Social Psychology, 63*, 452–59.

Butcher, J. N., & Rouse, S. V. (1996). Personality: Individual differences and clinical assessment. *Annual Review Psychology, 47*, 87–111.

Campbell, D. T., & Fiske, D. W. (1959). Convergent and discriminant validation by the multitrait-multimethod approach. *Psychology Bulletin, 56*, 81–105.

Cattell, R. B. (1963). Concepts of personality growing from multivariate experiment. In J. M. Wepman & R. W. Heine (eds). *Concepts of Personality*. Aldine: Chicago.

Gardner, R. W., Holzman, P. S., Klein, G. S., Linton, H. B., & Spence, D. P. (1959). Cognitive control: A study of individual consistencies in individual behavior. *Psychology Issues, 1*, 1–186.

Goldberg, L. R. (1990). An alternative "description of Personality": The Big Five factor structure. *Journal of Personality and Social Psychology, 59*, 1216–1229.

Holtzman, W. H. (1964). Recurring dilemmas in personality assessment. *Journal of Projective Techniques and Personality Assessment, 28*, 144–150.

Holtzman, W. H. (1965). Personality structure. *Annual Review of Psychology, 16*, 119–156.

Hundleby, J., Pawlik, K., & Cattell, R. B. (1964). *Personality factors in objective test devices.* Knapp: San Diego.

Jackson, D. (1989). *Basic personality inventory manual.* Port Huron: Sigma Assessment System.

Loevinger, J. (1994). Has psychology lost its conscience? *Journal of Personality Assessment, 62,* 2–8.

McCrea, R. R. & Costa, P. T. Jr. (1997). Personality trait structure as a human universal. *American Psycholigst, 52,* 509–516.

Messick, S. (1961). Personality structure. *Annual Review of Psychology, 12,* 93–128.

Millon, T. (1994). *Manual for the Millon clinical multiaxial inventory-III.* Minneapolis: National Computer Systems.

Morey, L. C. (1991). *Personality assessment inventory: Professional manual.* Odessa, FL: Psychological Assessment Resources.

Spielberger, C. D. (1983). *State-Trait Anxiety Inventory (Form Y) Manual.* Palo Alto: Consulting Psychologists Press.

Wiggins, J. S. & Pincus, A. L. (1992). Personality: Structure and assessment. *Annual Review of Psychology, 43,* 473—504.

Witkin, H. A., Dyk, R. B., Faterson, H. F., Goodenough, D. R., & Karp, S. A. (1962). *Psychological differentiation.* New York: Wiley.

4

Socially Desirable Responding: The Evolution of a Construct

Delroy L. Paulhus
University of British Columbia

OVERVIEW

Socially desirable responding (SDR) is typically defined as the tendency to give positive self-descriptions. Its status as a response style rests on the clarification of an underlying psychological construct. A brief history of such attempts is provided. Despite the growing consensus that there are two dimensions of SDR, their interpretation has varied over the years from minimalist operationalizations to elaborate construct validation. I argue for the necessity of demonstrating departure-from-reality in the self-reports of high SDR scorers: This criterion is critical for distinguishing SDR from related constructs. An appropriate methodology that operationalizes SDR directly in terms of self-criterion discrepancy is described. My recent work on this topic has evolved into a two-tiered taxonomy that crosses degree of awareness (conscious vs. unconscious) with content (agentic vs. communal qualities). Sufficient research on SDR constructs has accumulated to propose a broad reconciliation and integration.

INTRODUCTION

I define *response biases* as any systematic tendency to answer questionnaire items on some basis that interferes with accurate self-reports. Examples are tendencies to choose the desirable response or the most moderate response, or to agree with statements independent of their content (for a review, see Paulhus, 1991). Following Jackson and Messick (1958), I distinguish *response styles*—biases that are consistent across time and questionnaires—from *response sets*— short-lived response biases attributable to some temporary distraction or motivation.

The topic of this essay is restricted to one response bias—*socially desirable responding* (SDR)—defined here as the tendency to give overly positive self-descriptions. Note that my qualification—*overly*—is seldom included in definitions of SDR, but is of central importance in this essay. Indeed, I will argue that no SDR measure should be used without sufficient evidence that high scores indicate a departure from reality.

This essay begins with a selective review of the wide variety of constructs held to underlie SDR scores. Coverage of the early developments is particularly selective because that history has already been reviewed elsewhere (Messick, 1991; Paulhus, 1986). The latter part of the essay emphasizes the recent developments with which I have been associated. Although my approach departs from theirs in some respects, my understanding of the topic of SDR draws liberally from the substantial empirical and theoretical contributions of the team of Sam Messick and Doug Jackson (e.g., Jackson & Messick, 1962; Messick & Jackson, 1961). And specific to this volume, my depiction of the interplay between response styles and personality can be traced to Messick's insightful analyses (Damarin & Messick, 1965; Messick, 1991).

A PLETHORA OF OPERATIONALIZATIONS

Assessment psychologists have agreed, for the most part, that the tendency to give socially desirable responses is a meaningful construct. In developing measures of SDR, however, they have used a diversity of operationalizations. A singular lack of empirical convergence was the unfortunate result. Commentators who were already wary of the very concept of SDR have exploited this disagreement to buttress their skepticism (e.g., Block, 1965; Kozma & Stones, 1988; Nevid, 1983). And the skeptics have a point in that the allegation that SDR contaminates personality measures is difficult to substantiate without a clarification of the SDR construct itself. This chapter aims to provide such a clarification. I argue that the attention given to SDR research cannot be dismissed as a red herring (Ones, Viswesvaran, & Reissa, 1996), but represents a process of construct validation that has now accumulated to the point where a coherent integration is possible. Accordingly, my review of the literature begins by laying out the three approaches that require integration.

1. Minimalist Constructs. A number of contributors have erred on the cautious side by using a straightforward operationalization of SDR with minimal theoretical elaboration. One standard approach entails (a) collecting social desirability ratings of a large variety of items, and (b) assembling an SDR measure consisting of those items with the most extreme desirability ratings. (e.g., Edwards, 1953; Jackson & Messick, 1961; Saucier, 1994). The rationale is that individuals who claim the high-desirability items and disclaim the low-desirability items are likely to be responding on the basis of an item's desirability rather than its accuracy.

The validity of such SDR measures has been supported by demonstrations of consistency across diverse judges in the desirability ratings of those items (Edwards, 1970; Jackson & Messick, 1962[1]). Moreover, scores on SDR scales developed from two different item domains (e.g., clinical problems, personality) were shown to be highly intercorrelated (Edwards, 1970). In short, the same set of respondents was claiming to possess a variety of desirable traits.

Exemplary of the minimalist approach was the psychometrically rigorous but theoretically austere creation of the SD scale by Allen Edwards (1957, 1970). Throughout his career, Edwards remained cautious in representing SD scores as "individual differences in rates of SD responding" (Edwards, 1990, p. 287).[2] At the same time, the prominence of his work derived undoubtedly from the implication that (a) high SD scores indicate misrepresentation and that (b) personality measures correlating highly with his SD-scale were contaminated to the point of futility (Edwards & Walker, 1961). Such inferences were easily drawn from his frequent warnings about the utmost necessity that personality measures be uncorrelated with SD (Edwards, 1970, p. 232; Edwards, 1957, p. 91).

An important alternative operationalization of SDR has been labeled *role-playing* (e.g., Cofer, Chance, & Judson, 1949; Wiggins, 1959). Here, one group of participants are asked to "fake-good", that is, respond to a wide array of items as if they were trying to appear socially desirable. The control group does a "straight-take": That is, they are asked simply to describe themselves as accurately as possible. The items that best discriminate the two groups' responses are selected for the SDR measure. This approach led to the construction of the MMPI Malingering scale and Wiggins's Sd scale, which is still proving useful after 30 years (see Baer, Wetter, & Berry, 1992).

Both of the above operationalizations seemed reasonable yet the popular measures ensuing from the two approaches (e.g., Edwards's SD-scale and Wiggins's Sd-scale) showed notoriously low intercorrelations (e.g., Holden &

---

1 Nonetheless, both authors noted elsewhere that multiple points of views SD must be recognized to understand the role of SD in personality (Jackson & Singer, 1967; Messick, 1960).

2 On the few occasions where he lost his equanimity, his opinion was clear: "Faking good on personality inventories, without special instructions to do so, I would consider equivalent to the tendency to give socially desirable responses in self-description" (Edwards, 1957, p.57).

Fekken, 1989; Jackson & Messick, 1962; Paulhus, 1984; Wiggins, 1959). Although both measures comprise items with high desirability ratings, a critical difference is that the endorsement rate of SD items (their communalities) were relatively high (e.g., "I am not afraid to handle money") whereas the endorsement rate for Sd items (e.g., "I never worry about my looks") was relatively low. To obtain a high score on the Sd scale, one must claim many rare but desirable traits. Thus the Sd scale (and similarly-derived measures) incorporated the notion of exaggerated positivity.

2. Elaborate Constructs. Some attempts to develop SDR measures have involved more theoretical investment at the operationalization stage and, in varying degrees, have provided a detailed construct elaboration. Here, item composition involved specific hypotheses regarding the underlying construct (e.g., Crowne & Marlowe, 1964; Eysenck & Eysenck, 1964; Hartshorne & May, 1930; Sackeim & Gur, 1978). The items were designed to trigger different responses in honest responders than in respondents motivated to appear socially desirable. In short, these measures incorporated the notion of exaggerated positivity.

In the earliest example, Hartshorne and May's (1930) monumental program of research on deceit included the development of a lie scale. The items asked about behaviors that "have rather widespread social approval but . . . are rarely done" (p. 98). High scores on the lie scale were assumed to mark a dishonest character. A more influential lie scale, the MMPI Lie, scale was written with a similar rationale to identify individuals deliberately dissembling their clinical symptoms (Hathaway & McKinley, 1951). Eysenck and Eysenck (1964) followed a similar rational procedure in developing the Lie scale of the Eysenck Personality Inventory.

The most comprehensive program of construct validity was that carried out by Crowne and Marlowe (1964) in developing their social desirability scale. Like the above, they assembled items claiming improbable virtues and denying common human frailties. In contrast to the purely empirical methods, high scores were accumulated by self-descriptions that were not just positive, but improbably positive.

Crowne and Marlowe (1964) fleshed out the character of high scorers by studying their behavioral correlates in great detail. The authors concluded that a need for approval was the motivational force behind both (a) high scores on the Marlowe-Crowne scale and (b) public-behavior that was both conforming and socially harmonious. Further resolution of this character was provided by Crowne (1979). Thus the construct had evolved appropriately in response to accumulating data.

3. Accuracy Constructs. Serious consideration must be given to the theorists who argue that those scoring high on SDR instruments should be taken at their word: That is, they actually do possess an abundance of desirable traits (Block, 1965; McCrae & Costa, 1983; Milholland, 1964). To support the accuracy position, these researchers showed that the self-reports on SDR instruments correlated with reports by knowledgeable observers. More recent analyses, however, have revealed that the evidence regarding the accuracy of the claims made by high SDR respondents is mixed, at best (Paulhus & John, 1998).

The most prominent example of the accuracy position is Block's (1965) book, the *Challenge of Response Sets*. His view was that high scores on Edwards's SD scale (as well as the first factor of the MMPI) represented a desirable personality syndrome called *ego-resiliency*. His evidence included the confirmation by knowledgeable observers (e.g., spouses) of many of the desirable qualities that were self-ascribed on the SD scale. No doubt there is some degree of accuracy in SD scores, but my recent analysis of Block's Ego Resiliency measure confirmed that it also includes a demonstrable degree of distortion (Paulhus, 1998a).

McCrae and Costa (1983) articulated a similar argument for the accuracy of self-descriptions on the Marlowe-Crowne (MC) scale. They showed that spouses sustained many of the claims by high scorers that they possessed a variety of desirable traits. In apparent contradiction, a series of studies by Millham and Jacobson (1978) showed that high-MCs would lie and cheat to impress experimenters with their character. These conflicting depictions can be reconciled within the construct of need for approval. High scorers on MC may realize that socially conventional behavior is usually the best way to gain approval yet believe that deceit works better in a number of situations where detection is very unlikely. In short, the data do not support the naive claim that high MCs (or high-SDs) are simply those with desirable character.[3]

In sum, the two most popular measures of SDR (SD and MC) appear to tap both reality and distortion. Confirmation of the distortion component makes it easier to understand why some respondents describe themselves in consistently positive terms across a variety of trait dimensions.

TWO-FACTOR MODELS OF SDR

The notion that SDR appears in two distinct forms was recognized by a number of early researchers (Cattell & Scheier, 1961; Edwards, Diers, &

---

[3] See Paulhus and John (1998) for other reasons why the claims of high MC scores cannot be taken at face value.

Walker, 1962; Jackson & Messick, 1962; Messick, 1962; Wiggins, 1959). Factor analyses revealed two relatively independent clusters of measures non-committally labeled *Alpha* and *Gamma* by Wiggins (1964). The Alpha factor was clearly marked by Edwards SD-scale and the Gamma factor by Wiggins's Sd scale. Subsequent research positioned other measures on the first factor including the MMPI K-scale, Byrne's (1961) Repression–Sensitization scale and Sackeim and Gur's (1978) Self-Deception Questionnaire. Measures falling on the second factor included Eysenck's Lie scale and Sackeim and Gur's Other-Deception Questionnaire. A third set of measures loading largely, but not exclusively, on the second factor included the Marlowe-Crowne scale, the Good Impression scale (Gough, 1957), and the MMPI Lie scale (Hathaway & McKinley, 1951). With a growing consensus regarding two empirical factors, the conceptual task was now doubly challenging—what are the psychological constructs underlying these two SDR factors?

Damarin and Messick

It was not until the review by Damarin and Messick (1965)[4] that a detailed theoretical interpretation of the two factors was offered (see Figure 4.1a). Factor 1 was said to involve the defensive distortion of one's private self-image to be consistent with a global evaluative bias. As a substantive label for this factor, they proposed *autistic bias in self-regard*. Associated personality traits included self-esteem and ego-resiliency. Factor 2 was labeled *propagandistic bias* to indicate a naive tendency to promote a desirable public reputation. Here, the underlying motivation was linked to factors varying from social approval to habitual lying. For the first time, a detailed characteriological analysis had been provided for both factors.

Sackeim and Gur

Perhaps the most clear-cut example of the rational approach to SDR scale development was the work by Sackeim and Gur (1978; Gur & Sackeim, 1979; Sackeim, 1983). They applied to the process of questionnaire responding a distinction between the constructs of *self-deception* and *other-deception*. Some respondents report unrealistically positive self-depictions about which they appear to be convinced; other respondents consciously and deliberately distort their self-descriptions to fool an audience (See Figure 4.1b).

---

4 This was a technical report with limited circulation but much of the material was reviewed in the subsequent chapter by Messick (1991).

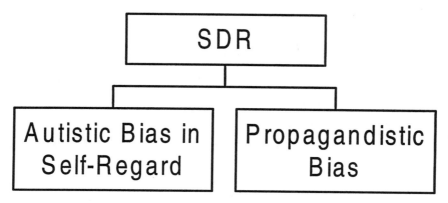

FIG. 4.1a. Two Constructs proposed by Damarin-Messick.

To compose a set of items indicating self-deception, the authors drew on the psycho-dynamic notion that sexual and aggressive thoughts are universally experienced yet often denied. If respondents overreact to questions with offensive content (e.g., "Have you ever thought about killing someone?"), then they are assumed to have self-deceptive tendencies. To measure other-deception, the authors wrote items describing desirable behaviors that are so public and blatant that they are not subject to self-deception (e.g., "I always pick up my litter"). According to the authors' reasoning, then, excessive claims of such commendable behaviors must involve conscious dissimulation.

The result of Sackeim and Gur's rational item composition was the "dynamic" duo of measures labeled the Self-Deception Questionnaire and the Other-Deception Questionnaire. Use of the word "deception" in both labels made it clear that exaggeration was an integral part of both conceptions. But to ensure that this exaggeration tendency was captured by the items, they recommended a scoring procedure that gave credit only for exaggeratedly positive item responses: Specifically, only responses of '6' or '7' on a 7-point scale were counted.

Early Paulhus

My early work was essentially an attempt to link and integrate the provocative concepts and instruments developed by Sackeim and Gur with the integrative structure provided by Damarin and Messick (see Paulhus, 1984; 1986). My

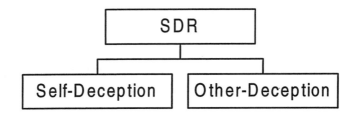

FIG. 4.1b. Sackeim and Gur's two deception constructs.

and Gur scales was revealing: Those two scales clearly marked the two factors suggesting a theoretical interpretation of the factors that was consistent with, but more theoretically trenchant than, the labels provided by Damarin and Messick. I settled on the labels, *self-deception* and *impression management* (see Figure 4.1c). The term, *other-deception*, was replaced because its implication of deliberate lying seemed presumptuous. Instead I argued, following Damarin and Messick, that habitual presentation of a specific positive public impression could be construed as an aspect of personality, rather than a deception (see also Hogan, 1983). Hence, the term, *impression management*, was judged to be more apt.

I also devoted some effort to evaluating the psychometric properties of Sackeim and Gur's Self- and Other-Deception Questionnaires, with some dismaying conclusions. To begin with, all the items on the former measure were negatively keyed and all items on the latter measure, positively keyed. Because the measures were thus confounded in opposite directions with acquiescence, their observed intercorrelation of .30 was likely to have

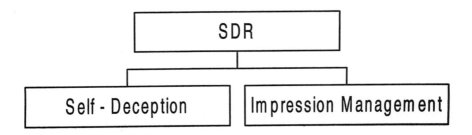

FIG. 4.1c. Two constructs proposed by Paulhus (1984).

underestimated the true value. As feared, when reversals were added to each scale, the intercorrelation exceeded .50. Although the balanced versions of these measures still loaded on their original factors, the high intercorrelation negated their advantage over single-factor measures. Moreover, some of the items on the Self-Deception Questionnaire were blatantly confounded with adjustment. To say the least, this state of affairs was discouraging for the two-factor conception.

A New Look at Socially Desirable Responding

Instead of conceding to the one-factor conception, my research group embarked on a new phase of item-writing. An extensive range of items were rationally composed to tap every conceivable form of self-deception and impression management (Paulhus, Reid, & Murphy, 1987). A swarm of factor analyses consistently revealed one factor of impression management and two factors of self-deception. The impression management items that cohered were largely the same items from earlier versions of the measure going back to Sackeim and Gur (1978). The two clusters of self-deception items appeared to involve *enhancement* (promoting positive qualities) and *denial* (disavowing negative qualities; Paulhus & Reid, 1991). Figure 4.2 shows the resulting subscales labeled Impression Management (IM), Self-Deceptive Enhancement (SDE), and Self-Deceptive Denial (SDD): They were incorporated into Version 6 of the *Balanced Inventory of Desirable Responding (BIDR)*, which I began distributing in 1988. Table 4.1 provides examples of the three types of items.

Construct Validity of the BIDR. The SDE and IM scales, in particular, form a useful combination of response style measures because they are relatively uncorrelated but capture the two major SDR dimensions (Paulhus, 1988, 1991). Their utility was demonstrated recently in a study of self-presentation during a job application situation (Paulhus, Bruce, & Trapnell, 1995). The IM scale, but not SDE, was extremely sensitive to faking instructions requesting various degrees of self-presentation. The sensitivity of the IM scale also far exceeded that of any of the NEO-FFI measures of the Big Five personality traits (Costa & McCrae, 1989). A similar pattern was observed in a study of job applicants vs. incumbents (Rosse et al., 1998)

In other studies, the SDE scale, but not the IM, predicted various kinds of self-deceptive distortions, for example, hindsight bias (Hoorens, 1995; Paulhus, 1988). More than 40 other studies, most outside of our laboratory, have added to the construct validity. For a more extensive review, see Paulhus (1998b).

TABLE 4.1
Sample items from the Balanced Inventory of
Desirable Responding
Version 6

Subscale	Items
Self-Deceptive Enhancement	My first impressions always turn out to be right.
Self-Deceptive Denial	I have never thought about killing someone.
Impression Management	I always pick up my litter on the street.

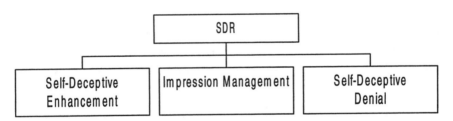

FIG. 4.2. Refined constructs proposed by Paulhus (1988).

Personality and Adjustment Correlates of the BIDR. One argument against interpreting SDR factors as personality constructs is that they rarely appear as independent factors in comprehensive factor analyses of personality. One possible explanation is that the BIDR response styles are simply disguised measures of normal personality. To clarify the interrelationships, my colleagues and I administered both kinds of measures to the same student samples under relatively anonymous conditions (Meston, Heiman, Trapnell, & Paulhus, 1998). Table 4.2 provides the correlations of the three response styles with Costa and McCrae's (1989) measures of the Big Five personality traits.

Although the response styles do not line up directly with any of the Big Five, the two self-deception subscales, SDE and SDD, do seem to pervade all five personality factors. Given the anonymous conditions of administration, the

TABLE 4.2
Correlations of BIDR Subscales with the Big Five personality factors.

	Self-Deception		Impression Management
	Enhancement	Denial	
Extraversion	.40	.16	.10
Openness	.48	.10	.11
Stability	.29	.32	.13
Conscientiousness	.19	.41	.29
Agreeableness	-.10	.50	.25

overlap suggests that self-deceptive bias plays a role in all personality dimensions. Correlations with the Impression Management scale are weaker but the fact that they are non-zero is noted here and discussed later.

The adjustment correlates of these response style measures have also been examined. In general, SDE, but not IM, is positively related to self-perceptions of mental health (e.g., Bonanno et al., in press; Brown, 1998; Nichols & Greene,1997; Paulhus & Reid, 1991; Paulhus, 1998b). High SDE can also have a positive impact on performance in certain circumstances (Johnson, 1995). In a recent study of interpersonal adjustment, however, high SDE scorers were perceived negatively after 7 weeks of interaction. Moreover, high-SDE but not high-IM or high-SDD participants exhibited a discordance with reality as indicated by an inflation in self-ratings relative to ratings by fellow group members (Paulhus, 1998a).

That research bears directly on the debate about whether positive illusions are adaptive (Taylor & Brown, 1988; Yik, Bond, & Paulhus, 1998) or maladaptive (Colvin, Block, & Funder, 1995; John & Robins, 1994). The SDE scale (along with measures of narcissism) represents a trait operationalization of positive illusions, that is, trait self-enhancement. The two studies by Paulhus (1998a) indicated, in short, that trait self-enhancement was adaptive in promoting high self-esteem and positive first impressions, but had negative interpersonal consequences (see also, Bonanno et al., in press).

THE STRUCTURE OF SELF-FAVORING BIAS

Disentangling these sources of variance will be no easy task, but a splendid beginning might be made by providing a right-answer key for each subject's answer to each item. (Damarin & Messick, 1965, p. 63).

The implication of this understated comment was that researchers making allegations about response bias must do the work of demonstrating departures from reality: This task requires the collection of credible measures of personality to be partialed from self-reports. Damarin and Messick (1965) went on to lay out the statistical partitioning necessary to isolate the residual bias component (p. 21).

This recommendation proved invaluable in my work with Oliver John on determining the structure of self-favoring bias (John & Paulhus, 2000; Paulhus & John, 1998). We needed a unit of bias to represent each part of the personality space.[5] For each personality variable, we collected self-ratings to compare with a more objective criterion, namely, ratings by knowledgeable peers (i.e., friends, family). In the case of intelligence, we also used IQ scores as a criterion. Each self-rating was regressed on its corresponding criterion to create a residual score representing the departure of the self-rating from reality. Factor analysis of a comprehensive set of such residuals should uncover the structure of self-favoring bias.

Using the Big Five dimensions of personality plus intelligence to represent personality space, our factor analyses of residuals revealed a smaller space than the 5-space of either self- or peer-ratings. The first two major dimensions appeared as in Figure 4.3. Factor 1 was marked by the Extraversion and Openness residuals whereas Factor 2 was marked by the Agreeableness and Conscientiousness residuals. Apparently, the structure of bias bears little resemblance to the standard Big Five structure. If anything, these factors look more like agency and communion (see Bakan, 1966; Wiggins, 1991). [6]

A replication study helped to clarify the meaning of the bias factors through the addition of a wide variety of self-report measures. These included traditional measures of SDR (Marlowe-Crowne scale) as well as related measures of self-enhancement (e.g., Narcissistic Personality Inventory). The additions allowed us to project a variety of bias and personality measures onto the two bias factors. The resulting projections (correlations with the factors) are depicted in Figure 4.4.

---

5 The last 15 years of work on the Five Factor Model suggests that it captures the 5 most important dimensions of personality (Wiggins, 1996). There is some dispute, however, about which rotation is optimal.

6 The results were more clear when we separated Conscientiousness into Dutifulness and Ambition following Paunonen and Jackson (1996). It is the Dutifulness measure that is most faithful, conceptually and empirically, to the Gamma factor.

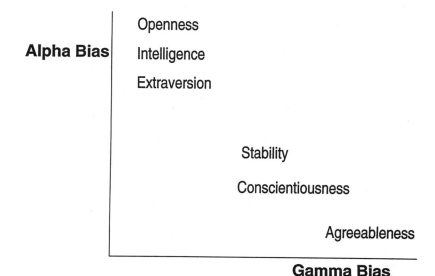

FIG. 4.3. Structure of Big Five Residuals.

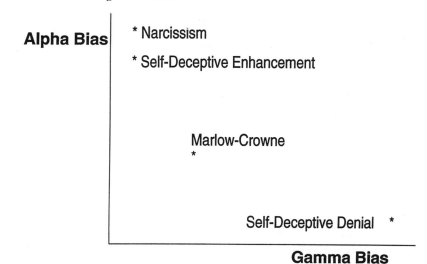

FIG. 4.4. Response style correlates of Alpha and Gamma.

Note first the striking match of the two BIDR subscales (SDE and SDD) to the two bias dimensions. Immediately, we have reason to believe that the factors represent Alpha and Gamma, the bias factors named by Wiggins (1964) and explicated by Damarin and Messick (1965). Note further that narcissism, as measured by the Narcissistic Personality Inventory (Raskin & Hall, 1981), marks Factor 1 along with SDE[7]. Factor 2 resembles earlier studies in being well-marked by the IM and SDD scales and less well by Eysenck's Lie scale, the MMPI Lie scale and the Marlowe-Crowne scale.

Remarkably, the venerable Alpha and Gamma SDR factors (noted above) have been re-generated via a novel technique requiring only personality content measures. The convergence of results across the two techniques adds substantial credibility to the Alpha and Gamma factors. In particular, the new technique provides evidence that both Alpha and Gamma assess departure-from-reality. That is, high scores on both SDR factors involve overly positive self-descriptions (Q.E.D.).

One remaining puzzle is the fact that two conceptually different response style measures, Self-Deceptive Denial and Impression Management, fall on the same SDR factor, Gamma. How can the response styles previously held to tap conscious and unconscious distortions (Paulhus, 1986; Sackeim & Gur, 1978) now coalesce at this point? In anonymous student samples, where pressure for self-presentation is minimal, SDD and IM appear to be capturing similar personality content. Yet IM is more responsive to instructional manipulations. In short, Gamma subsumes both conscious and unconscious aspects of common content. Apparently, I have to question my previous contention that level of consciousness is the core difference between Alpha and Gamma factors of SDR (e.g., Paulhus, 1986). This theoretical revision makes it easier to explain why the Gamma loading of an allegedly conscious deception measure (IM) does not disappear entirely in anonymous responses. With Gamma as a content factor, it is now quite understandable that IM should appear even when there is no audience to motivate impression management.

CONTENT VERSUS STYLE REDUX

In a more recent set of experiments, we sought to clarify the Alpha and Gamma factors via a series of studies varying self-presentation instructions (Paulhus & Notareschi, 1993). First we wondered why Gamma measures were

---

7 A number of recent reports on narcissism and self-deceptive enhancement suggests substantial overlap in both the constructs and the primary measures, NPI and SDE (McHoskey, Wortzel, & Szyarto, 1998; Paulhus, 1998a; Raskin, Novacek, & Hogan, 1991).

so sensitive to instructional manipulations (e.g., Paulhus, 1984). When given standard instructions to respond in a socially desirable fashion, respondents reported that they interpreted the instruction to mean that they should respond like a "nice person" or "good citizen." It struck us that this interpretation of social desirability was rather narrow, focusing on content related to agreeableness and dutifulness, i.e., communal traits. Accordingly we tried a more agentic form of instruction to respondents: "Respond to the questionnaire in a way to impress an experimenter with how strong and competent you are." Lo and behold, the SDE was more sensitive than the IM scale[8] to these instructions (Paulhus, Tanchuk, & Wehr, 1999). In retrospect, these findings seem embarrassingly obvious; yet they have dramatic implications for previous research on SDR.

First, it is now apparent why the items on Wiggins's Sd and other Gamma factor scales contained those socially desirable but distinctively conventional items.[9] Recall that these measures were developed using role-playing instructions that emphasized communion-related desirability. Second, it now seems obvious why Gamma-related scales were so responsive to instructions. They contain the very content that is implied by the instructions. Third, Alpha-related measures may be no more unconscious (and therefore self-deceptive) than Gamma measures.

Then what, after all, can we make of these two factors? Both appear under anonymous conditions. Both respond to faking instructions. Both have conscious and unconscious aspects to them. At least we don't have to withdraw the (thankfully noncommittal) labels, *Alpha* and *Gamma*.

The "final" two-tier conception suggests that (a) Alpha and Gamma be distinguished in terms of personality content, and that (b) each involves a self-deceptive style and an impression management style (see Figure 4.5). Alpha and Gamma are held to be two constellations of traits and biases that have their origins in two fundamental values, agency and communion (Paulhus & John, 1998). Excessive adherence to these values results in self-deceptive tendencies, which we label *egoistic bias* and *moralistic bias*.

Associated with Alpha is an *egoistic bias*, a self-deceptive tendency to exaggerate one's social and intellectual status. This tendency leads to unrealistically positive self-perceptions on such agentic traits as dominance, fearlessness, emotional stability, intellect, and creativity. Self-perceptions of

---

8 When subjects were notified that their answers could land them a summer job (emphasizing competence), then both scales showed significant increases (Paulhus, Lysy, & Yik, 1994).

9 The items were also low in communality (Wiggins, 1964).

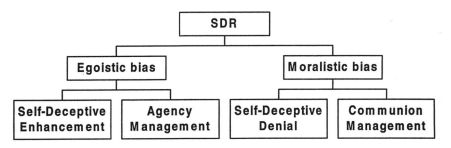

FIG. 4.5. Proposed two tier system.

high scorers have a narcissistic, "superhero" quality. Associated with Gamma is the *moralistic bias*, a self-deceptive tendency to deny socially-deviant impulses and claim sanctimonious, "saint-like" attributes. This tendency is played out in overly positive self-perceptions on such traits as agreeableness, dutifulness, and restraint.

At the impression management level, people are often motivated to deliberately exaggerate their attainment of agency and communion values. Thus the same two clusters of traits are involved but the exaggeration is more conscious. At this level, Alpha involves *Agency Management*, that is, asset-promotion or bragging. Such deliberate promotion of competence, fearlessness, physical prowess, etc. are most commonly seen in job applicants or in males attempting to impress a dating partner. Deliberate exaggeration of Gamma is termed Communion Management and involves excuse-making and damage control of various sorts. Such deliberate minimization of faults might also be seen in religious settings, or in employees who are trying to hold on to the status quo, or legal defendants trying to avoid punishment.

To fully assess the two-tiered system of SDR constructs, four types of measures are needed. Fortunately, three out of the four have been available for some time. Self-deceptive enhancement can be measured with its namesake (SDE) or the Narcissistic Personality Inventory (see Paulhus, 1998a). Self-deceptive denial can also be measured by its namesake scale (SDD). Communion management may be assessed using the traditional Impression Management scale, which has varied little since Sackeim and Gur (1978). Tentatively, it is renamed Communion Management.

The fourth type of desirable responding construct, agency management, required the development of a new instrument by the same name (AM). It consists of items related to agency content but with low endorsement rates in straight-take administrations. The low communalities permit room for manipulators to deliberately enhance impressions of their agency. Examples are

"I am very brave" and "I am exceptionally talented". Such items tend not to be claimed, even by narcissists, under anonymous conditions. But the endorsement rate is higher under agency-motivated conditions than under anonymous conditions.

In recent studies, we have found that the impression management scales, AM and CM, are more useful as response sets than response styles. They were designed for the purpose of capturing instructional sets to appear agentic or communal and they perform that task very well. These measures do not perform very well as styles, presumably because impression management has so many sources and is so sensitive to situational demands.[10] To the extent that a response bias is self-deceptive, the motivation for bias is more trait-like and therefore consistent with the definition of response style.

CONCLUSIONS

The fact that theories evolve is not a deficiency of science. Indeed, its responsiveness to new data can be seen as science's greatest asset. In this light, the evolution of constructs underlying SDR should be viewed as inevitable rather than distressing. At the same time, science should exhibit net progress rather than veer haphazardly. The ideas about SDR presented here are the result of such progress: They were founded on and developed from earlier work. In particular, the earlier writings by Messick (1991; Damarin & Messick, 1965) were a necessary precursor for many of the ideas presented here.

For example, Messick's writings emphasized the necessity of demonstrating departure-from-reality in assessing SDR. To this end, he suggested the statistical analysis of partial correlations. That notion and that method proved to be central to the development of our residuals method of determining the structure of bias in self-reports (Paulhus & John, 1998).

Yet those earlier ideas could not account for all the newly-collected data. In particular, the new data required a more elaborate structural model of SDR. This final two-tiered system incorporates a content-level (agency vs. communion) as well as a process level (conscious vs. unconscious). All four types of SDR were shown to involve the departure from reality that distinguishes response biases from content dimensions of personality. And they reaffirm the continuing challenge of response biases to valid assessment.

---

10 Promising new methods for measuring individual differences in impression management include the overclaiming technique (Paulhus & Bruce, 1990) and response latencies (Holden & Fekken, 1993).

REFERENCES

Baer, R. A., Wetter, M. W., & Berry, D. T. (1992). Detection of underreporting of psychopathology on the MMPI: A meta-analysis. *Clinical Psychology Review, 12*, 509–525.

Bakan, D. (1966). *The duality of human existence: Isolation and communion in Western man.* Boston: Beacon.

Block, J. (1965). *The challenge of response sets.* New York: Century.

Bonanno, G. A., Field, N. P., Kovacevic, A., & Kaltman, S. (in press). Self-enhancement as a buffer against extreme adversity. *Journal of Personality and Social Psychology.*

Brown, J. D. (1998). *The self.* Boston: McGraw-Hill.

Byrne, D. (1961). The repression-sensitization scale: Rationale, reliability, and validity. *Journal of Personality, 29*, 334–349.

Cattell, R. B., & Scheier, I. H. (1961). Extension of meaning of objective test personality factors: Especially into anxiety, neuroticism, questionnaire, and physical factors. *Journal of General Psychology, 61, 287–315.*

Cofer, C. N., Chance, J., & Judson, A. J. (1949). A study of malingering on the Minnesota Multiphasic Personality Inventory. *Journal of Psychology, 27*, 491–199.

Colvin, C. R., Block, J., & Funder, D. C. (1995). Overly-positive self-evaluations and personality: Negative implications for mental health. *Journal of Personality and Social Psychology, 68*, 1152–1162.

Costa, P. T., & McCrae, R. R. (1989). *Manual for the NEO Personality Inventory: Five Factor Inventory/NEO-FFI.* Odessa, FL: PAR.

Crowne, D. P. (1979). *The experimental study of personality.* Hillsdale, NJ: Lawrence Erlbaum Associates.

Crowne, D. P., & Marlowe, D. (1964). *The approval* motive. New York: Wiley.

Damarin, F., & Messick, S. (1965). *Response styles as personality variables: A theoretical integration* (ETS RB 65–10). Princeton, NJ: Educational Testing Service.

Edwards, A. L. (1957). *The social desirability variable in personality assessment and research.* New York: Dryden.

Edwards, A. L. (1970). *The measurement. of personality traits by scales and inventories.* New York: Holt-Rinehart-Winston.

Edwards, A. L. (1990). Construct validity and social desirability. *American Psychologist, 45*, p. 287–289.

Edwards, A. L., Diers, C. J., & Walker, J. N. (1962). Response sets and factor loadings on sixty-one personality scales. *Journal of Applied Psychology, 46, 220–225.*

Edwards, A. L., & Walker, J. N. (1961). A short form of the MMPI: The SD scale. *Psychological Reports, 8*, 485–486.

Eysenck, H. J., & Eysenck, S. B. G. (1964*). The manual of the Eysenck Personality inventory.* London: U of London Press.

Gough, H. C. (1957). *Manual for the California Psychological Inventory.* Palo Alto: Consulting Psychologists Press.

Gur, R. C., & Sackeim, H. A. (1979). Self-deception: A concept in search of a phenomenon. *Journal of Personality and Social Psychology, 37*, 147–169.

Hartshorne, H., & May, H. A. (1930). *Studies in the nature of character.* New York: MacMillan.

Hathaway, S. R., & McKinley, J. C. (1951). *MMPI manual.* New York: Psychological Corporation.

Hogan, R. (1983). A socioanalytic theory of personality. In M. M. Page (Ed.), *Nebraska Symposium on Motivation* (pp. 336–55), Lincoln, NE: University of Nebraska Press.

Hogan, R., & Nicholson, R. A. (1988). The meaning of personality test scores. *American Psychologist, 43*, 621–626.

Holden, R. R., & Fekken, G. C. (1989). Three common social desirability scales: Friends, acquaintances, or strangers? *Journal of Research in Personality, 23*, 180–191.

Holden, R. R., & Fekken, G. C. (1993). Can personality test item responses have construct validity? Issue of reliability and convergent and discriminant validity. *Personality and Individual Differences, 15*, 243–248.

Hoorens, V. (1995). Self-favoring biases, self-presentation, and the self-other asymmetry in social comparison. *Journal of Personality, 63*, 793–818.

Jackson, D. N., & Messick, S. (1958). Content and style in personality assessment. *Psychological Bulletin, 55*, 243–252.

Jackson, D. N., & Messick, S. (1961). Acquiescence and desirability as response determinants on the MMPI. *Educational and Psychological Measurement, 21*, 771–792.

Jackson, D. N., & Messick, S. (1962). Response styles on the MMPI: Comparison of clinical and normal samples. *Journal of Abnormal and Social Psychology. 65*, 285–299.

Jackson, D. N., & Singer, J. E. (1967). Judgements, items, and personality. *Journal of Experimental Research in Personality, 2*, 70–79.

John, O. P., & Paulhus, D. L. (2000). *The structure of self enhancement*. Unpublished ms., University of California, Berkeley.

John, O. P., & Robins, R. (1994). Accuracy and bias in self-perception: Individual differences in self-enhancement and the role of narcissism. *Journal of Personality and Social Psychology, 66*, 206–219.

Johnson, E. A. (1995). Self-deceptive coping: Adaptive only in ambiguous contexts. *Journal of Personality, 63*, 759–792.

Kozma, A., & Stones, M. J. (1988). Social desirability and measures of subjective well-being: Age comparisons. *Social Indicators Research, 20*, 1–14.

McCrae, R. R., & Costa, P. T. (1983). Social desirability scales: More substance than style. *Journal of Consulting and Clinical Psychology, 51*, 882–888.

McHoskey, J. W., Worzel, W., & Szyarto, C. (1998). Machiavellianism and psychopathy. *Journal of Personality and Social Psychology, 74*, 192–210.

Messick, S. (1960). Dimensions of social desirability. *Journal of Consulting Psychology, 24*, 279–287.

Messick, S. (1962). Response style and content measures from personality inventories. *Educational-and Psychological Measurement, 22*, 41–56.

Messick, S. (1991). Psychology and methodology of response styles. In R. E. Snow & D. E. Wiley (Eds.), *Improving inquiry in social science*. (pp. 161–200). Hillsdale, NJ: Erlbaum.

Messick, S., & Jackson, D. N. (1961). Desirability scale values and dispersions for MMPI items. *Psychological Reports, 8*, 409–414.

Meston, C. M., Heiman, J. R., Trapnell, P. D., & Paulhus, D. L. (1998). Socially desirable responding and sexuality self-reports. *Journal of Sex Research, 35*, 148–157.

Milholland, J. E. (1964). Theory and techniques of assessment. *Annual Review of Psychology, 15*, 311–346.

Millham, J., & Jacobson, L .I. (1978). The need for approval. In H. London & J. E. Exner (Eds.), *Dimensions of Personality* (pp. 365–390). New York: Wiley.

Nevid, J. S. (1983). Hopelessness, social desirability, and construct validity. *Journal of Consulting and Clinical Psychology, 51*, 139–140.

Nichols, D. S., & Greene, R. L. (1997). Dimensions of deception in personality assessment: The example of the MMPI-2. *Journal of Personality Assessment, 68*, 251–266.

Ones, D. S., Viswesvaran, C., & Reiss, A. D. (1996). Role of social desirability in personality testing for personnel selection: The red herring. *Journal of Applied Psychology, 81,* 660–679.

Paulhus, D. L. (1984). Two-component models of socially desirable responding. *Journal of Personality and Social Psychology, 46,* 598–609.

Paulhus, D. L. (1986). Self-deception and impression management in test responses. In A. Angleitner & J. S. Wiggins (Eds.), *Personality assessment via questionnaire* (pp. 143–165). New York: Springer-Verlag.

Paulhus, D. L. (1988). *Manual for the Balanced Inventory of Desirable Responding* (BIDR-6). Unpublished manual, University of British Columbia.

Paulhus, D. L. (1991). Measurement and control of response bias. In J.P. Robinson, P.R. Shaver, & L.S. Wrightsman (Eds.), *Measures of personality and social psychological attitudes* (pp. 17–59). New York: Academic Press.

Paulhus, D. L. (1998a). Intrapsychic and interpersonal adaptiveness of trait self-enhancement: A mixed blessing? *Journal of Personality and Social Psychology, 74,* 812–820.

Paulhus, D. L. (1998b). *Manual for the Balanced Inventory of Desirable Responding* (BIDR-7). Toronto/Buffalo: Multi-Health Systems.

Paulhus, D. L., & Bruce, M. N. (1990, June). *The Over-Claiming Questionnaire (OCQ).* Presented at the meeting of the Canadian Psychological Association, Ottawa, Canada.

Paulhus, D. L., Bruce, M. N., & Trapnell, P. D. (1995). Effects of self-presentation strategies on personality profiles and structure. *Personality and Social Psychology Bulletin, 21,* 100–108.

Paulhus, D. L., & John, O. P. (1998). Egoistic and moralistic bias in self-perceptions: The interplay of self-deceptive styles with basic traits and motives. *Journal of Personality, 66,* 1024–1060.

Paulhus, D. L., Lysy, D., & Yik, M. (1994). *Self-presentation on a real-world job application.* Unpublished manuscript, University of British Columbia.

Paulhus, D. L., & Notareschi, R. F. (1993). *Varieties of faking manipulations.* Unpublished data, University of British Columbia.

Paulhus, D. L., & Reid, D. B. (1991). Enhancement and denial in socially desirable responding. *Journal of Personality and Social Psychology, 60,* 307–317.

Paulhus, D. L., Reid, D. B., & Murphy, G. (1987). *The Omnibus Study of Desirable responding.* Unpublished data, University of British Columbia.

Paulhus, D. L., Tanchuk, T., & Wehr, P. (1999, August). *Value-based faking on personality questionnaires: Agency and communion rule.* Presented at the meeting of the American Psychological Association, Boston.

Paunonen, S., & Jackson, D. N. (1996) The Jackson Personality Inventory and the five-factor model of personality. *Journal of Research in Personality, 30,* 42–59.

Raskin, R. N., & Hall, C. S. (1981). The narcissistic personality inventory: Alternative form reliability and further evidence of construct validity. *Journal of Personality Assessment, 45,* 159–160.

Raskin, R. N., Novacek, J., & Hogan, R. T. (1991). Narcissism, self-esteem and defensive self-enhancement. *Journal of Personality, 59,* 19–38.

Rosse, J. G., Stecher, M. D., Miller, J. L., & Levin, R. A. (1998). The impact of response distortion on pre-employment testing and hiring decisions. *Journal of Applied Psychology, 83,* 634–644.

Sackeim, H. A. (1983). Self-deception, self-esteem, and depression:The adaptive value of lying to oneself. In J. Masling (Ed.), *Empirical studies of psychoanalytic theories* (pp. 101–157). Hillsdale, NJ: Lawrence Erlbaum Associates.

Sackeim, H. A., & Gur, R. C. (1978). Self-deception, other-deception and consciousness. In G.E. Schwartz & D. Shapiro (Eds.), *Consciousness and self-regulation: Advances in research* (Vol. 2; pp. 139–197). New York: Plenum Press.

Saucier, G. (1994). Separating description and evaluation in the structure of personality attributes. *Journal of Personality and Social Psychology, 66,* 141–154.

Taylor, S. E., & Brown, J. D. (1988). Illusion and well-being: A social-psychological perspective on mental health. *Psychological Bulletin, 103,* 193–210.

Wiggins, J. S. (1959). Interrelationships among MMPI measures of dissimulation under standard and social desirability instructions. *Journal of Consulting Psychology, 23 ,*419–427.

Wiggins, J. S. (1964). Convergences among stylistic response measures from objective personality tests. *Educational and Psychological Measurement, 24,* 551–562.

Wiggins, J. S. (1991). Agency and communion as conceptual coordinates for the understanding and measurement of interpersonal behavior. In W. Grove & D. Cicchetti (Eds.), *Thinking clearly about Psychology: Essays in honor of Paul Meehl* (Vol.2; pp. 89–113). Minneapolis: University of Minnesota Press.

Wiggins, J. S. (Ed.). (1996). *The Five Factor Model.* New York: Guilford.

Yik, M. S. M., Bond, M. H., & Paulhus, D. L. (1998). Do Chinese self-enhance or self-efface?: It's a matter of domain. *Journal of Research in Personality 24,* 399–406.

II

INTELLECT—
THEORY AND ASSESSMENT

5

Measurement From a Hierarchical Point of View

Jan-Eric Gustafsson
Göteborg University

There is ample empirical evidence that the structure of individual differences in cognitive abilities may be described in terms of a hierarchical model with three strata (Carroll, 1993; Gustafsson, 1988, Gustafsson & Undheim, 1996; Messick, 1992). From a taxonomic point of view the hierarchical approach has important advantages (Gustafsson, 1988), and it makes it possible to unite conflicting models that emphasize either one general ability (e.g., Spearman, 1927) or many specific abilities (e.g., Thurstone, 1938). But the hierarchical approach also may have implications for the measurement of cognitive abilities, and for measurement in general, which so far seem largely unexplored. The purpose of this chapter is to discuss possible implications of the hierarchical approach for measurement.

Coan (1964) introduced the term *referent generality* to refer to the scope of reference of a construct, or "the variety of behaviors or mental activities to which it relates and the degree to which it relates to them" (p. 138). Snow (1974) emphasized the referent generality of constructs representing outcomes of experimental designs, and Messick (1989) made frequent reference to the construct of referent generality in his treatise on validity. The idea that measures and constructs differ in referent generality has, of course, close affinity to the hierarchical model of the structure of individual differences (Coan, 1964; Gustafsson & Undheim, 1996; Messick, 1992; Snow, Corno & Jackson, 1996). For example, the construct general cognitive ability is more general than is the construct spatial ability, in the sense that the latter ability is only one among many abilities that may be subsumed under general cognitive ability. Similarly, it is obvious that a broad spatial ability subsumes a large set of more narrowly defined abilities, such as Vizualization, Flexibility of Closure, or Spatial Relations (see, e.g., Carroll, 1993; Gustafsson, 1988).

At a general, theoretical level distinctions between ability constructs of low and high referent generality are easy to make. It is not immediately obvious, however, how measurement of constructs of different referent generality should be accomplished. The issue how to best measure the high referent generality construct general cognitive ability has, thus, been extensively discussed since the days of Binet and Spearman (Gustafsson, 1997). There has been less controversy about measurement of low referent generality constructs, such as the Thurstonian "Primary Mental Abilities," but it will be argued that there may be complications worthy of attention in such measurement situations too. Before going any further there is reason, however, to describe the hierarchical conception of individual differences somewhat more closely.

THE HIERARCHICAL CONCEPTION OF ABILITY

Correlations between scores on tasks measuring knowledge and skills in different domains typically are larger than zero and lower than unity. As was observed by Wiley (1991) the pattern of covariation among a set of tasks may be due to several different factors, such as features of the test tasks, the pattern of previous learning experiences of the individuals, and "the structural constraints on the actual abilities or skills possessed by the individuals" (p. 84). For about a century now, researchers have applied different methods of multivariate analysis to matrices of correlations of task performance, aiming to disclose the structure of cognitive abilities. Some may have had the rather naive hope of being able to disclose an "inborn" structure of human cognitive abilities, but the complexity of the pattern of results has been all too obvious. Even today, there is far from perfect agreement about how the cumulated evidence should be interpreted (see Gustafsson & Undheim, 1996).

The construct of general cognitive ability (or general intelligence, or a number of other synonyms) has a prominent place in many models of the structure of individual differences, and it is by some regarded to be one of the great achievements of psychology. Indeed, as Scarr (1989) observed " . . . no concept in the history of psychology has had or continues to have as great an impact on everyday life in the Western world." (p. 75). However, both from a scientific and from a practical point of view general intelligence is a highly controversial construct.

The history of research on intelligence is too well known to be described here (see, e.g., Carroll, 1982, 1993; DuBois, 1970; Thorndike & Lohman, 1990), but there may be reason to make a quick review of the psychometric research on the construct. During the first few years of the 20th century major progress was thus made both with respect to the theory of measurement through the work of Spearman (1904a, 1904b), and in the development of practically useful tests intelligence through the contributions of Binet and Simon (1905).

Spearman's (1904b) major theoretical contribution was the Two-Factor theory, which states that performance on any intellectual task is affected by two factors: one general, which is common to all tasks (g); and one which is specific to the task (s). He also contributed the first crude forms of factor-analysis, and tested the model on empirical data, generally obtaining support for the existence of the g-factor.

At about the same time as Spearman made his contribution, Binet and Simon (1905) developed a scale of mental ability, based on developmental concepts. The scale was composed of a quite varied set of tasks of increasing complexity and difficulty, and it proved to be practically useful, for example, in diagnosing learning problems. The Binet scales were translated into other languages (e.g., Terman, 1916), and new intelligence scales were constructed along similar lines (e.g., Wechsler, 1939).

One might expect that Binet's work on intelligence scales and Spearman's work on the g-factor would be mutually supportive. However, Binet critized Spearman's work as empirically inadequate (Binet, 1905), and Spearman (1927) complained that the theoretical basis of Binet's tests, as well as the procedures used in development of the tests were weak and insufficient.

The practice of intelligence testing has from time to time been critically discussed (e.g., Cronbach, 1975), and there certainly has been misuse and misguided applications, but there is no doubt that the technology of intelligence testing is regarded as a useful tool in much psychological work. The tests are revised to keep a modern look, and to keep up with the trend toward increased performance in the population (e.g., Flynn, 1987). There are, thus, no signs that the interest in intelligence testing is diminishing, so Binet's early contribution certainly has had a lasting influence.

The scientific status of the construct of general intelligence has, however, been challenged, and for long periods during the 20th century, Spearman and his g-construct has been in scientific disrepute. One reason for this is that his Two-Factor theory met with empirical difficulties when confronted with empirical data, and that the crude factor-analytic model used by Spearman was superseded by the considerably more advanced multiple-factor analysis developed by Thurstone (1947). Another reason for the reluctance to accept general intelligence as a scientific construct is probably that the heterogeneous intelligence tests have not been accepted as measures of a single construct, because they have not fulfilled the ideal of homogeneity and unidimensionality demanded both by classical (e.g., Gulliksen, 1950) and modern (e.g., Lord, 1980) measurement theories. Furthermore, such tests have had difficulties meeting the criterion of "face validity" when being scrutinized (e.g., Neisser, 1976, Gould, 1981). Spearman (1927) did try to solve the measurement problem through development of more pure g-factor tests. John Raven was thus inspired by Spearman to develop the Progressive Matrices test as a g-test. This test has met with considerable success, but it has not generally been accepted as an alternative to the heterogenous intelligence tests in practical work, and it has not generally been accepted as *the* measure of g in scientific studies.

Compared to Binet's practical contribution, it thus seems that Spearman's theoretical and methodological contributions have had less of an impact during large periods of the 20th century. It seems, however, that the 1980s and 1990s have implied a renewed scientific interest in the construct of general intelligence, and in Spearman's work (Carroll, 1996; Dennis & Tapsfield, 1996).

One reason for this revitalization of theoretical interest in general intelligence is probably the growing popularity and success of reductionistic, biologically based, models to explain individual differences in general intelligence (see, e.g., Anderson, 1992; Brody, 1992). Another reason may be the research conducted during the 1980s and 1990s on hierarchical models of intelligence that has restored the g-factor as the apex factor (see, e.g., Carroll, 1993; Gustafsson, 1988, Gustafsson & Undheim, 1996; Undheim, 1981). A third likely reason for the interest in general intellegence is that there has accumulated a massive amount of empirical evidence of the ubiquitous importance of this dimension of individual differences (see, e.g., Lubinski & Humphreys, 1997). Reviewing the literature on relations between a variety of behavioral, medical, and social phenomena, and individual differences in general intelligence, these authors concluded that the relations are so obvious and strong that they must be taken into account. If that is not done the researchers commit the logical fallacy of the "neglected aspect," because they fail to include all relevant evidence. According to Lubinski and Humphreys general intelligence has been a "neglected aspect" in too much research, and they argued that: "Ignoring the *possibility* that general intelligence holds causal status for a variety of critically important behaviors is no longer scientifically respectable. We must let general intelligence compete with other putative causes. We must answer questions concerning its scientific status empirically" (Lubinsky & Humphreys, 1997, p. 190). Let me also add that another well established principle of scientific work, namely "Occam's razor," dictates that a more narrow concept should not be introduced if there already exists a more general concept with the same explanatory power.

There is, thus, considerable evidence that we must accept general intelligence as a construct, and later on in this chapter I revisit the measurement issues associated with this construct. But there is also ample evidence that structural models that only include one single, general, factor fail to account for the correlations among performance measures. It would, thus, be equally wrong to neglect specific abilities, as it is to neglect general intelligence.

For many decades Thurstone's (1938) approach of describing Primary Mental Abilities, using Multiple Factor analysis (Thurstone, 1947) on large test batteries, dominated the research on the structure of abilities. The approach was successful in yielding a large number of ability dimensions, which in one sense are equally important (or having equal referent generality), but which also show varying degrees of overlap. Much of the work in the field of differential psychology from 1950 and onward was conducted with the purpose to come to grips with the problems caused by multiple correlated abilities.

The Guilford (1967) "Structure-of-Intellect" (SI) model may be seen as an attempt to create a taxonomy of PMA's. However, although it was Guilford's intention to organize and understand the growing number of individual difference factors, he actually contributed substantially to the proliferation of ability dimensions by assuming all factors to be orthogonal. It does not seem that the SI model has been theoretically productive either.

During the 1960s other approaches to reducing the number of abilitity dimensions were developed, in which the correlations among PMAs were analyzed in terms of broad ability constructs. Cattell and Horn (e.g., Cattell, 1963; Horn & Cattell, 1966) used second-order factor analysis of factors or tests representing primary abilities to identify several broad abilities. Recently Carroll (1993) has formulated a hierarchical model with factors of three degrees of generality on the basis of results of his reanalysis of almost

500 correlation matrices collected thoughout the history of research on human cognitive abilities, and which may be regarded as an extension of the Cattell and Horn model. The three-stratum division corresponds to a classification of abilities in the categories narrow, broad, and general. The PMA's belong to the category of narrow abilities. Carroll also has identified some 10 broad abilities. In addition to *General Intelligence* (G), these are the same factors as were identified in the Cattell-Horn model, namely *Fluid Intelligence* (Gf), *Crystallized Intelligence* (Gc), *Broad Visual Perception* (Gv), *Broad Retrieval Ability* (Gr), and *Broad Auditory Perception* (Ga). In addition Carroll identified a broad memory factor (*General Memory and Learning*, Gy) as well as three factors reflecting *Broad Cognitive Speediness* (Gs, Gt, and Gp). A major difference between Carroll's model and the Cattell-Horn model is, however, that the former includes a general factor (G), whereas the latter does not.

There is a major difference between models that have a general factor at the apex of the hierarchy, and models that have multiple apexes. With the exception of Carroll (1993) the latter type of hierarchical models has been favored in American research, and the Cattell-Horn model has become increasingly popular. However, in British research there is also another tradition of hierarchical models, which may be regarded as extensions and elaborations of Spearman's Two-Factor Model, and which thus include a general factor.

The British researchers have relied on factoring techniques, which start by extracting the general factor, and then extract group-factors that successively get more and more narrow. Using such techniques Burt (1949) and Vernon (1950) have proposed hierarchical models that at first sight seem quite different from the Cattell-Horn model, and from the Carroll model.

However, it seems that the difference is more apparent than real. Comparisons between the American and British hierarchical models using confirmatory factor analysis (e.g., Gustafsson, 1984, 1988; Undheim, 1981; Undheim & Gustafsson, 1987) have shown that the correlation between the Gf-factor and the *g*-factor is so close to unity that these factors must be considered identical. Thus, in the Vernon model there is no broad group factor that corresponds to Gf because the *g*-factor accounts for all the systematic variance in the tests, leaving no variance that may define a subordinate Gf-factor.

The differences in the patterns of results of the American and the British hierarchical factorists thus are due to the way in which the analyses have been performed. In the American research the narrow factors have been seen as building blocks for the broader factors and the analysis is conducted from bottom going up, using what Gustafsson and Balke (1993) labeled a *higher order* modeling approach. In the British factor-analytic tradition the analysis has started at the top, going down, using a *nested-factor* modeling approach (Gustafsson & Balke, 1993). If, however, these approaches are carried through to yield a hierarchical model with three levels, similar results are obtained (Gustafsson, 1997).

There remains, however, an important conceptual difference between the two approaches. According to the bottom-up, higher order, modelling approach the lower order factors are undivisible, and there is no direct involvement of the higher order factors in the lower order factors. However, in the top-down approach factors at lower levels in the hierarchy are automatically freed from the variance due to the broader factors. Thus, the lower order factors are split up into two or more parts: one due to the lower order factor, and one due to the higher order factors. These two ways of looking at the lower order factors (i.e., the low referent generality factors) have, as will be shown below, important implications for how to go about measuring the factors.

AN EXAMPLE: THE HOLZINGER AND SWINEFORD STUDY

Discussions about alternative models of the structure of abilities tend to become both complex and abstract, so there is need for a concrete example. In order to be able to discuss measurement issues in concrete terms we also need an example, and I rely on the Holzinger and Swineford (1939) study for both these purposes. This study certainly deserves much more attention than it has gained so far. It seems, in fact, that this study, which was conducted in the 1930s, presented all the important results about hierarchical structures of ability that have been obtained in recent years. A second reason for selecting this study for reanalysis is that it includes a large test-battery, which covers a wide spectrum of broad and narrow abilities. The test-battery was administered to a reasonably large group ($N = 301$) of 7th- and 8th-grade students from two Chicago schools. These data thus provide material for discussion about many interesting measurement issues.

Holzinger, who was an American, studied for several years at the University of London with Pearson and Spearman. After returning to

Chicago he did methodological work on factor analysis, and he also did a considerable amount of substantive work. One line of work focused on the structure of mental abilities, and Holzinger in particular was oriented toward extending the Spearman model to accomodate the fact that the Two-Factor model had been proven too simplified. This work was done under the auspices of the so called Unitary Traits Committee, which was established in 1931 by E. L. Thorndike, under the enthusiastic support by Spearman, who was also a member of the committee.

During the 1930s, Holzinger published a series of preliminary technical reports on the "Spearman-Holzinger Unitary Trait Study." The last report in the series was the Holzinger and Swineford (1939) study, the purpose of which was to extend the Spearman Two-Factor theory into a full-fledged hierarchical model with factors of three degrees of generality: a general factor, group factors, and specific factors.

The test battery comprised 24 tests, and many of these are close to tests still in use. The battery was designed to measure abilities in five broad areas: spatial, verbal, memory, speed and mathematical deduction. The results presented by Holzinger and Swineford (1939) supported the hypothesized structure, except that no group factor representing mathematical deduction was found. This was because the general factor accounted for all the variance in the mathematical deduction factor, and Holzinger and Swineford (1939) concluded that "the general factor may be just such a deductive factor as these tests were expected to measure" (p. 8).

The Holzinger and Swineford study was reanalyzed by Gustafsson (1997) who used two different approaches of fitting hierarchical confirmatory factor models to the Holzinger and Swineford data. The main purpose of these reanalyses was to investigate the hypothesis of equivalence between general intelligence and fluid intelligence.

In one approach a higher order model (see, e.g., Gustafsson, 1988; Gustafsson & Balke, 1993) was fitted that included five first-order factors (Gc = verbal, Gv = spatial, Gf = mathematical deductive, Gm = memory and Gs = speed) and one second-order factor (G). The higher order models showed quite clearly that there is a relation of unity between G and Gf, whereas the relations between G and the other factors all were significantly lower than unity.

In the other approach a so-called nested-factor model (Gustafsson & Balke, 1993) was fitted. This model included a G-factor with relations to all 24 tests, and residual factors representing Gc, Gv, Gm and Gs. The nested-factor model also supported the hypothesis of equivalence between G and

Gf, because in this model it was not possible to introduce a residual Gf-factor, after G was included into the model.

What is even more interesting is that the results of the nested-factor model were very close to the results originally presented by Holzinger and Swineford. For their analyes they used the so called bi-factor method developed by Holzinger (see Holzinger, 1944; Holzinger & Swineford, 1939). The essence of the bi-factor solution is that it includes a general factor, uncorrelated group factors, and unique factors. The bi-factor solution can directly, and relatively simply, be computed from the correlation matrix. It does, however, require that the tests are brought together in groups before the analysis, so in this sense it is similar to confirmatory factor analysis. The technique is described in great detail in Harman's (1967) book on factor analysis.

Table 5.1 presents the estimates originally obtained by Holzinger and Swineford, and the results computed with the confirmatory nested-factor model.

As may be seen, the results are generally quite close. The reanalysis of the Holzinger and Swineford data with a modern form of factor analysis thus gives excellent support to the original bi-factor analysis, and it also supports the hypothesis that reasoning is of central importance to the general factor (see Gustafsson, 1997, for an extended discussion about the substantive implications of these findings).

MEASUREMENT IMPLICATIONS OF THE HIERARCHICAL APPROACH

I now consider some measurement issues that are associated with the hierarchical model, using the empirical results presented above. In the discussion I rely on a statistical model for relating observed test-score variance to the dimensions of a factor-analytic model. This model is closely associated with the nested-factor model, and may be regarded as an extension of classical test-theory to deal with multidimensionality.

Reuterberg and Gustafsson (1992) demonstrated that the internal-consistency measures of reliability (e.g., Cronbach's alpha) may be formulated in terms of confirmatory factor analytic models, and that reliability measures may easily be computed from the parameters estimated in such models. Thus, given a factor model in which a set of components is related to one common factor, the amount of true variance in the sum of components is the square of the sum of unstandardized factor loadings

Table 5.1
Estimated Loadings in the Original Analysis (HS) and in the Reanalysis (NF)

Test	g		Gv		Gc		Gs		Gy	
	HS	N	HS	NF	HS	NF	HS	NF	HS	NF
VISPER	.59	.63	.40	.34						
CUBES	.25	.30	.43	.36						
FRMBRD	.22	.29	.50	.44						
LOZENG	.45	.53	.44	.36						
GENINF	.36	.43			.78	.72				
PARCOMP	.52	.57			.61	.58				
SENCOMP	.38	.47			.82	.75				
WRDCLS	.50	.50			.51	.48				
WRDMEA	.56	.60			.60	.59				
ADD	.31	.26					.51	.57		
CODE	.57	.48					.43	.51		
CNTDOT	.32	.29					.54	.53		
SCCAPS	.40	.40					.37	.39		
WRDREC	.18	.22							.68	.67
NUMREC	.12	.14							.55	.58
FIGREC	.51	.52							.33	38
OBJNUM	.27	.23							.48	.48
NUMFIG	.19	.18							.47	.42
FIGWRD	.37	.39							.30	.28
DEDUCT	.51	.49								
NUMPUZZ	.69	.62								
PRBREAS	.68	.64								
SERCOM	.77	.76								
MIXFUND	.67	.60								

multiplied with the factor variance. The error variance of the component sum is the sum of the error variances of the components. As is shown below this basic formula generalizes straightforwardly to multidimensional, orthogonal, models of the nested-factor type.

Assume that observations are available on m variables for N individuals. The observations for an individual are assembled into the vector y. An ordinary factor model may then be written:

$$y = \Lambda\eta + \varepsilon$$

In this equation η is a vector of k latent variables, Λ is a matrix of factor loadings, and ε a vector of residuals in observed variables. Under the usual assumptions of independence of residuals and factors this model generates the following covariance structure (e.g., Jöreskog, 1971):

$$\Sigma = \Lambda\Psi\Lambda' + \Theta$$

Here Ψ is the covariance matrix of the latent variables and Θ the covariance matrix of the residuals in manifest variables. Assuming that we restrict attention to nested-factor models, Ψ will be diagonal, and Θ is also assumed to be orthogonal.

Here our primary interest is on properties of functions of the observed variables. Let us assume that we construct a simple unit-weighted sum (T, for total) of the individuals' scores on the m variables, which are assumed to be centered around the mean. Because the variance of a sum of components is equal to the sum of all the elements of the covariance matrix for the components it follows that:

$$\text{Var}(T) = \sum_{j=1}^{k}\left(\sum_{i=1}^{m}\lambda_{ij}\right)^2 \psi_{jj} + \sum_{i=1}^{m}\theta_{ii}$$

This formula thus achieves a decomposition of the total observed variance of T into different components due to the different latent variables and to errors of measurement. The contribution of each of the orthogonal latent variables simply is the square of the sums of loadings, times the factor variance. The algorithms for this decomposition of the total variance have been implemented in the STREAMS system (Gustafsson & Stahl, 1997) and will be applied here.

Let me start by putting down three propositions about measurement that more or less immediately follow from the hierarchical approach, given that we accept the assumptions involved in constructing such models:

1. To measure constructs with high referent generality it is necessary to use heterogenous measurement devices.
2. A homogenous test always measures several dimensions.
3. To measure constructs with low referent generality it is also necessary to measure constructs with high generality.

At first sight these three propositions may seem to conflict with current thinking about measurement, which emphasizes unidimensionality and homogeneity as prerequisites for interpretability (e.g., Pedhazur & Pedhazur Schmelkin, 1991). I try to show, however, that there is little conflict, but that the notion of measurement at different levels of generality makes it necessary to elaborate the meaning of the concepts unidimensionality and homogeneity.

Proposition 1: Measurement of High Generality Constructs Requires Heterogenous Instruments

The first proposition will be examined using measurement of general intelligence as an example of a construct with high referent generality. One way to create a heterogenous test is to use a simple unweighted sum of all the tests in the Holzinger and Swineford battery. Such a composite score would approximate an IQ score, or a score on a very heterogenous test. Assuming that standardized scores (i.e., z-scores) are summed together, the total observed variance for the sum would be 165.9. According to the formula presented above no less than 127.0, or 77 %, of the total variance is due to G. Another way of putting this information is that there is a correlation of .88 (i.e., the square root of .77) between G and the total score. This is a somewhat paradoxical result, given that the amount of relations between G and the individual tests are not particularly high. The standardized loadings (i.e., correlations) range between .14 and .76, but most of the loadings are quite low. Often the relation between the broad factor and a test is, furthermore, higher than is the relation between the G-factor and the test. However, there is a rather obvious reason why the G-factor is the dominating source of variance in the sum of scores, and it is that it is, to some extent, present in every test. According to the formula presented above the contribution of a latent variable is a function of the square of the number of variables to which it is related. Because the general factor is present in every one of the 24 tests it gets a weight, as it were, of $24^2 = 576$, whereas the Gv-factor, for example, to which only 4 tests are related only gets a weight of 16. The contribution of Gv to the variance in the sum of scores is 3.1, or 1.9%. From Gc (5 tests) the contribution is 8.7 (5.2%); from Gs (4 tests) it is 3.1 (1.9%) to Gs; and from Gy (6 tests) it is 6.4 (3.9%). These results thus show a striking dominance of the G-factor in the sum of scores, and quite limited contributions from the group-factors.

The influence from the residuals also is very much reduced in the sum, and together they only account for 6.9% of the variance.

It is interesting to compare the properties of the total sum of scores as a measure of Gf with the properties of the Gf-tests. The single best Gf-test is the SERCOM test, with a loading of .76 on G. This implies that about 58% of the variance in this test is due to G, and it seems that this is about as high as it is possible to get with a single measure (Gustafsson, 1998). The other Gf-tests have loadings on G around .6, which implies that no more than some 40% of the variance in these is due to G (or Gf). However, a sum of scores on the five Gf-tests in the Holzinger and Swineford battery has a variance which to 76% is due to Gf, and this is close to what is obtained from the entire testbattery. Such a score has a better face validity as a measure of reasoning ability than has the sum of scores on the entire testbattery, but it still would be derived from quite different types of tasks.

It may, in passing, be noted that these results explain the success of Binet's approach to measuring general ability with heterogenous tests, as compared to the relatively modest amount of success met by Spearman's attempts to measure general intelligence with a single Gf-test.

The total sum of scores on the test battery thus is a fairly homogenous measure of G, and also of Gf. The fact that a heterogenous mixture of task types may yield a fairly pure measure of a single ability, much like mixing all the colors yields white, is not easily realized, and it certainly is not obvious from an ocular inspection of a testbattery. Heterogenous tests thus are seriously lacking in face validity. It should, however, be emphasized that the principle of aggregation demonstrated here has been identified before. Thus, Humphreys (1962, 1985) argued that measurement of general intelligence is best done with heterogenous tests, because such tests do provide a homogenous measure of general intelligence.

It also may be pointed out that a similar line of reasoning as that used here can be applied to explain why the general factor is so highly predictive of performance over a wide range of situations. Although any single task performed in school, on the job, or in daily life has a low relation to G, the fact that there are so many tasks on which performance to some extent depends on the general factor explains why, in the long run, there will be a relation between aggregated measures of performance and test performance.

Proposition 2: A Homogenous Test Measures Several Abilities

This statement seems to be completely at odds with current views on the nature of measurement, in which homogeneity is seen as a prerequisite for measuring a single ability. When the test score is interpreted as a sample (Loevinger, 1957) this view makes sense, but when test performance is seen as a sign of one or more abilities it may, or may not, depending on which particular framework is used for constructing relations among the sign and the signified. If a hierarchical model is applied it seems, however, that the conclusion that any (homogenous) test simultaneously measures multiple abilities is inescapable (see also Vernon, 1961). This point can easily be demonstrated with any of the tests in the Holzinger and Swineford (1939) study, such as for example the VISPER test.

According to the model there are three sources of variance in this test (see Table 5.1), namely the G-factor, the Gv-factor, and the residual. The G-factor accounts for 39.7% of the variance, and the Gv-factor for 11.6%, so in spite of the fact that this test is classified and interpreted as a measure of Gv, it is in fact a better indicator of G. The largest source of variance in the test is the residual that accounts for 48.6% of the variance. This component of variance is, however, composed of at least two parts, a test-specific component of systematic variance, and a random error component. To decompose these components of variance, further information, such as half-test scores, would be needed.

It is, thus, quite obvious that the VISPER test measures more than one ability, and in the hierarchical model this is true for every other test as well. It seems that the only way to avoid this is to create heterogenous tests in which all the narrow abilities cancel, and the general factor becomes the dominant source of variance. But as long as the tests are homogenous tests of a cognitive ability it is inevitable that they will, to a smaller or larger extent, measure the general factor, and most likely a broad ability as well.

Proposition 3: Measurement of Low Generality Constructs Also Requires Measurement of High Generality Constructs

The third proposition is closely related to the second one. It states that if our intention is to measure one or more narrow abilities, it is necessary to partial out, or in some other way control for, the influence of the general factor and of other broad factors that may be related to performance, but which we are not interested in measuring. This may easily be done through computing factor scores, for example (Gustafsson & Snow, 1997), but this cannot be done unless test scores are available that allow estimation of the more general dimensions. Thus, to measure a narrow ability it does not suffice to measure a single ability, but as a minimum we also need to measure the general factor, which may be done with a set of Gf-tasks, or a heterogenous test.

When the focus of interest is not on the profile of ability of single individuals but on groups of persons we may use structural equation modeling methods for solving the measurement problems. This brings the advantage, among others, that errors of measurement is not a serious source of problems, which otherwise may be the case. A simple example is presented below.

An Example: Group Differences in Ability Profiles

The Holzinger and Swineford sample included 7th- and 8th-grade students from two Chicago schools. One (The Grant-White Elementary School, N = 145) was a suburban middle-class school, in which most pupils had native English speaking parents. The other school (Pasteur Elementary School, N = 156) was serving a working-class area. Many of the Pasteur parents were foreign born, and many were still using their native language at home. The profile of mean scores on the tests was quite different for the two schools: On the verbal tests and on the deductive tests the Grant-White group excelled, whereas the Pasteur group excelled on the speed tests, and on some of the spatial and memory tests (Holzinger & Swineford, 1939, p. 8).

These data may be used for purposes of illustrating analysis of group differences in latent variables when a hierarchical model is assumed, and when a non hierarchical model is assumed. The hierarchical model is the higher order model presented by Gustafsson (1997), and the non hierarchical model is an oblique five factor model, which includes Gf, Gv, Gc, Gs and Gm as correlated factors. Both these models fit the data quite well. Table 5.2 presents the estimates of group differences in latent variables.

For Gf the two models yield identical results, there being a higher mean in the Grant-White school. But for all the other abilities the results under the two models are dramatically different. Thus, for Gv the hierarchical model yields a significantly higher mean in the Pasteur school, but according to the oblique model there is no difference between the two

Table 5.2

Standardized Mean Differences between Schools on Latent Variables in Oblique and Hierarchical Models

	Oblique Model		Higher Order Model	
	Estimate	t-value	Estimate	t-value
Gf	.56	4.06	.56	3.97
Gv	-.10	-0.77	-.54	-4.49
Gc	.71	5.75	.34	3.15
Gm	.02	0.16	-.25	-1.83
Gs	-.09	-0.64	-.43	-3.10

Note. Positive values indicate a higher mean for the Grant-White Elementary School, and negative values a higher mean for the Pasteur Elementary School.

schools with respect to Gv. The observed level of performance on the Gv-tests thus is more or less the same in the two schools. However, according to the hierarchical model the Gv-tests are related both to Gf and to Gv, so the higher mean on Gf in the Grant-White school is compensated for by a lower mean on Gv. This is why the hierarchical model estimates a higher level on the residual Gv-factor for the Pasteur school. For the same reason the very large difference in favor of the Grant-White school on Gc according to the oblique model is considerably reduced in the hierarchical model. For Gm there is no significant difference under either of the two models, and the similarity in the pattern of results for this factor is because these tests have rather low relations to Gf. For Gs, finally, the pattern of results is similar to that obtained for Gv.

These results indicate that quite profound differences in the pattern of results may be obtained when a hierarchical measurement model is used (see also Rosén, 1995). It must be stressed, however, that the results presented in Table 5.2 assume that the test scores are interpreted as signs of the underlying system of abilities, whereas the oblique model is closer to a conception of the test score as a sample of performances from a domain. But it is, of course, possible to transform the hierarchical model into a model that makes statements about level of performance on particular tests through taking all the latent variables into account.

DISCUSSION

The somewhat paradoxical implications of the hierarchical approach to measurement, along with the strikingly different results obtained in the empirical illustration, raises many questions about the nature of different approaches to measurement. Some of these issues are discussed below. Because the discussion deals with interpretation and use of measures it does seem quite appropriate to carry the discussion in terms of validity (Messick, 1989).

It has already been concluded that measurement of high generality constructs requires heterogenous measurement devices. This conclusion may be rephrased in terms of one of the two major threats to construct validity discussed by Messick (1989), namely construct underrepresentation. Messick (1989) also argued that heterogeneity of tests may be necessary to avoid construct underrepresentation. As a hypothetical example he discussed in terms of a complex construct involving three facets, A, B, and C. Different aspects of the construct are measured by three measures: one taps facets A and B; another facets B and C; and the third facets A and C. Messick observed that:

> By virtue of the overlapping components, the three measures will intercorrelate positively and appear to converge in the measurement of 'something,' presumably the overall complex construct. Yet each measure is underrepresentative of some aspect of the construct. A composite of the three measures would cover all three aspects and, furthermore, the construct-relevant variance would contribute to the composite score while the irrelevant variance would not. (p. 35)

This line of reasoning is almost identical with the one presented here. There is, however, a subtle difference in conceptualization that may be worthwhile to discuss somewhat further. Thus, in Messick's formulation the construct is defined in terms of the different facets, much like in a componential model (see Gustafsson & Balke, 1993). In this model a set of low referent generality contructs together define a high referent generality construct. However, in the conceptual model relied on here the high generality construct is explicitly introduced along with the low generality constructs, and the variance in each observed measure is seen as being determined by both high and low generality constructs. This conceptual model thus is similar to the "reflective" model of the relation between observed and latent variables that is adopted in the factor analytic model

(Gustafsson & Balke, 1993). According to this model the observed variables are exchangeable indicators of the latent construct, and there is only a probabilistic relation between the observed and latent variables. For a construct such as general intelligence such a reflective, "open," model seems more appropriate than a componential, "closed," model.

These subtleties aside, it seems that construction of heterogenous measures is a way of avoiding the problem of construct under-representation in the measurement of high referent generality constructs. The problem of construct-irrelevant variance, which is the other major threat to construct validity discussed by Messick (1989), does not, however, seem to be a major problem in a well constructed heterogenous measure, because of the aggregation effects. However, when a more or less homogenous test is used to measure a high generality construct, such as when the Raven Progressive Matrices Test is used to measure the g-factor, the problem of construct-irrelevant variance, in the form of test-specific variance, seems to be the major threat to validity.

When a low generality construct is the intent of measurement (Wiley, 1991) construct-irrelevant variance seems to be the major problem, but now contributed by more general sources of variance. At least this follows if a reflective, hierachical, measurement model is assumed, because according to such a model variance from high referent generality constructs such as g contribute variance in the measure. If the measure is interpreted in terms of the low referent generality construct only, the variance due to the more general constructs takes the form of construct-irrelevant variance.

General sources of variance are only rarely conceptualized in terms of construct-irrelevant variance. It is, however, interesting to observe that Thorndike (1951) in the chapter on reliability in the first edition of *Educational Measurement* made a classification of sources of variance in test scores in terms of referent generality, from general to specific, and in term of lastingness. This model is close to the one presented here, and it follows that when a low generality construct is in the focus of interest, variance from more general sources of variance would be irrelevant.

The fact that measures of low referent generality constructs may capture more general sources of variance is, fortunately enough, often realized when substantive interpretations of findings is made. If, for example, a study establishes a correlation between a measure of spatial visualization ability and reading comprehension performance, the interpretation would typically not be couched in terms of, say, the demands on spatial visualization ability by the processing of letters and symbols of punctuation as figural elements. A more reasonable interpretation would be that the correlation is accounted for in terms of an unobserved third variable, such a general cognitive ability, which is related both to performance on the spatial visualization test and the reading comprehension test.

Thus, as long as measures of the more general abilities are included, the construct irrelevant variance may be kept under control, and even when the more general sources of variance have not been measured they may be brought in via theoretical deliberations. But much may be gained if we also conceptualize the problem as a problem of construct validity, because this would make the interpretational problems more obvious, and it would stimulate development of appropriate methods of controlling for the more general sources of variance (cf Gustafsson & Snow, 1997).

Before leaving this topic it must be emphasized, however, that the line of reasoning presented here is meaningful only when the measures of low referent generality constructs are interpreted as signs (Loevinger, 1957) of unobservable abilities. If the test scores instead are seen as samples from a domain, it does not make much sense to divide the variance in performance into sources of different degrees of generality. Thus, in this case we have to regard the performance measures as measures of an undivisible construct.

Let me, finally, make a few comments about choice of a hierarchical measurement instead of a more traditional measurement model. It must, thus, be emphasized that compared to an oblique measurement model a hierarchical model is more restrictive, and it is based on an additional set of assumptions. Thus, if the hierarchical model fits the data, and the assumptions are not being violated, such a model is to be preferred because it is more informative than is a less restrictive model. The problem is, of course, that it is not always clear which assumptions are imposed, and how they may be tested. The ordinary first-order factor model for relations between observed and latent variables is an additive, linear and compensatory model, and a higher order model imposes the same assumptions for the relations between higher order and lower order factors. Normally, however, a factor analyst does not test these assumptions, and carrying the factor analysis into the higher order realms does not typically imply any increased concern with these problems. In future work these issues should, however, be given more attention.

The measurement issues discussed here are implications of a particular theoretical model of the structure of cognitive abilities, and if this theoretical model is not accepted, these measurement implications will also be challenged. In fact, the question whether general intelligence exists or not has been one of the most controversial issues in the history of psychological research, and it still is. The hierarchical model explicitly introduces the general factor, and the model discussed here even goes as far as to make the assumption that the general factor is equivalent with Gf. Thus, anyone who does not believe in the existence of the general factor would be hesitant to adopt a hierarchical model for measuring cognitive abilities. But all measurement models embody theoretical conceptions, so this is not a unique feature of hierarchical models. It rather seems that this is made conspicuously clear in the present case because of the controversial nature of the construct of general intelligence.

As was observed by Messick (1989) each different theory of intelligence carries a particular view of the world, which embodies different assumptions and ideological premises. Adopting a theoretical perspective thus also implies adoption of a particular view of the world. The theoretical ladenness of measurement models also has been recognized for long, and it does make for a healthy relativism when it comes to comparisons of theoretical perspectives. But the relativism should be kept within limits, and although the possibilities of empirical testing and rejection of theoretical models are limited, any science that uses empirical methods must have some belief that knowledge gained in empirical work may be theoretically informative as well. Although these processes are slow and cumbersome (cf Cronbach, 1988) there is little doubt that the results from the empirical research conducted during the 20th century have had a profound effect on current thinking about intelligence. And I expect that this process will continue during the coming century.

REFERENCE

Anderson, M. (1992). *Intelligence and development. A cognitive theory.* Oxford: Blackwell.

Binet, A. (1905). Analyse de C. E. Spearman, "The proof and measurement of association between two things" et "General intelligence objectively determined and measured." *L' Année Psychologique, 11*, 623–624.

Binet, A., & Simon, T. (1905). Méthodes nouvelles pour le diagnostic du niveau intellectuel des anormaux (New methods for diagnosing the intellectual level of abnormals). *L' Année Psychologique, 11*, 191-336.

Brody, N. (1992). *Intelligence (2nd ed.).* San Diego, California: Academic Press.

Burt, C. (1949). The structure of the mind: A review of the results of factor analysis. *British Journal of Educational Psychology, 19*, 100–111, 176–199.

Carroll, J. B. (1982). The measurement of intelligence. In R. J. Sternberg (Ed.), *Handbook of human intelligence* (pp. 29–120). New York: Cambridge University Press.

Carroll, J. B. (1993). *Human cognitive abilities.* Cambridge: Cambridge University Press.

Carroll, J. B. (1996). A three-stratum theory of intelligence: Spearman's contribution. In I. Dennis & P. Tapsfield (Eds.) *Human abilities. Their nature and measurement* (pp. 1–17). Mahwah, New Jersey: Lawrence Erlbaum Associates.

Cattell, R. B. (1963). Theory of fluid and crystallized intelligence: A critical experiment. *Journal of Educational Psychology, 54,* 1–22.

Coan, R. W. (1964). Facts, factors and artifacts: The quest for psychological meaning. *Psychological Review, 71,* 123–140.

Cronbach, L. J. (1975). Five decades of public controversy over mental testing. *American Psychologist, 30,* 1–14.

Cronbach, L. J. (1988). Five perspectives on the validity argument. In H. Wainer & H. I. Braun (Eds.) *Test validity* (pp. 3–17). Hillsdale, New Jersey: Lawrence Erlbaum Associates.

Dennis, I., & Tapsfield, P. (1996). *Human abilities. Their nature and measurement.* Mahwah, New Jersey: Lawrence Erlbaum Associates.

DuBois, P. H. (1970). *A history of psychological testing.* Boston: Allyn & Bacon.

Flynn, J. R. (1987). Massive IQ gains in 14 nations: What IQ tests really measure. *Psychological Bulletin, 101,* 171–191.

Gould, S. J. (1981). *The mismeasure of man.* New York: Norton.

Guilford, J. P. (1967). *The nature of human intelligence.* New York: McGraw-Hill.

Gulliksen, H. (1950). *Theory of mental tests.* New York: John Wiley.

Gustafsson, J.-E. (1984). A unifying model for the structure of intellectual abilities. *Intelligence, 8,* 179–203.

Gustafsson, J.-E. (1997, July 14–16). On the hierarchical structure of ability and personality. Paper presented at the Second Spearman Seminar, Plymouth, England.

Gustafsson, J.-E. (1988). Hierarchical models of individual differences in cognitive abilities. In R. J. Sternberg, *Advances in the psychology of human intelligence. Vol. 4,* (pp. 35–71). Hillsdale, New Jersey: Lawrence Erlbaum Associates, Inc.

Gustafsson, J.-E. (1998). Measuring and understanding *G*: Experimental and correlational approaches. In P. L. Ackerman, P. C. Kyllonen, & R. D. Roberts (Eds.) *Learning and individual differences. Process, trait and content determinants* (pp. 275–291). Washington, D.C.: American Psychological Association.

Gustafsson, J.-E., & Balke, G. (1993). General and specific abilities as predictors of school achievement. *Multivariate Behavioral Research, 28,* 407–434.

Gustafsson, J.-E., & Snow, R. E. (1997). Ability profiles. In R. F. Dillon, (Ed.) *Handbook on testing* (pp. 107–135). Westport, Connecticut: Greenwood Press.

Gustafsson, J.-E., & Stahl, P. A. (1997). *STREAMS User's Guide,* Version 1.7. Mölndal, Sweden: MultivariateWare.

Gustafsson, J. E., & Undheim, J. O. (1996). Individual differences in cognitive functions. In D. Berliner & R. Calfee (Eds.), *Handbook of Educational Psychology* (pp. 186–242). New York: Macmillan.

Harman, H. H. (1967). *Modern factor analysis. 2nd edition.* Chicago: The University of Chicago Press.

Holzinger, K. J. (1944). A simple method of factor analysis. *Psychometrika, 9,* 257–262.

Holzinger, K. J., & Swineford, F. (1939). A study in factor analysis: The stability of a bi-factor solution. *Supplementary Educational Monographs,* No. 48. Chicago: Department of Education, University of Chicago.

Horn, J. L., & Cattell, R. B. (1966). Refinement and test of the theory of fluid and crystallized intelligence. *Journal of Educational Psychology, 57,* 253–270.

Humphreys, L. G. (1962). The organization of human abilities. *American Psychologist, 17*, 475–483.

Humphreys, L. G. (1985). General intelligence. An integration of factor, test and simplex theory. In B. B. Wolman (Ed). *Handbook of intelligence. Theories, measurements, and applications* (pp. 201–224). New York: John Wiley & Sons.

Jöreskog, K. G. (1971). Statistical analysis of sets of congeneric tests. *Psychometrika, 36*, 109–133.

Loevinger, J. (1957). Objective tests as instruments of psychological theory. *Psychological Reports, 3*, 635–694 (Monograph Supp. 9).

Lord, F. M. (1980). *Applications of item response theory to practical testing problems.* Hillsdale, NJ: Lawrence Erlbaum Associates.

Lubinski, D., & Humphreys, L. G. (1997). Incorporating general intelligence into epidemiology and the social sciences. *Intelligence, 24*(1), 159–201.

Messick, S. (1989). Validity. In R. L. Linn (Ed.) *Educational Measurement* (3rd ed., pp. 13–103). New York: Macmillan.

Messick, S. (1992). Multiple intelligences or multilevel intelligences? Selective emphasis on distinctive properties of hierarchy: On Gardner's *Frames of Mind* and Sternberg's *Beyond IQ* in the context of theory and research on the structure of human abilities. *Psychological Inquiry, 3*(4), 365–384.

Neisser, U. (1976). General, academic, and artificial intelligence. In L. Resnick (Ed.), *The nature of intelligence*, (pp. 134–144). Hillsdale, NJ: Lawrence Erlbaum Associates.

Pedhazur, E. J., & Pedhazur Schmelkin, L. (1991). *Measurement, design, and analysis. An integrated approach.* Hillsdale, NJ: Lawrence Erlbaum Associates.

Reuterberg, S.-E., & Gustafsson, J.-E. (1992). Confirmatory factor analysis and reliability: Testing measurement model assumptions. *Educational and Psychological Measurement, 52*, 795–811.

Rosén, M. (1995). Gender differences in structure, means and variances of hierarchically ordered ability dimensions. *Learning and Instruction, 5*, 37–62.

Scarr, S. (1989). Protecting general intelligence: Constructs and consequences for interventions. In R. L. Linn (Ed.), *Intelligence. Measurement, theory and public policy*, (pp. 74–118). Urbana: University of Illinois Press.

Snow, R. E. (1974). Representative and quasi-representative designs for research on teaching. *Review of Educational Research, 44*, 265–291.

Snow, R. E., Corno, L., & Jackson III, D. (1996). Individual differences in affective and conative functions. In D. Berliner & R. Calfee (Eds.), *Handbook of Educational Psychology* (pp. 243–310), New York: Macmillan.

Spearman, C. (1904a). The proof and measurement of association between two things. *American Journal of Psychology, 15*, 72–101.

Spearman, C. (1904b). "General intelligence," objectively determined and measured. *American Journal of Psychology, 15*, 201–293.

Spearman, C. (1927. *The abilities of man.* London: MacMillan.

Terman, L. M. (1916). *The measurement of intelligence.* Boston: Houghton-Mifflin.

Thorndike, R. L. (1951). Reliability. In Lindquist, E. F. (Ed.) *Educational Measurement* (pp. 560–620). Washington, D. C.: American Council on Education.

Thorndike, R. M., & Lohman, D. F. (1990). *A century of ability testing.* Chicago: Riverside Publishing Company.

Thurstone, L. L. (1938). Primary mental abilities. *Psychometric Monographs*, No. 1.

Thurstone, L. L. (1947). *Multiple factor analysis.* Chicago: The University of Chicago Press.

Undheim, J. O. (1981). On intelligence II: A neo-Spearman model to replace Cattell's theory of fluid and crystallized intelligence. *Scandinavian Journal of Psychology, 22*, 181–187.

Undheim, J. O., & Gustafsson, J. E. (1987). The hierarchical organization of cognitive abilities: Restoring general intelligence through the use of linear structural relations (LISREL). *Multivariate Behavioral Research, 22*, 149–171.

Vernon, P. E. (1950). *The structure of human abilities.* London: Methuen.

Vernon, P. E. (1961). *The structure of human abilities. 2nd edition.* London: Methuen.

Wechsler, D. (1939). *The measurement of adult intelligence.* Baltimore: Williams & Wilkins.

Wiley, D. E. (1991). Test validity and invalidity reconsidered. In R. E. Snow & D. E. Wiley (Eds.). *Improving inquiry in social science* (pp. 75–107). Hillsdale, New Jersey: Lawrence Erlbaum Associates.

6

The Five-Factor Personality Model: How Complete and Satisfactory Is It?

John B. Carroll
University of North Carolina at Chapel Hill

OVERVIEW

This chapter concerns the five-factor personality model proposed by Costa and McCrae (1985), Digman (1990), Goldberg and Digman (1994), and others as a basis for a comprehensive view of the structure of human personality. It briefly specifies the major features of the model, outlines its history, and alludes to criticisms of it offered by such writers as Block (1995a), Boyle, Stankov, and Cattell (1995), Eysenck (1992), Pervin (1994), and Tellegen (1993). Although the author sees merit in the model as a provisional foundation for further research, he concludes that it is necessarily incomplete or otherwise unsatisfactory in several ways: (a) Partly by virtue of previously unrecognized technical deficiencies in its research basis, it is essentially a model limited to second-stratum factors and thus far does not adequately address either lower order dimensions or possible third-stratum factors; (b) it is already evident that the model does not cover several major second- or higher order dimensions that can be found to exist; and (c) the model fails to come to grips with the motives, attitudes, and beliefs that may underlie personality dimensions defined by typical questionnaire items. These points are illustrated through reanalysis of a correlation matrix originally analyzed and interpreted by Digman and Inouye (1986). The reanalysis reveals, in addition to the "domain" factors proposed in the standard five-factor model, five dimensions at the first-order "facet" level, and two third-order "superfactors" that account for a large proportion of the covariance among the standard five factors, or certainly a large proportion of the covariance among the items on which the study was based.

THE BACKGROUND

A reader may well wonder how I came to explore the field of personality research, given that in recent years I have devoted most of my efforts to research on the structure of cognitive abilities. Several years ago I was asked to review for *Contemporary Psychology* a large volume, *International Handbook of Personality and Intelligence*, edited by Saklofske and Zeidner (1995). With this volume, Saklofske and Zeidner hoped to promote the integration of personality and intelligence as fields of research. In my review (Carroll, 1997), I noted that the contributors of essays in the volume often had difficulty in bringing the fields together, neglecting to point out similarities and differences between them or ways in which they might cooperate. Indeed, some of the contributors treated the fields as if they were almost completely separate. Few if any of them concerned themselves with comparing them, as they might have done, for example, with respect to the treatment of cognitive ability. In the field of intelligence per se, the development of multilevel or hierarchical structures has been a prevalent strategy. In the field of personality, intellect has often been treated as one of the factors in a so-called Big Five model favored by many researchers. In any case, through reading and studying Saklofske and Zeidner's edited book with the hope of writing a competent review, I became aware of a major controversy about the place of the Big Five model in personality research.

This controversy has been brought to a head in various ways. First, there has been a long series of publications promoting the Big Five model by Costa and McCrae (1988, 1992a, 1995; McCrae & Costa, 1987), who appear to be among its major proponents. They (Costa & McCrae, 1985, 1989, 1992b) have published a personality questionnaire (with a revision, and a shortened form) based on the five-factor model (FFM), the *NEO Personality Inventory*. This questionnaire has been widely used in clinical practice and research. A book published by the American Psychological Association (Costa & Widiger, 1994) seeks to show how the FFM applies to the classification and treatment of personality disorders and how it can be helpful as a supplement to the *Diagnostic and Statistical Manual of Mental Disorders (DSM-III)*(American Psychiatric Association, 1980). Several information-packed reviews in the *Annual Review of Psychology* (Digman, 1990; Wiggins & Pincus, 1992; Ozer & Reise, 1994) have given attention to the model as a highly favored basis for the analysis of personality; only the authors of the most recent of these reviews, Butcher and Rouse (1996), are strongly critical, presenting various arguments and empirical evidence against the five-factor model. According to them, "[m]any recognize the Five-Factor Model as too superficial to help much in clinical assessment, which requires more refined and broadened personality and symptom foci than are provided through the narrow lens of only five factors" (p. 103). Only in later phases of my literature review did I come across the most useful references I have found: edited volumes by Strack and Lorr (1994) and by Wiggins (1996), the former devoted to differentiating normal and abnormal personalities by means of various trait models, including the Big Five, and the latter expressly concerned with defending the five-factor model against its critics. My only complaint about the book edited by Wiggins is that the authors neglect to say enough about possible criticisms of the FFM. Finally, an impressive treatise on personality (Hogan, Johnson, & Briggs, 1997) devoted five of its 36 chapters to the Big Five model and its claimed dimensions, and McCrae and Costa (1997b) suggested that the five-factor personality trait structure is a human universal because it has been found to occur in a number of different languages, Indo-European and others. They even cite the linguist Edward Sapir (1921) as arguing that reality is structured by the language one speaks, just missing citing my early mentor Benjamin Lee Whorf and the "Whorfian hypothesis" (Carroll, 1956).

In preparing my review of the Saklofske and Zeidner volume, I noted that Boyle et al., (1995) took a strong position against the FFM, in stating that "both Cattell and Eysenck are in complete agreement that studies of the so-called big five are scientifically unacceptable" (p. 431). The authors of several other chapters in this book, however, devoted considerable space to the FFM, without expressing any major reservations about it. In fact, these authors (especially Bouchard, 1995; Lohman & Rocklin, 1995; Most & Zeidner, 1995) seemed to feel that the FFM constitutes a truly valuable contribution to research in personality structure.

I was sufficiently intrigued by this controversy to decide to study the literature about the FFM (and other models) for myself, in order to form an independent opinion about it. In my review (Carroll, 1997) of the Saklofske and Zeidner book I complained that it failed to contain material that would serve to resolve the controversy. When I received an invitation from Educational Testing Service to participate in a conference honoring Samuel Messick, the topic seemed tailor-made to discuss at that conference, considering Messick's interest in the study of personality. I felt that my contribution might be especially useful if I could develop my views from the standpoint of work I have done in the cognitive ability domain.

I quickly found that the literature on the structure of personality, or more particularly, the FFM, has burgeoned tremendously since Digman's (1990) review. I was easily able to identify several dozen articles about it, or using it, published in the last 3 or 4 years; through consulting these articles and their reference lists, I have amassed and studied more than 200 relevant references.

I also found, going back to the literature on personality structure from around 1945, that this literature is much more difficult to deal with than the literature from a comparable period on the structure of cognitive abilities. Whereas in my work in the cognitive ability realm (Carroll, 1993) I had been able to find numerous instances where original correlation matrices had been published, there were hardly any instances of this in the personality field, perhaps partly because the matrices often concerned many more variables than were usually dealt with in the cognitive ability domain. Published articles rarely mentioned anything about the availability of original data or correlation matrices, and even when results were published in matrix form, it was not always possible to tell, for example, whether a matrix was based on orthogonal or on oblique rotation. Even when a matrix of correlations among factors was published, it was difficult or impossible to use this in doing further rotations, performing higher order analyses, or conducting confirmatory factor-analyses, because of the unavailability of the original correlation matrices. Consequently, I have been able to do only limited reanalysis of datasets in the personality field.

Like many published articles in the cognitive ability domain, research studies in the personality domain often reported only the higher loadings, that is, those with an absolute value greater than about .30 (e.g., Gorsuch & Cattell, 1967). Failure to report the other loadings made it impossible to use the corresponding matrices in any reanalyses, or even to evaluate the results adequately. One would hope that eventually the practice of reporting only higher loadings would be abandoned. It takes no more space to report complete results; higher loadings can be emphasized by printing them in boldface.

One other problem surfaced. The very language in which the methodology was described was subtly different from that in the cognitive ability field. Authors frequently wrote about "higher order factors" or even "superfactors" when it was obvious from other evidence that they were not describing higher order factors based on correlations among lower order factors or variables. They were referring merely to factors based on variables at a higher level of aggregation than the original item or raw score data. Furthermore, I could not find a single instance in which data were treated with Schmid and Leiman's (1957) procedure for orthogonalizing higher order matrices—a procedure that I had frequently employed in dealing with cognitive ability data. However, with the help of Lewis Goldberg (personal communication, October 1997) I was able to identify at least one study in the personality domain that used the Schmid-Leiman procedure to demonstrate hierarchical properties of measures of anxiety (Zinbarg & Barlow, 1996).

THE BIG-FIVE, OR FIVE FACTOR MODEL (FFM)

Thus far I have not described the so-called "big five" or "five-factor" model, as I need to do for the benefit of those readers who may not have encountered it. In essence, the FFM is a statement of what are regarded by its proponents as five major independent and "robust" dimensions of personality that can be identified, by factor analysis or otherwise, in a number of instruments for measuring personality, with the further implication that these five factors encompass the overwhelming majority of the variance needed to describe individual differences in personality. Digman (1990, p. 424) gave names for these factors that were intended to indicate their meanings in a concise manner; these names, with single-letter abbreviations for them, are as follows:

I:	Extraversion/introversion, or Surgency ...	E
II:	Friendliness/hostility, or Agreeableness .	A
III:	Conscientiousness, or Will	C
IV:	Neuroticism/Emotional Stability (or Emotional Stability)	N
V.	Intellect (or Openness)	O

Several students have suggested the mnemonics OCEAN and CANOE for this set of five factors, named as shown above, allowing one to decide whether the personality domain can be regarded as an OCEAN or just a CANOE! The basic question, however, is whether five factors are sufficient, for practical purposes, to describe personality, and to provide guides for diagnosis and treatment of personality disorders.

Digman's (1990) review was entitled *Personality Structure: Emergence of the Five-Factor Model.* As one who favored (or had been converted to favoring) the FFM, he pointed out that the model was exemplified in a number of early studies, but that it tended to be ignored by reviewers and textbook writers, perhaps because they became diverted by Cattell's (1957) 16-factor model and Eysenck's (1970) 2- or 3-factor model. Thus, the model could be said to have recently "emerged" in studies of the personality domain because, from about 1988, a number of investigators came to accept and support the idea that a FFM is a useful conceptual framework for the study of personality.

Some writers (e.g., Digman, 1996, p. 16fn) have urged that a distinction be made between the "Big Five" model based on word-meanings and the "Five Factor Model" espoused by Costa and McCrae (1992b) for self-reports of personality trait ratings. Although this distinction may be useful, it has made little difference for factor-analytic methodology in personality research, and may be disregarded for the present purposes.

In his Table 1 of the review article mentioned earlier (Digman, 1990, p. 423), Digman sought to show how these factors appeared in structures found by various investigators from the time of Fiske (1949). Inspection of the tables underlying each of the studies cited by Digman indicates that at least some of these studies could be regarded as having found five factors, and that these same five factors recurred across the studies. The idea of "recurrent factors" was originated by Fiske (1949), but it was emphasized in the work of Tupes and Christal (1961), who reanalyzed data from four Air Force samples, two samples from Cattell (1947, 1948), and two studies from Fiske (1949). Various numbers of factors (up to eight) were found in these samples, but for comparison purposes, Tupes and Christal reported loadings on only "five fairly strong rotated" factors (p. 232 in the 1992 reprinting of the article) that emerged and that were "recurrent" across samples. Among other studies mentioned by Digman, as far as can be ascertained from published materials, there were clearly just five factors found in the studies by Norman (1963), Borgatta (1964), Hogan (1986), Costa and McCrae (1985), and Lorr (1986). But some of the other studies found fewer than five factors (Eysenck, 1970; Buss & Plomin, 1984; Tellegen, 1985), whereas others found more than five factors in one or more samples (Cattell, 1957; Guilford, 1975; Peabody & Goldberg, 1989). Thus, Digman might be accused of a certain amount of disingenuousness in claiming that all the cited studies supported a five-factor model. Certainly it was incorrect to assume that the work of Cattell and Eysenck supported a five-factor model, particularly because both Cattell (Boyle et al., 1995) and Eysenck (1991, 1992) have expressed disagreement with it (see also Cattell & Krug, 1986; Krug, 1994). It could more properly be claimed that all the cited studies showed fit with a five-factor model if occasional failures to match all five factors are ignored. These failures could usually be attributed to differences among studies in the sampling of variables.

More importantly, one must raise the question of how well the various factors, and the lower order variables that support them, can be matched across studies and samples. For the most part, the names assigned to the five factors by Digman (1990) are similar to those assigned by Tupes and Christal (1961): (a) Surgency, (b) Agreeableness, (c) Dependability, (d) Emotional Stability, and (e) Culture. But even Digman's Table 1 shows substantial variation across studies in the names assigned to factors. For the first factor, for example, it might be difficult to conclude that factors named *social adaptability, extraversion, surgency, assertiveness, power, activity, positive emotionality,* and *interpersonal involvement* are all the same basic factor.

There is great variation across factors in different studies in the lower order variables that are claimed to define the factors, but I cannot undertake here any detailed examination of this variation. My impression is that small variations in the phrasing of these lower order variables can make for considerable variation in factor interpretations.

There has been controversy about the interpretation of factors other than Extraversion, particularly the factor O, variously interpreted as *intellect, culture,* and *openness,* that is, *openness to experience.* In a chapter devoted to this factor, McCrae and Costa (1997a) admitted that "[t]he factor of Openness appears to be unusually difficult to grasp" (p. 826). They considered alternative interpretations: openness as *culture* and openness as *cognitive ability,* but rejected each of these. They favored a concept of openness as a psychic structure, as "a matter of inner experience, a mental phenomenon related to the scope of awareness or the depth and intensity of consciousness" (p. 835), also as "involving motivation, needs for variety, cognition, sentience, and understanding" (p. 839). They remarked that in interacting with psychologists and psychiatrists, people who are "imaginative, sensitive, empathic, flexible, inquisitive, and tolerant will respond quite differently from those who are practical, down-to-earth, rigid, and dogmatic" (p. 842). If this refined concept of *openness* is to be accepted, instruments for measuring it may need to be improved.

As one who has worked extensively in the cognitive ability domain, I feel that considerable confusion is introduced by characterizing the Openness factor in terms of intellect. To be sure, intellectual ability is an aspect of personality (in the broad sense of the term), but psychometrically, intelligence (or cognitive ability) is so different from personality (narrowly defined) that intelligence and personality can be regarded as the subject matters of two very different fields of individual-differences psychology. Measurements of cognitive ability are virtually always based on actual performance of tasks that differ not only in content but also in the amount of challenge they present, that is, in their "difficulty level." Often there is a chance success feature in cognitive ability tests, completely absent in personality inventories.

Variations occur in the interpretations of other components of the FFM. It is entirely possible that because of ambiguity in meaning, one or more of the factors could be found to require splitting into separate, new factors. This is perhaps more likely to occur if analyses are based on confirmatory methods, because traditional exploratory methods of factor analysis may not possess the required degree of power.

Before we can fully appraise the FFM, it may be useful to review criticisms that have already appeared in the literature.

CRITIQUES OF THE FFM

A major trend in the early investigations of personality was the attempt to classify and summarize, using factor analysis and other techniques, the thousands of personality traits that had been identified by Allport and Odbert (1936) in their studies of dictionaries of the English language. Thus, Cattell (1943, 1947, 1957), Fiske (1949), and Tupes and Christal (1961) based their studies on selected groups of Allport and Odbert traits. Tellegen (1993), however, pointed out that all these early investigators followed Allport and Odbert's counsel to rule out evaluative terms like *excellent*, *important*, and *evil*, thus excluding possibly hundreds or thousands of terms from the lexicon of personality. In a factor analysis of a 161-item measure that included some of these evaluative terms (including measures of what Tellegen, 1993, called *Positive Valence* and *Negative Valence*), seven factors were identified by Waller and Zavala (1993). From this and other research, Tellegen developed what he calls the Big Seven model of personality, essentially the Big Five plus the two new factors. Other investigators reporting the finding of these same seven factors are Benet and Waller (1995).

A slightly different set of seven factors emerged from a study by Jackson, Ashton, and Tomes (1996), including a Desirability factor that may have some similarity to Tellegen's Positive Valence. These authors argue, however, that their results support a six-factor model of personality. They do not mention Tellegen's model, but the six-factor model of personality proposed by these authors should be considered, along with Tellegen's model, in the attempt to identify a model that can be agreed on.

A still further seven-factor model, claimed to be suitable for differentiating normal and deviant personalities, has been proposed by Cloninger and Svrakic (1994).

Thus, presently available evidence suggests that the domain of personality traits needs at least seven second-stratum factors, and possibly more, to account for it. Indeed, Comrey (1980) provided for the measurement of eight hypothesized factors in a personality inventory that he constructed, and Krug (1994) has continued to insist that 16 factors are measured by Cattell's 16PF inventory (Cattell, Eber, & Tatsuoka, 1970; Cattell & Krug, 1986). However, some writers have claimed that this factor structure is not completely replicable. Noller, Law, and Comrey (1987) found only five factors in traits assembled from Comrey's inventory, the Cattell 16PF Inventory, and the Eysenck Personality Inventory. It should be remembered, however, that all these inventories started from a restricted set of Allport and Odbert's (1936) lexicon of personality terms, and thus it may not be surprising that only five factors emerged.

The FFM still retains an extraordinary amount of resilience to alternative suggestions. In one of the latest writings on personality structure that I can find (Wiggins & Trapnell, 1997), it is stated that "Hogan's competency perspective led him to formulate an alternative six-factor interpretation of the Big Five . . ." (p. 751), with six factors in which the Extraversion factor was split into two, *Sociability* and *Ambition*. Wiggins and Trapnell made no mention of Tellegen's seven-factor model. Indeed, Tellegen's model is nowhere mentioned in the large volume (Hogan, Johnson, & Briggs, 1997) in which Wiggins and Trapnell's chapter appeared. One can easily gain the impression, probably incorrect, that personality researchers who favor the FFM form a small but influential clique that does not communicate well with those who support expanded models.

The Tellegen model is treated, however, in a recent publication by Ackerman and Heggestad (1997); in fact, in that publication the Tellegen model is the basis of a proposed framework for depicting personality constructs and their relations. Ackerman and Heggestad regard Tellegen's framework as "essentially hierarchical" (p. 224), although they offer no evidence for hierarchical structure in personality traits similar to the hierarchical structures found in the ability domain.

In what he called "a critical analysis of current trait theory," Pervin (1994) raised many questions about the Big Five and other trait-based theories. He was impressed by claims that personality traits are influenced by genetics and that they are stable over time. He was particularly critical of claims for agreement on a "magic number five, plus or minus two" (p. 105). According to him, "despite heroic efforts to map traits from different schemes onto one another and suggestions that there is substantial agreement in this regard, questions remain concerning the comparability of factors across instruments and data sources" (pp. 105–106). Furthermore, "rather than being a serviceable system, the trait model is . . . fundamentally flawed in terms of its ability to come to grips with the issues of personality dynamics and personality pattern and organization" (p. 111).

Block (1995a) offered a strongly negative, "contrarian" view of what he called "the five-factor *approach* [FFA; my emphasis]" because he doesn't believe that it merits the term *model*. His review was published in the *Psychological Bulletin* along with replies by advocates of the FFM (Costa & McCrae, 1995; Goldberg & Saucier, 1995) as well as a rejoinder in which Block (1995b) continued to disparage the model. Block had misgivings about factor-analytic studies of personality. For one thing, he claimed that the algorithmic methods of factor analysis may not be conducive to the finding of personality structure: . . . It is the personality structure of an individual that, energized by motivations, dynamically organizes perceptions, cognitions, and behaviors so as to achieve certain "system" goals. No functioning psychological "system," with its rules and bounds, is designated or implied by the "Big Five" formulation; it does not offer a sense of what goes on within the structured, motivation-processing, system-maintaining individual.

> . . . the frequent presence and the powerful effects of "prestructuring" are often not sufficiently recognized by those using the method of exploratory factor analysis. ... [i]nfluential demonstrations of the sufficiency of the FFA may have been unduly influenced by prior prestructuring of the personality variables used in these analyses. If so, then the "recurrence" and "robustness" over diverse samples of factor structure may be attributable more to the sameness of the variable sets used than to the intrinsic structure of the personality-descriptive domain. (Block, 1995a, pp. 188–189)

Block further worried about often-cited problems with factor analysis— deciding on the proper number of factors, factor rotations, interpreting factors, the effects of merging samples from different populations, the selection of factorial models, and so forth. Actually, I believe that many of these problems (except that of assessing the number of factors; see the following) have been reasonably well resolved in current factor-analytic methodology. In my opinion, Block's mistrust of factor analysis goes·too far. Already several research studies (e.g., Saucier & Goldberg, 1996) have strongly suggested that biases resulting from what Block called *prestructuring* have not occurred. It is possible, however, that many current investigators in the personality domain may be unaware of technical problems with their analyses. Block correctly noted the problem that the Big Five dimensions may have been limited by the samples of adjective variables used—as Tellegen (1993) also suspected. As Block wrote:

> An infinite number of sets of descriptive variables can be formulated, each being preferred by its progenitor and contestable otherwise. What is needed is a basis for choosing among these alternative sets. Efforts to study or conceptualize the dynamics underlying intraindividual functioning might well move the study of personality toward such a basis. (p. 210)

These sound like good ideas, but in the minds of some of his critics (Goldberg & Saucier, 1995), Block failed to suggest how a reasonable basis for choosing appropriate sets of variables might be established.

SO WHAT DO WE DO ABOUT THE BIG FIVE?

I have a number of suggestions about personality research, looking at it from the standpoint of my experience with research in the cognitive ability realm.

First, I believe that there are lessons to be learned from that research, where the most successful and informative studies have come from efforts to find new factors and to determine the structure of new domains in relation to domains already established. This means that in the personality field, more attention needs to be paid to studying the factors already established—be they five, six, seven, or whatever—with the object of (a) determining whether any of the factors need to be more finely divided, and (b) determining what aspects of personality are poorly covered by those factors. This would presumably lead to the generation of lists of variables in the personality domain that hold promise of revealing new factors or dimensions of personality. Research should be directed not at confirming that personality is describable in terms of a given number of dimensions—such as five—but toward charting further dimensions until it becomes apparent that all the necessary dimensions are in hand. Do the Big Five factors really provide for all the varieties of personality described in chapters of a volume edited by London and Exner (1978)? That can be doubted—or at least investigated. There are already examples of studies that suggest that some of the factors need to be further divided. One of these is that of Cartwright and Peckar (1993), who propose a new "superfactor," *Purposefulness*, as a supplement or complement to factor C (*Conscientiousness*). I am also impresssed by Lykken's (1995) detailed studies of what he calls *antisocial personalities*. Some of the subtle ways in which various categories of antisocial personality differ from one another might constitute either new dimensions of personality that would supplement the Big Five, or new facets of selected domains.

Second, it appears that investigators in the personality realm have in general failed to utilize statistical methods that will properly handle the hierarchical nature of personality structure. Some investigators do not even seem to recognize this hierarchicality or are at least confused about the levels of the hierarchy at which they work. Fortunately, recent writings—for example, a tutorial by Goldberg and Digman (1994)—set forth the essentials of a hierarchical model in discussing "vertical" and "horizontal" perspectives on personality trait structure. Here (Figure 6.1) I reproduce a figure from Goldberg and Digman's tutorial that illustrates a hierarchical model for one of the standard five factors, including a facet level between the item level and the five-factor level. I have added to the figure a third-order level to indicate possible higher order factors suggested in recent work by Digman (1997), or reported in this chapter (see the following).

Goldberg and Digman did not, however, mention the procedure developed by Schmid and Leiman (1957) some years ago for dealing with hierarchical data in exploratory factor analysis. This procedure has been found highly useful in the cognitive ability realm, because it can compute loadings of variables on factors at different levels of the hierarchy beyond the lowest. As can be seen from Figure 6.1, it may be assumed that there are characteristically at least four levels in the personality measurement hierarchy. Three of these are what Goldberg and Digman (1994) and Costa and McCrae (1992b) call (a) the item level, (b) the facet level, and (c) the domain level. At the facet level, one can find first-order factors; at the domain level, one finds second-order factors. If some of the domains are intercorrelated to a significant degree, one may also find third-order factors, which could be called *superfactors*.

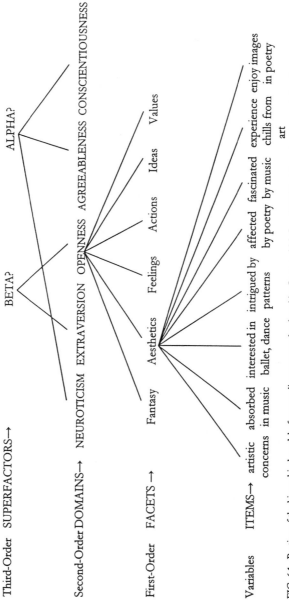

FIG. 6.1. Portion of the hierarchical model of personality structure developed by Costa and McCrae (1992b). Adapted, with permission, from Goldberg and Digman's (1994, p. 232) Figure 11.6.

Costa and McCrae (1992b) sought to measure the facet level in their *Revised NEO Personality Inventory*, but they established facet levels by item-analysis techniques rather than by more powerful factor-analytic procedures. They did, however, use factor analysis to establish factors at the domain level.

Essentially, the expanded FFM presents a set of five second-order factors—or perhaps one might call them second-*stratum* factors, analogous to the second-stratum factors in the cognitive ability domain—in addition to a series of first-order factors, facets, and possibly also one or more third-order superfactors.

The popularity of the FFM has prompted me to think that my work with cognitive abilities might have been more exciting to the psychometric community if I had dubbed the second-stratum factors in the cognitive domain the "Big Eight" --2F, 2C, 2Y, 2V, 2U, 2R, 2S, and 2T (Carroll, 1993, p. 626). But because I am uncertain about how many second-stratum factors actually exist in the cognitive domain, I do not like to commit myself to some definite number prematurely. Similarly, if I were working in the personality domain, I would not like to tie myself down to the idea that it contains only five second-order factors.

From the hierarchical perspective, it may be said that disagreements between Cattell (1957) and Eysenck (1970) in their theories of personality structure might be resolved by pointing out that Cattell was primarily concerned with first-stratum factors—what are elsewhere called facets—whereas Eysenck was concerned mainly with second-stratum or even third-stratum factors.

Treatment of hierarchical data is not limited to exploratory factor analysis. It can also be handled in confirmatory factor analysis by postulating and testing factor patterns that specify different levels of a hierarchy. This procedure has been pioneered in the ability realm by Gustafsson (1984, 1988). It can easily be applied in the personality realm.

Since delivering my address at the September 1997 ETS conference, I have had an opportunity to consider further the nature of data typically found in the personality realm and to formulate factor-analytic procedures suitable for analyzing such data. I have been able to test my procedures by applying them to a dataset supplied to me by Digman, previously analyzed and reported on in an article published by Digman and Inouye (1986; see also Digman, 1997).

As noted previously, typical data in the personality research realm can be hierarchically structured, with facets at the first order and domains at the second order (Goldberg & Digman, 1994). In investigating simulated data, I have discovered that when factor loadings of facets on domains are generally higher than factor loadings of variables on facets, as they can be in the personality realm, standard methods of estimating the number of factors that are worthwhile to analyze may give incorrect results. Specifically, the number of principal component roots that are greater than one may under these conditions give an estimate, not of the number of facets (first-order factors) in a set of data, but of the number of *domains* (second-order factors) in the data. Similarly, the Montanelli and Humphreys (1976) parallel analysis criterion may estimate the number of domains, not the number of facets, in a dataset. These facts imply that at least some published factor analyses of personality data may have been performed incorrectly and incompletely, in the sense that they have found loadings for domains, but not for facets. It may be the case that a given set of data has five "big factors" (second-order factors masquerading as first-order factors) but this does not inform one about facets (as true first-order factors).

To perform correct factor analyses in the personality realm, it is necessary first to estimate the number of facets (first-order factors) in the dataset. My results suggest that the number of facets can best be estimated by determining the maximum number of principal factors that properly and easily (with a relatively small number of iterations) converge to a strict epsilon criterion of .0005 for differences between successive communality estimates.

Further computations involve exploratory factor-analytic procedures required to perform a Schmid-Leiman orthogonalization of factor matrices produced at two or more levels of a hierarchy. Given results of this procedure, confirmatory factor analyses using LISREL or other appropriate computer programs are done to refine the total structure and to establish the statistical significance of the structure and its elements.

Specifying details of these procedures is beyond the scope of this chapter. However, the procedures may be illustrated as applied to the Digman and Inouye (1986) correlation matrix that was supplied by Digman.

REANALYSIS OF THE DIGMAN AND INOUYE (1986) DATASET

The data consisted of the matrix of Pearsonian correlations among 43 personality trait ratings (on 9-point scales) made by teachers on 499 6th-grade children in Hawaii. According to Digman and Inouye (1986, p. 118), the resulting distributions of ratings "may be described as quasi normal, generally symmetric, and with very comparable means and standard deviations."

Conventional procedures in the exploratory factor analysis of this matrix would have yielded five or possibly six factors, in that there were five principal component roots greater than unity, and the Montanelli and Humphreys (1976) parallel analysis procedure for principal factoring specified that there were six factors worth analyzing. However, on the basis of simulation studies mentioned earlier, it was conjectured that these estimates were for the number of second-order factors, not for the number of first-order factors. The number of first-order factors was estimated provisionally by performing exploratory factoring for 3 to 15 factors, choosing the number of useful factors as the highest number that provided convergence for estimated communalities without an excessive number of iterations. Convergence was defined as occurring if the maximum difference between successively estimated communalities was less than .0005. To illustrate with the Digman and Inouye dataset, for 7 to 12 factors, convergence occurred with 9, 13, 10, 9, 14, and 49 iterations, respectively. For 13, 14, and 15 factors, convergence occurred with 165, 14, and 115 iterations, respectively. A conservative estimate of the number of useful factors would have been 11 or 12, but initially the estimate, 14, was more liberal.

Using Jöreskog and Sörbom's (1989) LISREL 7 program, I estimated the number of *correlated* factors required to fit the underlying correlation matrix; thus, in the model parameter line, PH=ST was specified. Initially, a pattern of loadings on 14 factors was proposed, based on the pattern of high loadings in the corresponding Varimax-rotated matrix computed by exploratory procedures. This and some of the succeeding runs failed, presumably because it was impossible to fit the data when too many factors were specified. In successive LISREL runs, guided by the modification indexes provided by the program, it became apparent that no more than 10 first-order factors (facets) could be supported. With 10 factors, the value of chi-square with 796 degrees of freedom was 1774; Goodness of Fit Index (GFI) and Adjusted Goodness of Fit Index (AGFI) were .848 and .819 respectively; and the Root Mean Square Residual (RMSR) was .047, indicating relatively small differences between the correlations reproduced by the fitted matrix and the actual correlation matrix.

The resulting first-order factor matrix, with its second-order matrix of correlations among the 10 first-order factors, was used in the beginning stages of the computations for a Schmid and Leiman (1957) transformation whereby matrices at three factor levels were the input for an orthogonalized factor matrix giving loadings for all variables on the three levels of factors. The second-order correlation matrix was factored to produce a second-order factor matrix for five factors, which turned out to be the five factors of the standard five-factor model. Next, the correlations among these five factors were factored, producing a third-order factor matrix with two uncorrelated third-order factors. When the first-order, second-order, and third-order factor matrices were submitted to a program for the Schmid-Leiman procedure, there emerged an orthogonal matrix showing loadings for each of the 43 variables on each of 17 factors (2 superfactors, 5 domain factors, and 10 facets).

Nevertheless, the Schmid-Leiman matrix was regarded as only provisional because one could not be certain that all of its 17 factors were statistically significant. Moreover, a Schmid-Leiman transformation is subject to the limitation that its higher order factors are mathematically dependent on the lower order factors.

For this reason, a further series of computations was undertaken, again using the LISREL 7 program, to arrive at a factor matrix giving zero or nonzero loadings (coefficients) for all 43 variables on a certain number of mathematically independent factors. This involved computing LISREL estimates that best fitted patterns of proposed loadings that were supplied to the program under the condition that the resulting factors would be independent. (In the program, this required specifying PH=ID in the model parameter (MO) line.) Initially, the pattern supplied to the program consisted of a "1" for each loading in the Schmid-Leiman output that appeared to be significantly different from zero, and "0" (zero) otherwise. In subsequent runs, the choice of postulated pattern entries was based mainly on the "Modification Indices" supplied by the program in the immediately previous run. If difficulty was experienced in the estimation of the LISREL coefficients for a given factor, that factor was dropped unless there were good reasons to try a different pattern for the factor. This procedure is essentially what Jöreskog and Sörbom (1989, p. 251) term *specification search*, involving elimination of parameters with small *t*-values and addition of parameters with large modification indices. MacCallum (1986) found that specification searches should be viewed with caution because under some conditions (e.g., when N is not large), they are likely to produce an incorrect model. However, MacCallum's results were not for measurement model investigations such as the present one, and the sample used here ($N = 496$) was relatively large. Furthermore, in the final stage of the present analysis, the LISREL model was tested against a correlation matrix for each of two virtually random independent samples (i.e., the odd- and the even-numbered cases). Any nonzero parameter found to be nonsignificant in either of these two samples was dropped and replaced by a zero. The resulting factor matrix model, with 12 uncorrelated factors, is shown in Table 6.1. These factors, and their labels, are arranged to show their provenance in the Schmid-Leiman matrix that was used to start the computations. There were two superfactors, labeled SF1 and SF2; 5 domain factors, labeled +O, -N, +C, -E, and +A that were interpreted as identical or similar to the factors in the so-called five-factor model, and five facets, labeled f3, f4, f7, f8, and f12, concerned with highly specific varieties of behavior. It is interesting to note that the two superfactors accounted for by far the largest amounts of variance in the data, certainly more than the variance accounted for by the "standard" five factors. For this matrix, the fit to the data matrix was indicated by the following statistics: Chi-square with 759 degrees of freedom was 1370; GFI = .887; AGFI = .860; RMSR = .084.

The factor matrix shown in Table 6.1 is not subject to the restriction whereby higher order factors are dependent on lower order factors, because the LISREL procedure chosen insures that all factors are completely independent.

Interpretations of the Factors. The factor matrix shown in Table 6.1 indicates how much each of the 43 variables measures each of the 12 factors that were found to be significantly present in the data. That is, each row of the table specifies the "loading" of the particular variable on each of the 12 factors listed. The loadings, whether they are zero or nonzero, can be thought of as the estimated weights of the factors in producing the scores or ratings on a particular variable. Most variables are shown to measure several factors. For example, variable 8 ("knowledgeable") has nonzero loadings on three factors: .705 on the superfactor SF1, .524 on the domain factor O ("Openness"), and .261 on facet f3. The problem is to arrive at a reasonable interpretation of the meaning of each factor. Typically, this is done by comparing variables having high loadings on a factor with variables having low or zero loadings on the factor, seeking to induce some general rule or characteristic, variations in which would appear to explain the contrasts in loadings. It should be noted that some variables were reflected in the process of factoring; the names of these variables have negative signs prefixed to them. A negative sign thus means "opposite of"; for example, variable -13 (-lethargic) is taken to mean "the opposite of lethargic" or "active."

It may be useful to consider first the domain factors +O (factor 2), -N (factor 5), +C (factor 6), -E (factor 10), and +A (factor 11) and the facets associated with them. The symbols for these factors are found in the row, near the top of the table, labeled "Symbol for Factor." The sign of the factor shows how it is oriented. Factor +O is oriented positively in the sense that high scores on the factor indicate high degrees of "openness," whereas Factor -N is oriented negatively: high scores on the factor indicate *low* degrees of "neuroticism." In most cases, the variables loaded on a domain factor are listed in Table 6.1 in the order of the algebraic magnitudes of their loadings on it. Loadings greater than $|.30|$ are printed in **boldface**.

Factor +O is interpreted as "openness to experience"—the interpretation favored by a number of personality researchers (e.g., McCrae & Costa, 1997a). Some of the variables highly loaded on +O also have loadings on facet f3, "Knowledge," or on facet f4, "Creativity." For one of the variables loaded on facet f3, "sensible," the loading is significant and negative, though relatively small. It is hard to find an explanation for this result, which seems to indicate that persons rated as knowledgeable and "verbal" (with a large vocabulary), tend to be rated as less "sensible" than otherwise. All variables loaded highly on +O also have high loadings on the superfactor SF1, to be discussed below.

Factor -N is interpreted as "Not neurotic"; the loadings are relatively small. Associated with this factor is facet f12, possibly indicating lack of anxiety, in the sense that high scores on facet f12 indicate lack of fearfulness, not being "concerned," and not being nervous. Some of the variables with high loadings on -N (-12, "not rigid," and +9, "adaptable") have high loadings on SF1; others -43, "not restless", and -19, "not outspoken", have high loadings on SF2, discussed below.

Factor +C is the factor often interpreted as indicating Conscientiousness, but for these data it seems that this interpretation is not as appropriate as some other interpretation might be, because variable +2, "conscientious" has a relatively low loading on it. One may suggest a more general term, such as "Thoughtfulness." Note two facets associated with this factor: facet f7, which may be interpreted as either "neatness" or "non-eccentricity," and facet f8, possibly interpretable as "plodding."

TABLE 6.1
Confirmatory Reanalysis of the Digman and Inouye (1986) Dataset:
Loadings of 43 Variables on 12 Uncorrelated Factors (Decimals Omitted)

Order of Factors:	3	2	1	1	2	2	1	1	3	2	2	1	
Symbol for Factor:	SF1	+O	f3	f4	-N	+C	f7	f8	SF2	-E	+A	f12	
Hierarchical Factor No.:	1	2	3	4	5	6	7	8	9	10	11	12	h²
Var. No. Name													
+24 socially confident	**82**												73
+39 esthetic	**52**								-24				37
+8 knowledgeable	**70**	**52**	26	**32**									84
+5 perceptive	**75**	**49**											81
+7 verbal (large vocab.)	**73**	**42**	27										78
+38 original	**72**	**33**		**30**					-20				77
+36 imaginative	**68**	**32**		**63**					-20				99
+6 sensible	**72**	**31**	-27						19				72
+37 curious	**68**	29							-28		19		65
+21 planful	**66**	17				20		**30**	**34**				71
-13 lethargic	**66**	13					14		-27				54
-28 concerned	32	-16							28			**46**	42
-10 fearful	35				**45**							**33**	44
+9 adaptable	**76**	18			25								67
-12 rigid	**62**				23				17				48
-40 nervous	19				20				**44**			17	30
-19 outspoken	**-50**				-05				**76**				82
-43 restless	11				-12				**81**	12			69
+32 careful	29					**42**	27		**50**				58
-35 careless	**39**					**35**			**59**				62

													h²
+33 neat	30								25				39
-23 irresponsible	49							18	44				56
+22 persevering	54							39	43				71
-20 fickle	36							18	60			16	55
-42 impulsive									85				72
-41 fidgets	17								79		-13		67
-14 fluent (verbally)	-31								65			17	54
-25 gregarious	-29								54	60			74
-15 energetic	-45								53	28			56
-27 eccentric							47		36	-25			42
-26 seclusive	42								-31	-54			57
-31 touchy	17				27	14			54		50	-26	61
+1 considerate of others	17	-13									49	24	71
-30 jealous									58		46		70
-4 spiteful									66		42		77
-3 rude					29		16		77	-12	39		80
+11 happy	42										35	-30	43
+34 mannerly	45								56		31		57
+2 conscientious	42					21			65		26	31	60
-29 complaining									43		24		57
+17 submissive	-56								53		23		65
-18 assertive	-47								73		22		81
+16 self-minimizing	-32								76		17		70
Sum of Squares (X100):	965	119	23	59	54	72	47	27	1054	82	156	72	2731
Proportion of CFC¹:	.35	.04	.01	.02	.02	.03	.02	.01	.39	.03	.06	.03	1.00

¹Common Factor Covariance

Factor -E is the opposite of the factor E often cited in the factorial literature as "Extraversion," thus possibly justifying the label "Introversion." It is not particularly well defined in this dataset; the highest loadings are for ratings characterizing persons as gregarious, or as seclusive. It has no facets associated with it, and its variables often have high loadings on either or both of the superfactors SF1 and SF2.

Factor +A is the factor often cited in the literature as A, Agreeableness. Variables with high loadings on it include "not touchy," "considerate of others," "not jealous," and "mannerly." Some of the variables loading on it also load on facet f12, possibly interpretable as "Non-Anxious."

It is particularly important to find meaningful interpretations of the superfactors SF1 and SF2 because they account for large proportions (.353 and .386, respectively) of the common factor covariance (in contrast to the proportion, .261, contributed by all domain factors and facets). If one arranges all variables in order of their absolute loadings on factor SF1, the highest 20 of the loadings are for the following variables: socially confident (.82), adaptable (.76), perceptive (.75), verbal (.73), original (.72), sensible (.72), knowledgeable (.70), curious (.68), imaginative (.68), planful (.66), not lethargic (.66), not rigid (.62), not submissive (.56), esthetic (.52), persevering (.54), outspoken (.50), responsible (.49), assertive (.47), energetic (.45), and mannerly (.45). In contrast, variables with very low or zero loadings are: considerate of others (.17), doesn't fidget (.17), not restless (.11), rude (0), spiteful (0), eccentric (0), complaining (0), jealous (0), touchy (0), and impulsive (0). From these findings, it appears that superfactor SF1 refers to what may be called *General Social Competence*. The variables with high loadings describe various forms of social competence, whereas the variables with low or zero loadings are generally irrelevant to social competence.

Using a similar approach to the interpretation of superfactor SF2, one finds the variables with the 20 highest loadings on it (in absolute magnitude) to be as follows: not impulsive (.85), not restless (.81), not rude (.80), doesn't fidget (.79), not spiteful (.77), not outspoken (.76), self-minimizing (.76), not assertive (.73), not jealous (.66), not complaining (.65), not verbally fluent (.65), not careless (.59), considerate of others (.58), not fickle (.58), conscientious (.56), not gregarious (.54), not touchy (.54), submissive (.53), not energetic (.53), and careful (.50). In contrast, traits having zero loadings on the factor, and consequently irrelevant to it, are: perceptive, verbal (large vocabulary), knowledgeable, adaptable, fearful (or not fearful), and happy. One gets the impression that persons with high scores on this factor are simply "nice people" who don't draw attention to themselves and who don't act in any antisocial ways. They are considerate of others, conscientious, and thoughtful. Persons with low scores on this factor would be those who tend to be antisocial, too assertive, too talkative, or otherwise objectionable. One might call this factor *General Goodness of Personality*.

The above analysis of the Digman and Inouye (1986) dataset, yielding 12 factors at three levels of a hierarchy, appears to make sense. Because of the methodology used to arrive at it, its results are rather different from most of what may be seen in the personality trait literature, except, of course, with respect to the "recurrent" factors of the five-factor model. It is difficult to tell whether the two superfactors found here correspond, for example, to any of the factors found by Tellegen (1993) or others who have explored personality traits beyond those specified by the FFM. This is a question that needs to be investigated with further samples of individuals and variables using factorial methodology similar to that employed here.

Of interest is the fact that the interpretations of superfactors SF1 and SF2 offered here differ considerably from the interpretations of higher order factors *alpha* and *beta* offered by Digman (1997). Undoubtedly the differences arise from differences in methodologies. In this chapter, the methodology focuses on individual items to the extent that they play a role in defining factors, whereas Digman's (1997) methodology focused on factors without further consideration of individual items.

The factorial structure found in the reanalysis presented here is unfortunately more complex than that found in many recent studies of personality traits, because it appears that most variables in personality studies tend to measure, simultaneously, several different underlying factors. This will make for difficulty in estimating persons' scores on factors. Research will be needed on the best means of structuring assemblages of variables and computing reliable and construct-valid factor scores from them.

A FURTHER SUGGESTION

Research studies should attempt to come to better grips with the processes that underlie personality factors found in ensembles of behavioral traits (Revelle, 1989, 1995). Rather than simply describing personality in terms of common language adjectives or short phrases, the variables used in personality questionnaires should attempt to get at the motives, attitudes, and beliefs underlying observable behavior habits. According to Johnson (1997):

> [M]ost psychologists regard "outer" (behavioral) traits as descriptions that need explanation and they assume that "inner" (emotional and cognitive) traits generate and therefore explain outer traits. Behavioral traits or consistencies may be determined by the interaction of several emotional and cognitive traits. (p. 79)

Take the dimension labeled Conscientiousness. According to Wiggins and Pincus (1994, p. 82), characteristic questionnaire items measuring this dimension include the following:

> (On the positive side:) "When I make a commitment, I can always be counted on to follow through." "I am a productive person who always gets the job done." (And on the negative side:) "Sometimes I'm not as dependable or reliable as I should be." "I never seem to be able to get organized."

But these items pertain only to observable behaviors. Could it be that more informative items could be constructed around the possible motives, attitudes, and beliefs underlying these behaviors? I am not sure whether research in personality has adequately identified and listed the motives, beliefs, and attitudes that lead people to behave in conscientious or unconscientious ways. Nevertheless, a chapter on conscientiousness and integrity written by Hogan and Ones (1997) may be helpful. According to them, conscientiousness is a complex scale. It contains at least three themes: (a) control and lack of impulsiveness; (b) orderliness, tidiness, and methodicalness; (c) hard work and perseverance. (Note that two of these themes correspond to facets f7 and f8 in the reanalysis of the Digman & Inouye dataset.) Hogan and Ones appeal to socioanalytic theory (R. Hogan, 1983) for an explanation of these traits in terms of their value for social conformity, the maintenance of group structure, a hierarchy of social statuses, and accountability and dependability of group members. It might be possible, therefore, to construct scales whereby subjects could be asked to rate the importance to them of maintaining group structure and the individual accountability of group members. Possibly this is already done in certain questionnaires for measuring honesty and integrity. For example, subjects might be asked to rate each alternative in the following: "If I've agreed to do a job, it is important for me to get it done, because (a) people will think poorly of me if I fail, (b) it is important that people be able to plan whether I will get a job done, (c) things work out better if my commitments can be counted on." The intention would be to construct scales whereby one could detect the strength of the motives and beliefs underlying each of the Big Five (and other) factors. It would be interesting to factor-analyze these scales to see whether the factors would correspond in some way to the Big Five (or Seven) factors, or to a new set of factors quite different from the Big Five.

CONCLUSION

I see many good features in the Big Five model. It has been useful in bringing agreement on important and recurrent features of personality structure, and in organizing new research. But it is undoubtedly incomplete. In asking the question, "Is the five-factor model comprehensive from an evolutionary psychological perspective?" Buss (1996) opined, "From the current theoretical perspective, it is unlikely that the five factors alone will prove to be sufficient" (p. 203). As I have already mentioned, possibly the sixth and seventh factors of personality identified by Tellegen (1993) and others must be considered, and possibly there are still more factors of personality to be elevated to second stratum status similar to that of the Big Five. Several of the Big Five factors seem overly complex, such that they need to be split into further factors. In particular, the factor of Openness to Experience seems unnecessarily ambiguous and complex. The work of Ackerman and Heggestad (1997) and Goff and Ackerman (1992) on the role of intellect—or what they call *typical intellectual engagement*—needs to be further developed.

It will be important, also, in reanalyzing the factor-analytic literature on the structure of personality, to add information on facets underlying the Big Five and other second-order factors, such as those identified in the sample reanalysis offered here.

Above all, work on the three-level structure of personality—comprising facets, domains, and possible higher order factors—needs to be continued in the framework of normal science. I can eagerly endorse McCrae and Costa's (1996) assertion that the FFM is "desperately in need of elaboration" (p. 78). And there must be renewed focus on the motives, attitudes, and beliefs that may underlie different aspects of personality structure. Ten years from now, perhaps the Big Five model will have been laid aside, replaced by still another, more compelling model.

ACKNOWLEDGMENTS

I express thanks for the help of various researchers in personality structure who may have read earlier versions of this chapter or supplied me with useful materials and comments. These include Phillip L. Ackerman, A. Timothy Church, Andrew L. Comrey, Paul T. Costa, Jr., Donald W. Fiske, Lewis R. Goldberg, Wim Hofstee, Robert R. McCrae, Auke Tellegen, Niels G. Waller, and Richard E. Zinbarg.

I am particularly indebted to John M. (Jack) Digman, who supplied me with correlation matrices deriving from his studies with Jillian Inouye and permitted me to subject them to reanalysis. Unfortunately, with illness followed by his death on May 25, 1998, he did not live to give thorough consideration to the final results.

I am also grateful to my colleague Abigail T. Panter for her help with various aspects of the computations for the analyses presented here, and for her enthusiasm for the new methodological ideas introduced.

REFERENCES

Ackerman, P. L., & Heggestad, E. D. (1997). Intelligence, personality, and interests: Evidence for overlapping traits. *Psychological Bulletin, 121,* 219–245.

Allport, G. W., & Odbert, H. S. (1936). Trait-names:A psycho-lexical study. *Psychological Monographs, 47,* (Whole No. 211).

American Psychiatric Association (1980). *Diagnostic and statistical manual of mental disorders* (3rd ed.). Washington, DC: Author.

Benet, V., & Waller, N. G. (1995). The Big Seven factor model of personality description: Evidence for its cross-cultural generality in a Spanish sample. *Journal of Personality and Social Psychology, 69,* 701–718.

Block, J. (1995a). A contrarian view of the five-factor approach to personality description. *Psychological Bulletin, 117,* 187–215.

Block, J. (1995b). Going beyond the five factors given: Rejoinder to Costa & McCrae (1995) and Goldberg & Saucier (1995). *Psychological Bulletin, 117,* 226–229.

Borgatta, E. F. (1964). The structure of personality characteristics. *Behavioral Science, 9,* 8–17.

Bouchard, T. J., Jr. (1995). Longitudinal studies of personality and intelligence: A behavior genetic and evolutionary psychology perspective. In D. H. Saklofske & M. Zeidner (Eds.), *International handbook of personality and intelligence* (pp. 81–106). New York: Plenum.

Boyle, G. J., Stankov, L., & Cattell, R. B. (1995). Measurement and statistical models in the study of personality and intelligence. In D. H. Saklofske, & M. Zeidner (Eds.), *International handbook of personality and intelligence* (pp. 417–446). New York: Plenum.

Buss, A. K., & Plomin, R. (1984). *Temperament: Early developing personality traits.* Hillsdale, NJ: Lawrence Erlbaum Associates.

Buss, D. M. (1996). Social adaptation and five major factors of personality. In J. S. Wiggins (Ed.), *The five-factor model of personality: Theoretical perspectives* (pp. 180–207). New York: Guilford.

Butcher, J. N., & Rouse, S. V. (1996). Personality: Individual differences and clinical assessment. *Annual Review of Psychology, 47*, 87–111.

Carroll, J. B. (Ed.). (1956). *Language, thought, and reality: Selected writings of Benjamin Lee Whorf.* New York: John Wiley, and Cambridge, MA:The Technology Press of M.I.T.

Carroll, J. B. (1993). *Human cognitive abilities: A survey of factor-analytic studies.* New York: Cambridge University Press.

Carroll, J. B. (1997). Can personality and intelligence be "integrated"? Review of D. H. Saklofske, & M. Zeidner (Eds.), *International handbook of personality and intelligence* (New York: Plenum, 1995). *Contemporary Psychology, 42*, 215–217.

Cartwright, D., & Peckar, H. (1993). Purposefulness: A fourth superfactor. *Personality and Individual Differences, 14*, 547–555.

Cattell, R. B. (1943). The description of personality: Basic traits resolved into clusters. *Journal of Abnormal and Social Psychology, 38*, 476–506.

Cattell, R. B. (1947). Confirmation and clarification of primary personality factors. *Psychometrika, 12*, 197–220.

Cattell, R. B. (1948). The primary personality factors in women compared with those in men. *British Journal of Psychology, 1*, 114–130.

Cattell, R. B. (1957). *Personality and motivation structure and measurement.* New York: World Book.

Cattell, R. B., Eber, H. W., & Tatsuoka, M. M. (1970). *Handbook for the Sixteen Personality Factor Questionnaire.* Champaign, IL: Institute for Personality and Ability Testing.

Cattell, R. B., & Krug, S. E. (1986). The number of factors in the 16PF: A review of the evidence with special emphasis on methodological problems. *Educational and Psychological Measurement, 46*, 509–522.

Cloninger, C. R., & Svrakic, D. M. (1994). Differentiating normal and deviant personality by the seven-factor personality model. In S. Strack & M. Lorr (Eds.), *Differentiating normal and abnormal personality* (pp. 40–64). New York: Springer.

Comrey, A. L. (1980). *Handbook of interpretation for the Comrey Personality Scale.* San Diego, CA: Educational & Industrial Testing Service.

Costa, P. T., Jr., & McCrae, R. R. (1985). *The NEO Personality Inventory.* Odessa, FL: Psychological Assessment Resources.

Costa, P. T., Jr., & McCrae, R. R. (1988). Personality in adulthood: A six-year longitudinal study of self-reports and spouse ratings on the NEO Personality Inventory. *Journal of Personality and Social Psychology, 54*, 853–863.

Costa, P. T., Jr., & McCrae, R. R. (1989). *The NEO Personality Inventory/NEO Five-Factor Inventory manual supplement.* Odessa, FL: Psychological Assessment Resources.

Costa, P. T., Jr., & McCrae, R. R. (1992a). Four ways five factors are basic. *Personality and Individual Differences, 13*, 653–665.

Costa, P. T., Jr., & McCrae, R. R. (1992b). *The NEO Personality Inventory (Revised) manual.* Odessa, FL: Psychological Assessment Resources.

Costa, P. T., Jr., & McCrae, R. R. (1995). Solid ground in the wetlands of personality: A reply to Block. *Psychological Bulletin, 117*, 216–220.

Costa, P. T., Jr., & Widiger, T. A. (Eds.). (1994). *Personality disorders and the five-factor model of personality.* Washington, DC: American Psychological Association.

Digman, J. M. (1990). Personality structure: Emergence of the five-factor model. *Annual Review of Psychology, 41*, 417–440.

Digman, J. M. (1996). The curious history of the five-factor model. In J. S. Wiggins (Ed.), *The five-factor model of personality: Theoretical perspectives* (pp. 1–20). New York: Guilford Press.

Digman, J. M. (1997). Higher-order factors of the Big Five. *Journal of Personality and Social Psychology, 73*, 1246–1256.

Digman, J. M., & Inouye, J. (1986). Further specification of the five robust factors of personality. *Journal of Personality and Social Psychology, 50*, 116–123.

Eysenck, H. J. (1970). *The structure of human personality* (3rd ed.). London: Methuen.

Eysenck, H. J. (1991). Dimensions of personality: 16, 5, 3? Criteria for a taxonomic paradigm. *Personality and Individual Differences, 12*, 773–790.

Eysenck, H. J. (1992). Four ways five factors are *not* basic. *Personality and Individual Differences, 13*, 667–673.

Fiske, D. W. (1949). Consistency of the factorial structures of personality ratings from different sources. *Journal of Abnormal and Social Psychology, 44*, 329–344.

Goff, M., & Ackerman, P. L. (1992). Personality-intelligence relations: Assessment of typical intellectual engagement. *Journal of Educational Psychology, 84*, 537–552.

Goldberg, L. R., & Digman, J. M. (1994). Revealing structure in the data: Principles of exploratory factor analysis. In S. Strack & M. Lorr (Eds.), *Differentiating normal and abnormal personality* (pp. 216–242). New York: Springer.

Goldberg, L. R., & Saucier, G. (1995). So what do you propose we use instead? A reply to Block. *Psychological Bulletin, 117*, 221–225.

Gorsuch, R. L., & Cattell, R. B. (1967). Second stratum personality factors defined in the questionnaire realm by the 16 P F. *Multivariate Behavioral Research, 2*, 211–224.

Guilford, J. P. (1975). Factors and factors of personality. *Psychological Bulletin, 82*. 802–814.

Gustafsson, J.-E. (1984). A unifying model for the structure of intellectual abilities. *Intelligence, 8*, 179–203.

Gustafsson, J.-E. (1988). Hierarchical models of individual differences in cognitive abilities. In R. J. Sternberg (Ed.), *Advances in the psychology of human intelligence*, Vol. 4 (pp. 35–71). Hillsdale, NJ: Lawrence Erlbaum Associates.

Hogan, J., & Ones, D. S. (1997). Conscientiousness and integrity at work. In R. Hogan, J. A. Johnson, & S. R. Briggs (Eds.), *Handbook of personality psychology* (pp. 849–870). San Diego, CA: Academic.

Hogan, R. (1983). A socioanalytic theory of personality. In M. M. Page (Ed.), *The 1982 Nebraska Symposium on Motivation: Current theory and research* (pp. 59–89). Lincoln, NE: University of Nebraska Press.

Hogan, R. (1986). *Manual for the Hogan Personality Inventory 1 (HPI)*. Minneapolis, MN: National Computer Systems.

Hogan, R., Johnson, J. A., & Briggs, S. R. (Eds). (1997*). Handbook of personality psychology*. San Diego, CA: Academic.

Jackson, D. N., Ashton, M. C., & Tomes, J. L. (1996). The six-factor model of personality: Facets from the big five. *Personality and Individual Differences, 21*, 391–402.

Jöreskog, K. G., & Sörbom, D. (1989*). LISREL 7: User's reference guide*. Mooresville, IN: Scientific Software, Inc.

Johnson, J. A. (1997). Units of analysis for the description and explanation of personality. In R. Hogan, J. A. Johnson, and S. R. Briggs (Eds.), *Handbook of personality psychology* (pp. 73–93). San Diego, CA: Academic.

Krug, S. E. (1994). Personality: A Cattellian perspective. In S. Strack & M. Lorr (Eds.), *Differentiating normal and abnormal personality* (pp. 65–78). New York: Springer.

Lohman, D. F., & Rocklin, T. (1995). Current and recurring issues in the assessment of intelligence and personality. In D. H. Saklofske & M. Zeidner (Eds.), *International handbook of personality and intelligence* (pp. 447–474). New York: Plenum.

London, H., & Exner, J. E., Jr. (Eds.). (1978). *Dimensions of personality.* New York: Wiley.

Lorr, M. (1986). *International Style Inventory: Manual.* Los Angeles, CA: Western Psychological Services.

Lykken, D. T. (1995). *The antisocial personalities.* Mahwah, NJ: Lawrence Erlbaum Associates.

MacCallum, R. (1986). Specification searches in covariance structure modeling. *Psychological Bulletin, 100,* 107–120.

McCrae, R. R., & Costa, P. T., Jr. (1987). Validation of the five-factor model of personality across instruments and observers. *Journal of Personality and Social Psychology, 52,* 81–90.

McCrae, R. R., & Costa, P. T., Jr. (1996). Toward a new generation of personality theories: Theoretical contexts for the five-factor model. In J. S. Wiggins (Ed.), *The five-factor model of personality: Theoretical perspectives* (pp. 51–87). New York: Guilford.

McCrae, R. R., & Costa, P. T., Jr. (1997a). Conceptions and correlates of openness to experience. In R. Hogan, J. Johnson, & S. Briggs (Eds.), *Handbook of personality psychology* (pp. 825–847). San Diego, CA: Academic.

McCrae, R. R., & Costa, P. T., Jr. (1997b). Personality trait structure as a human universal. *American Psychologist, 52,* 509–516.

Montanelli, R. G., Jr., & Humphreys, L. G. (1976). Latent roots of random data correlation matrices with squared multiple correlations on the diagonal: A Monte Carlo study. *Psychometrika, 41,* 341–348.

Most, R. B., & Zeidner, M. (1995). Constructing personality and intelligence instruments: Methods and uses. In D. H. Saklofske & M. Zeidner (Eds.), *International handbook of personality and intelligence* (pp. 475–503). New York: Plenum.

Noller, P., Law, H., & Comrey, A. L. (1987). Cattell, Comrey and Eysenck personality factors compared: More evidence for the five robust factors? *Journal of Personality and Social Psychology, 53,* 775–782.

Norman, W. T. (1963). Toward an adequate taxonomy of personality attributes: Replicated factor structure in peer nomination personality ratings. *Journal of Abnormal and Social Psychology, 66,* 574–583.

Ozer, D. J., & Reise, S. P. (1994). Personality assessment. *Annual Review of Psychology, 45,* 357–388.

Peabody, D., & Goldberg, L. R. (1989). Some determinants of factor structures from personality-trait descriptors. *Journal of Personality and Social Psychology, 57,* 552–567.

Pervin, L. A. (1994). A critical analysis of current trait theory. *Psychological Inquiry, 5,* 103–113.

Revelle, W. (1989). Personality, motivation, and cognitive performance. In R. Kanfer, P. L. Ackerman, & R. Cudeck (Eds.). *Abilities, motivation, and methodology: The Minnesota Symposium on Learning and Individual Differences* (pp. 297–341). Hillsdale, NJ: Lawrence Erlbaum Associates.

Revelle, W. (1995). Personality processes. *Annual Review of Psychology, 46,* 295–328.

Saklofske, D. H., & Zeidner, M. (Eds.). (1995). *International handbook of personality and intelligence.* New York: Plenum.

Sapir, E. (1921). *Language: An introduction to the study of speech.* New York: Harcourt, Brace.

Saucier, G., & Goldberg, L. R. (1996). Evidence for the Big Five in analyses of familiar English personality adjectives. *European Journal of Personality, 10,* 61–77.

Schmid, J., & Leiman, J. M. (1957). The development of hierarchical factor solutions. *Psychometrika, 22,* 53–61.

Strack, S., & Lorr, M. (Eds.). (1994). *Differentiating normal and abnormal personality*. New York: Springer.

Tellegen, A. (1985). Structures of mood and personality and their relevance to assessing anxiety, with an emphasis on self-report. In A. H. Tuma & J. D. Maser (Eds.), *Anxiety and the anxiety disorders* (pp. 681–706). Hillsdale, NJ: Lawrence Erlbaum Associates.

Tellegen, A. (1993). Folk concepts and psychological concepts of personality and personality disorder. *Psychological Inquiry, 4*, 122–130.

Tupes, E. C., & Christal, R. E. (1961). *Recurrent personality factors based on trait ratings.* Technical Report, United States Air Force, Lackland Air Force Base, TX. (Reprinted, *Journal of Personality, 1992, 60*, 225–251).

Waller, N. G., & Zavala, J. D. (1993). Evaluating the Big Five. *Psychological Inquiry, 4*, 131–134.

Wiggins, J. S. (Ed.). (1996). *The five-factor model of personality: Theoretical perspectives.* New York: Guilford.

Wiggins, J. S., & Pincus, A. L. (1992). Personality structure and measurement. *Annual Review of Psychology, 43*, 473–504.

Wiggins, J. S., & Pincus, A. L. (1994). Personality structure and the structure of personality disorders. In P. T. Costa, Jr., & T. A. Widiger (Eds.), *Personality disorders and the five-factor model of personality* (pp. 73–93). Washington, DC: American Psychological Association.

Wiggins, J. S., & Trapnell, P. D. (1997). Personality structure: The return of the big five. In R. Hogan, J. A. Johnson, & S. R. Briggs (Eds.), *Handbook of personality psychology* (pp. 737–765). San Diego, CA: Academic.

Zinbarg, R. E., & Barlow, D. H. (1996). Structure of anxiety and the anxiety disorders: A hierarchical model. *Journal of Abnormal Psychology, 105*, 181–193.

7

Using Cognitive Measurement Models in the Assessment of Cognitive Styles

David F. Lohman
Anton Bosma
The University of Iowa

Somehow styles and abilities need to be disentangled to improve the valid measurement of each.

—Messick, 1996, p. 92

* * * * * * * * * * * * * * * * * * * *

Sam Messick long championed the cause of cognitive styles—at once carefully distinguishing entangled style constructs while simultaneously tracing their path through an immense field of research on the psychology of human differences (Gardner, Jackson, & Messick, 1960; Messick, 1984, 1987, 1996; Messick & Kogan, 1963). Indeed, the influence of cognitive styles extends well beyond the borders of differential psychology. Characteristic ways of perceiving and organizing experience represented in cognitive style constructs are important not merely for understanding how individuals differ, but for understanding belief and conflict in science itself. In other words, cognitive styles are not just an interesting subfield of differential psychology, but are more like foundational elements that help shape the sorts of theories we build, the methods we use to test them, and, perhaps most important, cause conflict among those who hold different beliefs. One of our themes will be the confusions that have resulted from failure to understand why investigators adhere so tenaciously to different research paradigms and procedures. In this chapter, however, we will discuss—not so much the broad sweep of theorizing about cognitive styles—but rather the much narrower topic of how they might be measured. We emphasize the limitations of trait-factor models and the

127

potential contributions of cognitive models for this task. We hope to hasten the arrival of the day when the sophistication of techniques for measuring style constructs catches up with the sophistication of theorizing about them that Messick championed. One avenue for improved measurement is through the use of measurement models derived from cognitive psychology.

However, before we discuss how such models can aid in the measurement of style constructs, it is necessary to understand why cognitively based have not had much impact on the measurement of ability constructs. Thus, first we discuss abilities, then styles.

Cognitive Psychology and Testing

A new enthusiasm invigorated discussions of ability measurement in the 1970s. For the first time in a very long time, experimental psychology saw more than error in individual differences. To name a few of the many contributors: Estes (1974) proposed studying cognitive tests as cognitive tasks; Hunt, Frost, and Lunneborg (1973) proposed using laboratory tests to clarify the meaning of ability constructs; Underwood (1975) proposed using individual differences as a crucible for theory construction; Chang and Atkinson (1976) investigated correlations among individual differences on a memory search task, a visual memory search task, and SAT scores. From the differential side, Carroll (1976) showed how an information-processing paradigm might help us understand ability factors and Royer (1971) showed that the Digit Symbol subtest of the WAIS could be studied as an information processing task. The new look held a particularly strong attraction for those such as Bob Glaser at Pittsburgh and Dick Snow at Stanford, who had long tried to keep a foot in both the experimental and differential camps. Finally, there were the freshly hatched new PhDs who developed these ideas into research programs of their own (again to name a few): Susan Embretson, Bob Sternberg, Jim Pellegrino, Pat Kyllonen, and Phil Ackerman. But what began with parades down Main Street eventually petered out in a hundred side streets. Some early enthusiasts—such as Earl Hunt—wondered aloud whether experimental psychology and differential psychology might indeed be fundamentally incompatible. After years of effort that produced, at best, a scattering of small correlations, Hunt (1987) concluded: "It does not seem particularly fruitful to try to derive the dimensions of a [trait model] of abilities from an underlying process theory" (p. 36). Although this surely overstates, we believe Hunt's pessimism is closer to the truth than the naive optimism of many would-be bridge builders, whether they begin their efforts from the precipitous cliffs that ring the tight little island of experimental psychology or from the sprawling beaches of the seemingly borderless empire of differential psychology (cf. Cronbach, 1957).

Of the many differences between the two disciplines that could be discussed, we believe two are central. The first concerns how researchers think about variation. One could call it a difference in philosophy or cognitive style. The second difference stems from the fact that constructs in the two disciplines are defined by quite different—often largely independent—aspects of score variation. We discuss each of these in turn.

Essentialism versus Population Thinking

In his efforts to explain the rift between experimental and evolutionary biology, Mayr (1982) distinguished between what he called *population thinking* and *essentialist thinking*. Variation and diversity are the stuff of population thinking; categories and typologies are the stuff of essentialist thinking. Population thinking uniquely characterized the Darwin-Wallace theory of natural selection, and later Galton's studies of the inheritance of mental and physical traits. Essentialist thinking, on the other hand, has ever guided experimentalists in biology, physics, and psychology. Essentialism, a philosophy originating with Plato and Aristotle, asserts that observable characteristics of objects in the world are but imperfect shadows of more perfect forms or essences. These essences are more permanent and therefore more real than the particular objects through which we conceive or deduce them. Variation among category members reflects error or imperfection in the manifestation of the essential form.

Essentialist thinking in psychology is perhaps most clearly evident in the seminal work of the Belgian statistician Quetelet and his conception of the mean of a distribution of anthropomorphic measurements as revealing the essential form of the average man (*l'homme moyen*). Variation about the mean reflected the action of accidental causes. So Quetelet reasoned that "there is no possibility of discovering anything about the important constant [or systematic] causes in nature from the character of the error distribution, since this distribution is related only to accidental causes" (Hilts, 1973, p. 217). In its purest form, this view endures in psychometrics in what Lord and Novick (1968) called a *Platonic true score*. In muted form, it characterizes all efforts to describe elements within a category by a single score, from Bacon's goal of carving nature at its joints to the more esoteric applications of the principle of exchangeability (see, e.g., Novick, 1982).

With the possible exception of quantum physics, the philosophy of essentialism has fitted well with the conceptual structure of the physical sciences. Carbon atoms are indeed alike; those that differ define new isotopes or ions (i.e., a new category). Budding chemists are not taught how to make distributions of "carbonness" from which they might infer something about the character of carbon. In psychology, those trained in experimental methods seem most comfortable with essentialist modes of thought. This is particularly evident in attempts of experimentalists to explain individual differences. Many, of course, do not get beyond the notion of individual differences as error and thus see no need to explain them. But for those who do, there is usually an attempt to impose a typology of some sort on the data. Thus, we have not one type of person in the world but two types, which on closer inspection, are further subdivided, as in stage-theoretic models of development or as in the early attempts of the Menniger group (Gardner, Holzman, Klein, Linton, & Spence, 1959) to investigate individual differences in cognitive controls. Indeed, as Kogan (1994) noted, the work of this group and others who investigated cognitive styles was anchored in the categories and tasks of experimental psychology, and in the typological thinking of Jung and other ego psychologists.

Probabilistic thinking about populations takes the opposite tack. Population thinkers stress the uniqueness of each individual. There is thus no *typical* individual; mean values are considered abstractions. Rather, variation is the most interesting characteristic of natural populations. Galton was the first to understand the error distributions of Quetelet in this way. In his memoirs he noted:

> The primary objects of the Gaussian Law of Error were exactly opposed, in one sense, to those to which I applied them. They were to get rid of, or to provide a just allowance for errors. But these errors or deviations were the very things I wanted to preserve and to know about. (Galton, 1908, p. 305)

Or, as Cronbach (1957) put it: "The correlational psychologist is in love with just those variables the experimenter left home to forget" (p. 674).

Differential psychology is, of course, grounded in population or probabilistic thinking. As such, its adherents are more concerned with variation than with means, with quantitative than with qualitative differences between individuals, and with relative rather than with absolute scales of measurement. Measuring the relative fit between persons and situations is what the discipline is all about. Even when absolute measures (such as response latency) are available, it is information about the relative standing of individuals that is its special concern. Thus, part of the difficulty in forging relationships between trait and process—that is, between differential and experimental psychology—is that adherents of the two disciplines tend to conceptualize problems and consequently to measure variables differently. Experimentalists generally prefer the neatly ordered categories of essentialism; differential psychologists prefer the unbounded multidimensional spaces of population thinking.

Construct Confusions

These differences in cognitive style translate into much more profound differences in the type of information (or variation) used to define constructs in the two domains. Consider, for example, the most important (or at least the most well-studied) construct in each domain: learning in experimental psychology and intelligence in differential psychology. Learning is defined by changes over trials (or columns in a basic person-by-item data matrix). Intelligence is defined by variation between persons (or rows in that same matrix). In other words, constructs in experimental and differential psychology are often defined by partitioning the basic data matrix in different ways. Failure to appreciate the statistical independence of row and column deviation scores has lead to much confusion in attempts to relate these two domains, from Woodrow's (1946) failure to find much relationship between learning on laboratory tasks and intelligence, to the efforts of Gulliksen and his students (e.g., Allison, 1960; Stake, 1961) to relate learning rate measures to a Thurstonian model of abilities, to the more recent efforts of Sternberg (1977) and Hunt et al. (1973) to correlate scores for component mental processes and ability constructs.

Intersections of the Sets

But the two disciplines do meet, or overlap. Nonindependence of row and column variation shows up in the interaction term. When considering the relationship between learning and intelligence, the most important cause of the interaction is an increase in score variation across trials, or what Kenny (1974) called the fan effect. Statistically, the fan effect occurs when true gain on the learning task is positively related to initial status on the learning task. If initial status on the learning task correlates with intelligence, then gains will also show a correlation.

There are, of course, other possibilities, but this is a common scenario. Thus, the interaction term is the key to a better understanding of styles. Unfortunately, both differential and experimental psychologists have been taught to minimize the interaction term. Differential psychologists evaluate the dependability or reliability of individual differences by the proportion of the between-person variance attributable to the person variance component (Cronbach, Gleser, Nanda, & Rajaratnam, 1972). A large person variance component and a comparatively small person $\times$ item interaction variance component are the goal. For the experimentalist, differences between conditions (or items, i) are judged relative to the size of the p by i interaction. But a small p by i interaction is not always the goal. Diagnostic information about how subjects solve tasks is most informative when the interaction term is large. In such cases, a single rank order of individuals or of conditions does not give all of the interesting information. Influential developmental psychologists have long built their psychology around tasks that induce subjects to reveal important, preferably qualitative differences in knowledge or strategy by the type or pattern of responses they give. Furthermore, these differences in knowledge or strategy must then be shown to generalize to other tasks or even to be indicative of broad thinking competencies. Piaget was particularly clever in inventing or adapting such tasks for use with children. Siegler (1988) and others have continued the tradition.

The primary contribution of an information-processing analysis of a task or problematic situation is information on how subjects understood that situation or solved that task. Although such analyses usefully inform interpretation of test scores even when all subjects follow a uniform strategy, process models are most useful for understanding individual differences when there are interesting differences in the way subjects perceive situations and in the strategies they deploy when attempting to solve tasks. However, most tasks studied by experimental psychologists and most tests developed by differential psychologists are not designed to elicit such qualitative differences in type of knowledge or strategy use or to reveal them when they do occur. In fact, tasks and tests are usually constructed with exactly the opposite goal in mind. When such tests or tasks are subjected to an information-processing analysis, the results are not exactly earth shaking. For example, information processing analyses of spatial tasks that require the mental rotation of figures tell us that a major source of individual differences on such tasks is to be found in the speed and accuracy of the rotation process. Did anyone seriously doubt this? What is news is when we find subjects who do not rotate stimuli, or who persist in rotating them in one direction when rotation in the other direction would be shorter, or when some rotate along rigid axes while others perform a mental twisting and turning at the same time. Yet even these strategy differences are of no enduring interest unless they can be related to more global indices of ability or some personological attribute such as conation.

Most research in the past 20 years attempting to relate cognitive and differential psychology has assumed that connections between the two disciplines would be more straightforward. Investigators fitted information processing models to each subject's data, then estimated component scores for different mental processes (such as the slope parameter from the regression of latency on angular separation between stimuli in the rotation paradigm), and then used these process-based parameters as new individual difference variables. However, individual differences that are consistent across trials are located in the intercepts of the individual regressions, not in the slopes or other component scores, as commonly assumed (Lohman, 1994). Such complexities complicate but by no means embargo traffic between the two disciplines of scientific psychology. The main avenue of contact is through tasks or measurement procedures designed to elicit rather than to prohibit (or obscure) differences in strategy or style, which brings us back to cognitive styles.

Cognitive Styles as Constructs

Cognitive styles include constructs such as field articulation, extensiveness of scanning, cognitive complexity versus simplicity, leveling versus sharpening, category width, reflection versus impulsivity, automatization versus restructuring, and converging versus diverging. Messick (1996) argued that cognitive styles reflect consistent individual differences in the manner or form of cognition as distinct from the content or level of cognition. As such, cognitive styles are often viewed as performance variables rather than as competence variables. The division is not sharp, however, because styles are generally thought to be interwoven with personological characteristics and to function mainly as conative mechanisms that regulate cognitive processes, learning strategies, and affect. In this way, styles may also impact competence as well as performance (Messick 1989). Within an information processing framework, however, cognitive styles are interpreted more narrowly as consistencies in modes of perception, memory, and thought (Miller, 1991). For example, field articulation, as a component of attention, would fall under the category of perceptual styles. Individuals with early perceptual attention control may be less prone to distraction by irrelevant information than those who do not exhibit such a level of control.

A variety of learning styles, or consistencies in strategies employed in learning and studying, have also been hypothesized (Weinstein, Goetz, & Alexander, 1988). The most general distinction concerns whether particular learning styles lead to learning strategies that produce deep versus surface processing during learning (Entwistle, 1987; Snow & Swanson, 1992). However, such strategies cannot be understood in isolation from motivation for learning (Ainley, 1993; Biggs, 1987). Furthermore, different subject-matter domains may also require or lead learners to develop different global strategies for organizing their knowledge (Pask, 1976).

Finally, defensive styles refer to consistent ways of organizing and channeling affect in cognition (Messick, 1987). As such, they are primarily ego-protective, but also serve the important adaptive function of maintaining cognition, often in the face of intense affect. Four broad defensive styles have been proposed: obsessive-compulsive, hysterical, paranoid, and impulsive, which, in the normal range of personality, are called rigid, impressionistic, suspicious, and unintegrated cognition, respectively.

Styles and Strategies

In one way or another, the notion of strategy enters into all of these style dimensions. What, then, is the relationship between the two? Style is clearly a more general term than strategy. Strategy may signify no more than a particular way of solving a task. When the term is used in this way, there is no requirement that individuals choose or even be aware of the strategies they adopt. However, strategy use can also imply choice in action or thought. When the term is used in this way, listing strategies as exemplars of styles implies the presence of some form of executive or self-regulatory processes. The range of situations in which particular processes are used and the flexibility with which they are used may depend on an individual's cognitive style. Therefore, cognitive styles contain conative and volitional components that have implications for their assessment. These components involve, in the case of volition, mechanisms for the self-control of cognition and affect in regulating action or behavior, or in the case of conation, mechanisms for the initiation and maintenance of action-appropriate thought. Thus, one way to observe styles is through consistencies in the application of strategies across tasks or situations. For example an obsessive–compulsive style may be inferred from consistencies in the coping strategies used to fend off the influence of negative affect.

The style-strategy distinction is perhaps most salient in the cognitive style constructs of field dependence and field independence. A crucial aspect of strategy control is not so much the purposeful disposition to facilitate performance through task-relevant cognitions but rather to inhibit irrelevant or misleading cognitions (see Kuhl, 1992, and Pascual-Leone, 1989, for two perspectives on the role of inhibition and facilitation in strategy use). Self-regulation suggests a situationally sensitive and adaptable approach to the planning, initiation, and maintenance of context appropriate (or disengagement from context inappropriate) intentions. Field-independent and field-dependent learners can be distinguished in this respect. The former are more able to make use of appropriate (inhibitory or facilitatory) strategies. The latter are more oriented toward situational cues and make less use of appropriate strategies, even when they are available. It is the differential effect of internal versus external cues that appears to distinguish between the obsessive–compulsive and field-dependent/field-independent dimensions. In the first case, internally generated affect influences strategy, whereas in the second case, the external cues influence strategy. In one, the individual keeps the world at bay by inhibiting external influences; in the other, the individual keeps inner demands at bay by inhibiting affect. In both cases, style facilitates cognition and so the type of strategy used can indicate broader dispositional style.

This brings us to the issue of conscious control or choice in strategy use, a topic briefly alluded to earlier. Control appears to be a question of degree, ranging from unconscious and automatic control to fully conscious control. For our purposes, we assume that control can be exerted at any of these levels and reflects the action of a higher order self-regulatory system. However, for the valid measurement of cognitive styles, there is no prerequisite that an individual be consciously involved in the application of any particular strategy.

Because strategies and—to a lesser degree—styles can be perceived as being part of a self-regulatory system, they can be situated within a larger cognitive-conative-affective framework (Snow, Corno, & Jackson, 1996; see also Miller, 1991). In Snow's taxonomy the conative domain is situated between the cognitive and affect domains, and represented by a motivation-volition continuum. Strategies are mostly subsumed under the more cognitive-volitional pole and, to a lesser degree, under the affective-motivational pole. Styles, on the other hand, are distributed more evenly across volition and motivation.

One advantage of Snow's scheme is that different style constructs (and their concomitant strategies) are not operationally dependent on an overarching and rather conceptually nebulous cognitive-personality system. Messick took a somewhat different approach. Whereas Snow argued for a specific set of variables spanning the space, but excluding the superordinate constructs of cognition and personality, Messick (1989) preferred a greater inclusion of personality variables. He wrote:

> The human personality is a system in the technical sense of something that functions as a whole by virtue of the interdependence of its parts.... Personality may influence the organization of cognition, the dimensionality and stability of structure, and the nature and course of cognitive processes, as well as that of level of measured ability. (p. 36)

Accordingly, styles should be treated, not as cognitive, affective, or behavioral variables related to personality, but as "manifestations of form-giving personality structures in cognition, affect, and behavior" (Messick, 1994, p. 133).

An important question then is, "Do we include personality characteristics when attempting to assess styles," and if we do, "At which point do we integrate them into our measures?" This question can be answered from either a top-down or bottom-up analysis, with the former linking personality to performance and the later performance to personality. From the top-down perspective, styles are considered the superordinate tier subsuming and instantiating strategies; most likely they do so differentially across situations and tasks, not unlike the personality constructs to which they are presumably affixed. Our tack will take us through the bottom-up analysis: We try to determine how individuals process information in particular contexts, and then look for consistencies in the strategies used.

Using Cognitive Measurement Models to Measure Styles

By definition, styles concern not *how much* but *how*. As Messick (1976) observed:

> Cognitive styles differ from intellectual abilities in a number of ways. . . . Ability dimensions essentially refer to the content of cognition or the question of what—what kind of information is being processed by what operation in what form? . . . Cognitive styles, in contrast, bear on the questions of how—on the manner in which behavior occurs. . . . (pp. 6–9)

Measures of style should yield scores that are bipolar and value differentiated rather than unipolar and value directed (Messick, 1984, 1996). Messick proposed that we examine typical performance (see also Goff & Ackerman, 1992) and use ipsative or contrasted scores to measure styles. There are a variety of ways to do this. However, most attempts to measure cognitive styles have inappropriately followed the ability-factor model, which is better suited to value directional questions about unipolar, maximal performance constructs that ask *how much*.

The subversion of questions about *how* by methods better attuned to *how much* is but one example of how the application of elegant statistical techniques that do not really answer the questions posed can unwittingly reshape a discipline. Early mental testers—particularly Binet, but others as well (see Freeman, 1926)—were as much concerned with how children solved problems as with the answers they gave. This concern with process was picked up by developmental psychologists, but gradually abandoned by psychometricians, especially with the rise of group-administered tests that could be scored by a clerk, and then later, by a machine. Tests became increasing efficient vehicles for identifying those who were more (or less) able, but increasing uninformative as to what abilities might be (Lohman, 1989). Issues of process were exiled to the land of cognitive styles. There, isolated from the mainstream of differential psychology, promising style constructs were gradually ground into traits already known to ability theorists, but by other names. When the redundancy was finally discovered, ability theorists claimed priority and style theorists were left with the residue.

The key to measuring style lies in measuring *how* rather than *how much*. But how can one measure *how*? First, one needs tasks in which individual differences are clearly reflected in measures of *how* rather than in measures of *can*, that is, tasks that everyone solves in some sense but which are amenable to different solution strategies. Second, one must have some way of making clear inferences about strategy from responses that are given. This is important. We often find that, even though there are different ways of solving a task, the different methods are not distinguishable with our dependent measures. For example, different ways of solving a problem that requires mental rotation of a figure may all show increases in response latency with amount of rotation required. It may be difficult or impossible to detect such strategy differences using response latencies. (Although other measures, such as self-reports, patterns of eye fixations, or response errors—particularly the nature of the foil chosen—may provide such evidence.) Third, one needs not only tasks that elicit strategy differences, and dependent measures that are sensitive to them, but also measurement models that can represent them. Measurement models developed in cognitive psychology to estimate consistencies in strategies are, in fact, much better suited to the task of measuring *how* (Lohman & Ippel, 1993). Therefore, one of the more straightforward contributions cognitive psychology can make to measurement is through improved measures of cognitive styles. Fourth, one needs a scheme (or, more formally, a measurement model) whereby different strategies can be mapped onto one or more style constructs. *Strategy* is a narrower term than *style*. Put differently, many different strategies could be classified as indicators of a particular style. There are many different ways to solve problems that might be termed *analytic* or *impulsive*. However, not all of these strategies will represent the style with equal clarity. Again, typological thinking would mislead us into trying to classify each strategy as belonging or not belonging to a particular style category. A spatial metaphor would envision strategies as distributed throughout a continuous, multidimensional space defined by different style constructs. Just as different birds are not equally good indicators of the category *bird*, so too are some strategies better indicators of particular style constructs. But even those strategies that well characterize a style cannot be equated with it. *Bird* implies more than *robin*, even though for most North Americans, *robin* exemplifies the category *bird*.

Observations Designs and Measurement Models

Every test may be described in terms of the observation design used to structure observations and the measurement model(s) used to map observations onto scores or categories. The observation design describes test items, their organization, and the type of responses required. The purpose of the observation design is to structure observations so as best to distinguish among categories or levels of the measurement model. When the goal is to distinguish among different ways of solving a task, the observation design must allow for such contrasts. The measurement model refers to the procedure used to assign a single value to an object of measurement. More concretely, the measurement model is used to specify the rules that will be used to score, classify, or combine objects of observation. For example, a single score for a person can be obtained by averaging performance over items. This is consistent with a measurement model that relegates variability in performance across items to a within-person error term. Information processing accounts of task performance should result in a more complex set of measurement models in which different solutions strategies may be explicitly represented and compared. These different measurement models can be evaluated for a given observation design by combining and contrasting performance on different item sets in different ways, using regression or other model fitting procedures to do this.

The Process Model as Target Variable

The process model itself can also be the object of measurement. If individuals solve items on a task in different ways, then they can be classified on the basis of the information processing model that best describes their performance. If these process models can be ordered, then the classification scheme for ordering models becomes a new measurement model. Developmental theories provide the most straightforward examples of how such second-order measurement models can be used to explain systematic variation in how individuals solve tasks (i.e., first-order process models). This is because they usually posit a single dimension along which information-processing models may be classified.

For example, Sternberg (1977) distinguished among four different validity models for analogical reasoning tasks. In Model I, all component processes were self-terminating, whereas in Model IV, all component processes were exhaustive. Models II and III distinguished intermediate cases. Performance of adult subjects was generally well fit by Models III or IV. In later work with children, Sternberg discovered that the performance of younger children was better fit by models with self-terminating processes, whereas that of older children was generally better fit by models that hypothesized more exhaustive processing (Sternberg & Rifkin, 1979). Thus, models could be ordered by amount of exhaustive processing required. Category score in this measurement model was then shown to be correlated with age or developmental level.

Sometimes more than one dimension is required, such as in attempts to relate strategy differences on cognitive tasks to ability constructs identified in dimensional theories. Siegler (1988) reported a nice example of how classification of measurement models along two dimensions might be accomplished. He administered addition, subtraction, and word identification tasks to two groups of first graders. Performance on each item was classified as based either on retrieval of a response or on construction of a response using a back-up strategy. Students were then classified in one of three groups depending on the pattern of response correctness overall, on retrieval problems, and on back-up strategy problems. Siegler labeled the groups good, not-so-good, and perfectionist students. Perfectionists were students who exhibited good knowledge of problems but set high confidence thresholds for stating retrieval answers. The distinction between perfectionist and good students thus mirrors the cognitive style dimension of reflectivity–impulsivity. Note, however, that the latter dimension is typically defined by performing a median split on latency and error scores on a figure-matching task and then discarding subjects in two of the four cells. Siegler, however, started with a model of strategy use that distinguished between strength of associations (a classic "cognitive" construct) and a confidence criterion for stating retrieval answers (a "conative" construct). Furthermore, the hypothesized style dimension was shown by examining response patterns across three tasks commonly used in the classroom.

The key assumption in both the Sternberg and Rifkin (1979) and Siegler (1988) studies is that individuals can be classified on the basis of which of several models best describes their data. Once again, this is an essentialist or typological way of thinking about the issue. When tasks admit a variety of solution strategies, individuals only rarely appear to solve all items in the same way. The problem is not "which strategy does the individual use?" or even "which strategy does the individual use most frequently?" but rather "what is the probability that the individual used each of the hypothesized strategies?" When stated in this way, it is obvious that individuals may differ not only in which strategy they typically use, but also in the propensity to use a variety of different strategies. Experts not only have a broader array of strategies at their disposal than do novices; they use them more appropriately. In other words, they are tuned to environmental constraints and affordances, and to metacognitive knowledge of self. Indeed, the continued application of an ineffective strategy is one hallmark of immature and disordered functioning.

Kyllonen, Lohman, and Woltz (1984) showed how to do this in a rough way in an investigation of the solution strategies subjects used on a spatial assembly task. Consider the case in which two strategies are hypothesized: Strategy 1 and Strategy 2. Kyllonen et al. tested models that presumed subjects solved different proportions of the item using each strategy: 0%, 25%, 50%, 75% or 100% of Strategy 1 with the complement solved using Strategy 2. Of course, 0% and 100% represent single strategy models. The investigators were able to distinguish among these different models, because the characteristics of items used to predict whether subjects synthesized or did not synthesize figures varied orthogonally in the observation design. Without this, it would not have been possible to distinguish among the different process or measurement models.

Kyllonen et al. (1984) found that subjects with extreme ability profiles were more likely to use a single strategy. In particular, subjects who scored much higher on reference spatial ability and visual memory tests than on other reference tests consistently synthesized component figures into a single shape, whereas those who showed the opposite profile seemed only able to combine figures actually in view. Those who where generally the most able showed the most flexible adaptation, changing solution strategies to meet changes in item demands. Brodzinsky (1985) claimed that this generalization also applies to the cognitive style construct of impulsivity–reflectivity. In particular, individuals who show extremely impulsive or reflective behavior are less able to modify their speed-accuracy trade-off across situations.

A much simpler example comes from the work of Riding and Dyer (1980). Children in their study first listened to a short story and then answered a series of questions about the passage, all of which required inference. Questions were of two types, those that depended on imagery and those that depended on semantic elaboration. For example, the story may have mentioned the fact that someone knocked on the door of a cottage. The question might be "What color was the door?" There was no right answer, because the color of the door was not specified. Response latency was recorded. However, the dependent variable of interest was an ipsative score that compared latencies on semantic and imagery questions. The idea was to identify children who were much quicker to answer one type of question than the other. Correlations were then computed between this ipsative score and the Junior Eysenck Personality Inventory. Correlations with the Extroversion scale were $r = -.67$ for boys ($n = 107$) and $r = -.76$ for girls ($n = 107$). Thus, children who showed a preference for imagistic processing were much more likely to be introverted, whereas those who showed a preference for verbal elaboration were more likely to be extroverted. One of the nice features of this study is that the correlations do not impose a typology, even though careless interpretation of them may.

Although different in many respects, the Siegler (1988), Kyllonen et al. (1984), and Riding and Dyer (1980) studies all show how consistent individual differences in strategy preference can, with proper observation designs and measurement models, define style constructs that provide one important bridge between the domains of personality and ability. Although all of these examples use latency as the only or the primary dependent measure, other dependent measures can also be used. For example, one can also follow the lead of Binet and Piaget and many others in the developmental tradition who have attempted to make inferences about the nature of cognition from a classification of the response given. Many of these schemes have failed because they sought to place the child unambiguously in a category rather than to estimate the probability that the child's responses fell in each of the categories used. A good measure of style would seek to capture rather than to discard or ignore information on the consistency of behavior across trials, tasks, or contexts. It is only our fondness for typological thinking that makes inconsistency in style or strategy seem problematic.

Implications

Style is a second-order family resemblance concept. Individuals generally cannot be typed by strategy, and strategies cannot be typed by style. Thus, the relationship between individual and style is distal. This means that attempts to make strong predictions about behavior in a particular context on the basis of a style will generally not succeed. This does not mean that style constructs are any less real than more proximal measures of behavior. A description of the general features of the landscape is valid even if it does not well describe a particular garden.

The measurement of cognitive styles can provide a fertile ground for interaction between the two disciplines of scientific psychology. Indeed, we believe there probably is greater promise for fruitful interaction between the two disciplines in the measurement of styles than in the measurement of abilities. For this to occur, however, trait models of cognitive styles that involve a simple aggregation of item scores must give way to models that reflect qualitative differences in strategy. Furthermore, these strategies must be mapped onto one or more style dimensions. The domain must also overcome its penchant for categorizing persons or strategies. The siren call of essentialist or typological thinking is as dangerous for the measurement of styles as is reductionism for psychology generally. Typological labels usually identify extremes on a continuum of normally distributed scores. In other words, the measurement of style must recognize that the category membership of responses or persons is a probabilistic affair. Categories are often nothing more than convenient fictions—arbitrary parsings of a continuous space that enable us to communicate with one another. But because of this need to communicate, we will always have a need for such category labels. The trick is to remember not to be misled into taking literally what we say.

REFERENCES

Ainley, M. D. (1993). Styles of engagement with learning: Multidimensional assessment of their strategy use and school achievement. *Journal of Educational Psychology, 85,* 395–405.

Allison, R. B. (1960). *Learning parameters and human abilities* (UM 60-4958). Unpublished report, Princeton, NJ: Educational Testing Service.

Biggs, J. B. (1987). *Student approaches to learning and studying.* Hawthorn, Victoria: Australian Council for Educational Research.

Brodzinsky, D. M. (1985). On the relationship between cognitive styles and cognitive structures. In E. D. Neimark, R. D. Lisi, & J. L. Newman (Eds.), *Moderators of competence.* Hillsdale, NJ: Lawrence Erlbaum Associates.

Carroll, J. B. (1976). Psychometric tests as cognitive tasks: A new "structure of intellect." In L. B. Resnick (Ed.), *The nature of intelligence.* Hillsdale, NJ: Lawrence Erlbaum Associates.

Chang, A., & Atkinson, R. C. (1976). Individual differences and relationships among a select set of cognitive skills. *Memory and Cognition, 4,* 661–672.

Cronbach, L. J. (1957). The two disciplines of scientific psychology. *American Psychologist, 12,* 671–684.

Cronbach, L. J., Gleser, G. C., Nanda, H., & Rajaratnam, N. (1972). *The dependability of behavioral measurements.* New York: Wiley.

Entwistle, N. (1987). Explaining individual differences in school learning. In E. DeCorte, H. Lodewijks, R. Parmentier, & P. Span (Eds.), *Learning and instruction: European research in an international context* (Vol. 1, pp. 69–88). Oxford: Pergamon Press.

Estes, W. K. (1974). Learning theory and intelligence. *American Psychologist, 29,* 740–749.

Freeman, F. N. (1926). *Mental tests: Their history, principles and application.* Boston: Houghton Mifflin.

Galton, F. (1908). *Memories of my life* (2nd ed.). London: Methuen.

Gardner, R. W., Holzman, P. S., Klein, G. S., Linton, H. B., & Spence, D. (1959). Cognitive control: A study of individual consistencies in cognitive behavior. *Psychological Issues, 1,* Monograph 4.

Gardner, R. W., Jackson, D. N., & Messick, S. (1960). Personality organization in cognitive controls and intellectual abilities. *Psychological Issues, 2,* Monograph 8.

Goff, M. & Ackerman, P. L. (1992). Personality-intelligence relations: Assessment of typical intellectual engagement. *Journal of Educational Psychology, 84*(4), 537–552.

Hilts, V. L. (1973). Statistics and social sciences. In R. L. Giere and R. S. Westfall (Eds.), *Foundations of the scientific method: The nineteenth century* (pp. 206–233). Bloomington: Indiana University Press.

Hunt, E. (1987). Science, technology, and intelligence. In R. R. Ronning, J. A. Glover, J. C. Conoley, & J. C. Witt (Eds.), *The influence of cognitive psychology on testing: The Buros-Nebraska symposium on measurement and testing* (Vol. 3, pp. 11–40). Hillsdale, NJ: Lawrence Erlbaum Associates.

Hunt, E. B., Frost, N., & Lunneborg, C. (1973). Individual differences in cognition: A new approach to intelligence. In G. Bower (Ed.), *The psychology of learning and motivation* (Vol. 7, pp. 87–122). New York: Academic Press.

Kenny, D. A. (1974). A quasi-experimental approach to assessing treatment effects in nonequivalent control group design. *Psychological Bulletin, 82,* 345–362.

Kogan, N. (1994). Cognitive styles. In R. J. Sternberg (Ed.), *Encyclopedia of intelligence* (pp. 266–273).

Kuhl, J. (1992). A theory of self-regulation: Action versus state orientation, self-discrimination, and some applications. *Applied Psychology: An International Review, 41*(2), 97–129.

Kyllonen, P. C., Lohman, D. F., & Woltz, D. J. (1984). Componential modeling of alternative strategies for performing spatial tasks. *Journal of Educational Psychology, 76,* 1325–1345.

Lohman, D. F. (1989). Human intelligence: An introduction to advances in theory and research. *Review of Educational Research, 59,* 333–373.

Lohman, D. F. (1994). Component scores as residual variation (or why the intercept correlates best). *Intelligence, 19,* 1–12.

Lohman, D. F., & Ippel, M. J. (1993). Cognitive diagnosis: From statistically-based assessment toward theory-based assessment. In N. Frederiksen, R. Mislevy, & I. Bejar (Eds.), *Test theory for a new generation of tests* (pp. 41–71). Hillsdale, NJ: Lawrence Erlbaum Associates.

Lord, F. M., & Novick, M. (1968). *Statistical theories of mental test scores.* Reading, MA: Addison-Wesley.

Mayr, E. (1982). *The growth of biological thought: Diversity, evolution, inheritance.* Cambridge, MA: Harvard University Press.

Messick, S. (1976). Personality consistencies in cognition and creativity. In S. Messick, (Ed.), *Individuality in learning: Implications of cognitive styles and creativity for human development.* San Francisco: Jossey-Bass.

Messick, S. (1984). The nature of cognitive styles: Problems and promise in educational practice. *Educational Psychologist, 19,* 59–74.

Messick, S. (1987). Structural relationships across cognition, personality and style. In R. E. Snow & M. J. Farr (Eds.), *Aptitude, learning, and instruction: Vol. 3. Conative and affective process analyses* (pp. 35–75). Hillsdale, NJ: Lawrence Erlbaum Associates.

Messick, S. (1989). *Cognitive style and personality: Scanning and orientation toward affect* (RR-89-16). Princeton, NJ: Educational Testing Service.

Messick, S. (1994). The matter of style: Manifestations of personality in cognition, learning, and teaching. *Educational Psychologist, 29*(3), 121–136.

Messick, S. (1996). Human abilities and modes of attention: The issue of stylistic consistencies in cognition. In I. Dennis & P. Tapsfield (Eds.), *Human abilities: Their nature and measurement* (pp. 77–96). Hillsdale, NJ: Lawrence Erlbaum Associates.

Messick, S., & Kogan, N. (1963). Differentiation and compartmentalization in object-sorting measures of categorizing style. *Perceptual and Motor Skills, 16,* 47–51.

Miller, A. (1991). *Personality types: A modern synthesis.* Calgary, Alberta, Canada: University of Calgary Press.

Novick, M. R. (1982). Educational testing: Inferences in relevant subpopulations. *Educational Researcher, 11,* 4–10.

Pascual-Leone, J. (1989). An organismic process model of Witkin's field-dependence—independence. In T. Globerson & T. Zelniker (Eds.), *Cognitive style and cognitive development* (pp. 36–70). Norwood, NJ: Ablex.

Pask, G. (1976). Styles and strategies of learning. *British Journal of Educational Psychology, 46,* 128–148.

Riding, R. J., & Dyer, V. A. (1980). The relationship between extroversion and verbal-imagery learning style in twelve-year-old children. *Personality and Individual Differences, 1,* 273–279.

Royer, F. L. (1971). Information processing of visual figures in a digit symbol substitution task. *Journal of Experimental Psychology, 87,* 335–342.

Siegler, R. S. (1988). Individual differences in strategy choices. Good students, not-so-good students, and perfectionists. *Child Development, 59,* 833–857.

Snow, R. E., Corno, L., & Jackson, D. (1996). Individual differences in conative and affective functions. In D. C. Berliner & R. C. Calfee (Eds.), *Handbook of educational psychology* (pp. 243–310). New York: Macmillan.

Snow, R. E., & Swanson, J. (1992). Instructional psychology: Aptitude, adaptation, and assessment. *Annual Review of Psychology, 43,* 583–626.

Stake, R. E. (1961). Learning parameters, aptitudes, and achievement. *Psychometric Monographs,* No. 9.

Sternberg, R. J. (1977). *Intelligence, information processing, and analogical reasoning: The componential analysis of human abilities.* Hillsdale, NJ: Lawrence Erlbaum Associates.

Sternberg, R. J., & Rifkin, B. (1979). The development of analogical reasoning processes. *Journal of Experimental Child Psychology, 27,* 195–232.

Underwood, B. J. (1975). Individual differences as a crucible in theory construction. *American Psychologist, 30,* 128–140.

Weinstein, C. E., Goetz, E. T., & Alexander, P. A. (Eds.). (1988). *Learning and study strategies.* San Diego, CA: Academic Press.

Woodrow, H. (1946). The ability to learn. *Psychological Review, 53,* 147–158.

8

Assessment in the Performing Arts

Nathan Kogan
New School University

INTRODUCTION

In a volume dedicated to the contributions and influence of Samuel Messick, it seems most appropriate that I begin this chapter with an account of the role that Sam played in my intellectual development and professional career. I joined the ETS Research Division in the Fall of 1959 and stayed for 10 years. My first year there was spent rather unhappily outside of Sam Messick's Personality Research Group, and I recall seriously contemplating the possibility of leaving for an academic position elsewhere. Sam, however, arranged a transfer to his Research Group, and made it possible for me to flourish at ETS for the remainder of my stay there.

I arrived at ETS with a keen interest in cognitive style, a topic that had engaged Sam as well ever since his postdoctoral stint at the Menninger Foundation. When Sam embarked on his NIMH-supported project devoted to the systematization of the cognitive controls and styles derived from the earlier Menninger studies, he invited my participation. Several joint publications on categorization and conceptualization styles evolved from this collaborative effort. Beyond this collaborative work, however, Sam created the kind of atmosphere in his research group that made it possible for me to continue working with my earlier collaborator, Michael Wallach, on studies of risk-taking behavior, and the convergent versus divergent thinking distinction.

I continued my research and writing on cognitive styles through the 1970s, 1980s and into the early 1990s. Sam was also publishing papers on this topic throughout this period, and I would like to think that I cited them all generously. After reading any of Sam's papers devoted to cognitive styles, I always came away with the impression that his contribution was better organized, more systematic, more analytic, and more critically constructive than anything I had written about the topic. Of course, Sam cited my work as well, and I am grateful for his praiseworthy comments about it.

As my engagement with the topic of cognitive styles approaches the 40-year mark, I am compelled to acknowledge that the peak of activity and interest in the field was reached some years ago, with a steady decline since that time. I am sure that Sam would have agreed with this assessment. It is quite disconcerting to discover that cognitive styles, on which one had focused only a short time ago, were now relegated to historical chapters representing older approaches (Cantor & Kihlstrom, 1987; Sternberg, 1997). The latter author claims that his work on thinking styles (based on a theory of mental self-government) will rejuvenate the field. Clearly, more time will have to pass before such a claim can be effectively evaluated.

Following my contribution to the cognitive-style literature in the form of an encyclopedia entry (Kogan, 1994), I vowed that it would be my final word on the subject. Breaking the vow for the purpose of this volume would have been possible, but I could not see the point of it. I would essentially find myself recycling ideas that I had previously committed to print. It was evident that I had to move in a different direction.

Throughout my career, I have derived much gratification from the construction of psychological measuring instruments tapping constructs for which no such instruments existed or where existent instruments were grossly inadequate. My initial engagement in such activity began before my arrival at ETS. The area of gero-psychology was quite underdeveloped at that time, and I accordingly took on the challenge of devising a series of instruments to measure attitudes toward and beliefs about the elderly (Kogan, 2000). In collaboration with Michael Wallach, the Choice Dilemmas Questionnaire was constructed (Kogan & Wallach, 1964), an enormously popular instrument that pervaded the research on risk-taking behavior (individual and group) for many years.

With the move to ETS, and the influence of Sam and the prevailing psychometric tradition, I became more aware of the subtleties and complexities of measurement, and I would like to believe that my instrument-construction activities became more sophisticated. In the 1970s, my graduate students and I devoted much effort to the construction and validation of the pictorial Metaphoric Triads Task, an instrument intended to assess individual differences in metaphoric sensitivity in both children and adults (Kogan, Connor, Gross, & Fava, 1980).

All of this is a prelude to the challenge that confronted me when I accepted a consultantship with the Lincoln Center Institute, an organization devoted to the facilitation of aesthetic education in public primary and secondary schools. Jack Carroll (a former ETS colleague and a contributor to this volume) had served in the role and recommended that I take over as his successor. The Institute wished to evaluate the success of their program, and it became evident to me that new and possibly unique instruments would have to be developed to accomplish that goal.

In the next section of this chapter, I describe the approach taken in the development of such instruments. The intent of the present chapter, however, is to go beyond the particulars of the Lincoln Center Institute evaluation to assessment in the performing arts more generally, and of performing artists more specifically.

AESTHETIC SENSITIVITY IN CHILDREN

How does one proceed to study children's sensitivity in the aesthetic domain? It is evident that we must place aesthetically relevant stimuli before the child, and then evaluate the responses offered to such stimuli. There are a number of ways such a goal can be accomplished. At one extreme, one can offer the child musical or dance works from the appropriate standard repertoire, and then ask a series of questions intended to tap his or her appreciation of such works. This is a direction that we deliberately chose not to take, given the premium such a procedure would place upon verbal ability, prior familiarity, and cultural sophistication. Accordingly, we adopted a more experimental trial-and-error approach to the construction of the required instruments.

Consider first the tasks developed for the dance assessment. We asked the following question: Are there aspects of dance of sufficient saliency and immediacy to lend themselves to at least partial apprehension by children naive to the dance field? If so, could tasks incorporating those aspects be pitched at a level of difficulty to allow for meaningful individual differences? In the case of dance, we settled on tasks assessing (1) sensitivity to the affective and descriptive qualities inherent in dance movements, and (2) the ability to translate a dance movement into a two-dimensional abstract design (that is not a floor pattern of dance steps).

Three improvisational dancers were available to us, and a particular test item was represented by one, two, or all three dancers. Thus, in the case of the first dance component indicated previously, the dancers were requested to produce a brief movement representing a specific descriptive–affective combination (e.g., sharp–angry). A test item was then constructed by adding four distractors (i.e., fast–happy, slow–strong, angular–strong, wiggly–exciting). Seven such items were developed. For the second component indicated earlier, a subset of items from the Welsh Figure Preference test (Welsh, 1980) was shown to the dancers, who chose those most readily adaptable to a movement representation. For each of these (eight in all) three distractor figures were added.

In constructing new instruments of the type described, there is bound to be a modicum of doubt regarding the answer keyed correct. Heavy reliance is placed on the dancers responsible for the construction and enactment of the items. To assuage our doubts, the instruments were first tried out on advanced dance students at the Juilliard school. Consensus on the correct answer was exceptionally high for the large majority of items. Distractors attracting more than 5% of the responses were replaced. All of this implies that, in the case of the Welsh figures, experienced dancers are able to take an unfamiliar abstract design and translate it into a sequence of movements that other dancers can then easily match to the figure that inspired the dance movement in the first place.

The task in the case of music required that the child match a particular musical selection with a visual pattern (again drawn from the Welsh Figure Preference Test). A professional music educator selected items to which a classical or ethnic music selection could be matched. Again, appropriate distractors for each item were chosen. Advanced music students at Juilliard were used to ensure a consensus on the item keyed correct, with popular distractors (more than 5% of responses) replaced.

A few words about the use of distractors is called for here. In initial pilot work, we employed distractors highly discrepant from the correct alternative, and obtained marked ceiling effects in children 8 to 9 years old. It is thus apparent that such children exhibit a basic veridical sensitivity to the affective–descriptive properties of dance movement, and are able to recognize the correspondences between dancers' movement through space and an abstract representation of that movement in the form of a design on paper. Such ceiling effects were less severe in the case of the musical stimuli, possibly due to the increased difficulty associated with crossing modalities—auditory and visual. Of course, as more subtle discriminations are required by virtue of less obviously discrepant distractors, individual variation is enhanced. Such variation is clearly essential for validation studies (see Kogan, 1989). At the same time, it is apparent that the figural skills at issue are likely to be present in at least rudimentary form at a fairly young age. Indeed, year-old infants demonstrate better-than-chance cross-categorical matching of auditory signals and visual line patterns (Wagner, Winner, Cicchetti, & Gardner, 1981). Such findings point to the primordial synesthetic and physiognomic linkages described by Werner and Kaplan (1963). The point at issue is that cross-categorical sensitivities can be demonstrated early in the life span, but with development, they become more subtle and differentiated. I should like to argue that the increasing subtlety of differentiation proceeds at different rates across children, hence generating the kinds of individual differences under discussion.

It is important to note that the aesthetic education program of the Lincoln Center Institute was not aimed at training performers, although many of the classroom exercises offered students the opportunity to perform. Rather, the intent was basically aimed at instilling an appreciation for and sensitivity to the performing arts through the demonstration and participation of experienced teacher-artists in the fields of music, dance, and drama. The performing arts world obviously requires sophisticated spectators as well as talented performers. To the degree that children are sensitized to the performing arts and exposed to some of its classic works in a supportive educational context, one can hopefully anticipate that they are more likely to become the engaged audiences of the future.

CAREERS IN THE PERFORMING ARTS

Of course, it is entirely possible that a small proportion of the children in the Lincoln Center program were stimulated to the point of aspiring toward a performing-arts career. Such children would naturally be expected to score high on measures of aesthetic sensitivity, but clearly this would be but a minimum requirement for the success or pursuit of a career in the performing arts. Ideally, we should follow the lives of such children through adolescence and young adulthood to see what happens to them. The research on teenagers by Csikszentmihalyi, Rathunde, and Whalen (1993) offers a model of how talent is developed or dissipated across the high school years in different domains (including music and the visual arts). That research does not, however, offer information on the fate of these teenagers after high school graduation, nor does it consider students talented in dance or acting. Although we learn a great deal about the forces—internal and external—that contribute to success and failure at the high school level, we would also like to know more about those individuals who have committed themselves to a career in the performing arts. Are there particular cognitive, personality, and motivational patterns that characterize musicians, dancers, and actors?

Innate Talent Versus Practice

To raise this question implies that we have entered the realm of talent and expertise, a realm that has been explored recently in considerable depth by K.A. Ericsson (1996). To oversimplify the issue for the moment, the crucial distinction concerns the role of deliberate practice in the acquisition of expertise—whether extent of practice is the primary causal agent of expert performance or whether a high level of talent, possibly innate, is causal, motivating extensive practice and subsequent expertise as an outcome.

Extreme positions regarding the origins of expertise are represented, on the one hand, by Sloboda (1996) who emphasizes the role of early parental involvement in fostering good practice habits in musical training, and on the other hand, by Winner (1996), who makes a strong case for exceptionally early precocity in the visual arts manifested independently of any extrinsic influences. It is possible to argue, of course, for domain differences, such that musical expertise is largely a function of skills developed through specific training and practice regimens, whereas expertise in the visual arts essentially reflects an inborn talent that assumes a distinctive artistic form over time. It is this author's impression, however, that those adhering to these extreme positions are uncomfortable with the domain-specificity argument. Winner (1996), for example, extends her argument for native talent from the visual arts to music, and, by contrast, Ericsson (1996) maintains that one must search further for "potential counterexamples documenting instances of confirmed exceptional performance that cannot be satisfactorily explained by practice and training." (p. 33). The approach taken in this chapter opts for neither extreme. Later in the chapter a schematic working model of careers in the performing arts will be offered that allows for both intrinsic and extrinsic determinants.

Athletic Aspects and the Role of Memory

A cursory glance at the contemporary research literature on the performing arts points to the very thin boundary separating that field from sports psychology. Indeed, James Sloan Allen, former Dean of the Juilliard School, commented as follows: "So demanding are the physical expectations of performance as to remove performers from the guild of artists and send them into the ranks of athletes." (1992, p. 201). Allen carries the analogy even further, noting how both performing artists and athletes rely on drill and practice, perform collectively in ensembles or teams, and engage in competitions with the aim of winning (victory for athletes and unreserved applause for performing artists). Such competition also takes the form of making it through an audition in the performing arts and qualifying for the team in athletics.

Can the analogy to sports and athletics be extended to the realm of memory? There can be no question that memory is critical for performing artists, and especially for actors and dancers (as well as singers). Musicians can, of course, perform from a visible score, but the gifted performer often does not feel in full possession of a work until it is committed to memory. But athletes (especially in competitive sports) memorize game plans and often are called on to remember the strengths and weaknesses of specific opponents. But much of what happens in an athletic contest cannot be anticipated, and the outcome often hinges on spur-of-the-moment decisions and actions. A losing effort is rarely characterized as a memory failure. On the other hand, a memory lapse by a performing artist can be very serious, and its anticipation can give rise to the "stage-fright" phenomenon.

Naturally, the symbol system specific to the particular art form will determine what is remembered—notes for musicians, words for actors, movements for dancers, notes and words for singers. For beginning students of the performing arts, we are referring to what has commonly been described as *rote memory*. This represents a skill, once highly valued in our schools, but now considered of much less importance than critical thinking and insightful problem-solving. Yet rote memory may play a major role in the education and training of performing artists, despite the negative implications assigned to it in current educational thinking.

It is possible, however, that the term *rote memory* does not do complete justice to what performing artists are striving to accomplish. The long hours of practice and rehearsal assure technical mastery, and in addition appear to transform mental into physical memories such that particular bodily actions feel just right. For actors, it may well be the emotional tone that feels just right. For musicians as well, emotional expressiveness in performance is all-important, and a major purpose of musical training is to strengthen the link between specific musical structures and congruent emotional responses (see Sloboda, 1991). It is the goal of teachers in the performing arts to facilitate such transformation. For the exceptionally gifted performer, the transformation will produce a personal performance style often distinguished by new interpretive insights.

A highly relevant study employing expert and novice ballet dancers was carried out by Janet Starkes and her associates (Starkes, Deakin, Lindley, & Crisp, 1987). The dancers were shown a videotaped sequence of eight ballet steps without accompanying music. In one case the sequence was selected by an experienced choreographer; in the other case, the sequence used the same elements randomly arranged. The dancers were required to reproduce the sequence of steps from memory. The results showed that the expert dancers did better at the task than did the novices, but only in the case of the sequences with choreographic structure. In addition, when music was added, the expert dancers' probability of recall showed a further increase. Of interest as well are the differences in the strategies of recall of the expert and novice dancers. The novices rushed to reproduce the sequences before the memories faded; the experts, by contrast, had encoded the movement sequences through a process called marking—where dancers substitute hand positions for foot and body positions. These hand positions are reinstated during recall, thereby facilitating retrieval of the sequence of steps. Verbal labels are also sometimes assigned to the particular movement sequences to enhance recall. It is thus evident that acquisition of ballet expertise entails a growing sensitivity to choreographic structure (of which music is an integral part), and the effective use of specialized memory techniques to encode movement sequence (see Allard & Starkes, 1991). Clearly, we have advanced well beyond *rote memory* as typically conceived. Indeed, as we have seen, removal of choreographic structure through randomization of ballet steps—essentially turning the task into one of rote memory—wipes out the advantage of expertise.

Comparable effects have been reported by Noice and Noice (1997) in their studies of the memory for dramatic script among professional actors. Professional actors and novices were randomly assigned to *rote* and *gist* instructional conditions. In the former, the task involved memorizing the lines by rote repetition without scanning forward or backward in the script; in the latter, the participants had to learn the role as if preparing for an imminent audition. Recall proved to be vastly superior in the gist relative to the rote condition for both the actors and novices, although the difference was surprisingly larger for the latter. Noice and Noice (1997) suggested that the actors were better able "to defeat the constraints of the rote strategy" (p. 45). In comments following the experiment, the actors talked about the extreme frustration they felt when not permitted to move freely through the script. No such anecdotal comments were offered by the novices according to the Noices. In sum, it is evident that rote memorizing does not work for either actors or dancers, for the reason that it does not permit access to the deeper structure or meaning of the material to be learned.

Personality, Motivation, and Socialization

Personality. As we depart from the study of the skills inherently demanded by the performing arts, and move to the personality correlates of choosing specific performing arts careers, we cannot anticipate findings distinguished by great statistical power. For we are essentially asking whether there are characteristics beyond the requisite talents that contribute to choosing particular performing arts careers. One can conceptualize the issue in multiple regression terms (i.e., what is the incremental contribution of personality dispositions to choice of and success in the performing arts, assuming that skills and talent factors constitute the strongest predictors)? There is also the possibility that the criteria employed—choice of a performing arts career and success in that career—may have distinct causal sources. Conceivably, different qualities are associated with success in the performing arts than with choosing to embark on such a career in the first place. Unfortunately, at the present time, we do not have answers to these questions for the reason that the kinds of studies required to answer them have not been conducted. Investigators who study the skill components of the performing arts are not especially interested in personality factors and vice versa.

A first approach, largely confined to actors, involves the construction of a theoretically based instrument on which actors are expected to achieve especially high scores. A good example is represented by Mark Snyder's (1987) construct of self-monitoring whose central feature concerns the extent to which individuals are able to achieve self-control, and accordingly, "are, in a sense, actors with a large repertoire of roles, willing and able to work from a wide range of scripts; they cast themselves in many different parts in life. By contrast, the low self-monitor may be likened to the performer who has the same part in every production, particularly the performer whose own personality seems to provide the script for his or her every role." (Snyder, 1987, p.186). Not surprisingly, the item that best differentiates high from low self-monitors on the Self-Monitoring scale reads as follows: "I would probably make a good actor."

What we seem to have here is an attempt to operationalize Goffman's (1959) dramaturgical metaphor, but with an emphasis on individual differences in the degree to which one's self-concept fits the metaphor. Essentially, Snyder is using acting and actors to validate his self-monitoring construct in the general population. The work does not really tell us anything new about actors or the acting profession. We already knew that actors must cultivate expressive self-control in order to play diverse roles on the stage or screen.

Another effort along similar lines is represented by the work of Friedman and his associates (Friedman, Prince, Riggio, & DiMatteo, 1980). These authors devised a self descriptive questionnaire (the Affective Communication Test), whose items reflect the degree to which a respondent manifests nonverbal emotional expressiveness in behavior. Whereas self-monitoring is concerned with the appropriateness of one's emotional behavior to the situation, the measure developed by Friedman and his associates is concerned with the nonverbal enhancers of emotional expressiveness quite apart from their appropriateness. Example items are "I can easily express emotion over the telephone," and "I often touch friends during conversations." But note that the item, "People tell me that I would make a good actor or actress," is also present, and again one finds that subjects who have been involved in acting generated higher scores on the instrument. The rationale for this link to acting is that a stage role is more effectively communicated to an audience if the performance in that role displays the appropriate level and quality of nonverbal emotional expressiveness. The relationships observed, although in the expected direction, were modest in magnitude, however, and the authors unequivocally state that sheer expressiveness as measured by the Affective Communication Test cannot be equated with acting ability. As in the case of self-monitoring, we find acting serving as a metaphor to assist in the development of an individual differences variable relevant to the general population. There are countless numbers of individuals who are high in self-monitoring and in emotional expressiveness, yet only a tiny percentage of such individuals become actors whether as students, amateurs, or professionals.

Rather than a single theoretically derived personality dimension, an alternative approach is multidimensional (i.e., a standardized battery of personality measures is administered to performing artists or students in the performing arts and sometimes to a control group of individuals who are not performing artists). Comparisons are then drawn between performing artists and control subjects, and among different kinds of performing artists. The guiding hypothesis behind this work is that the diverse performing arts constitute distinctive subcultures, each with its own atmosphere and requirements. The presumption is that individuals will be drawn to such subcultures to the extent that they possess a congruent personality profile. Bakker's (1988) research on young ballet students in The Netherlands is typical of the approach. That author observed that, relative to controls, dancers were more introverted, achievement-oriented, and inclined toward higher levels of emotionality. These traits are considered conducive to the world of classical ballet—the strong emphasis on individual performance during training as conducive to introversion, the focus on competition to succeed as consistent with achievement motivation, and the need to give emotional expression to music and choreography as benefiting dancers distinguished by high levels of emotionality. The fit is quite good, although one suspects that it is post hoc (i.e. the personality profiles were observed first and the requirements of the professional subculture rationalized to fit the profiles)

Clearly needed is a personality comparison within the same study of performing artists across different fields. Such a study has been carried out by Marchant-Haycox and Wilson (1992). The sample included British musicians, actors, singers, dancers, and nonartist controls, who volunteered to fill out a multitrait personality instrument—the Eysenck Personality Profile. The 21 traits assessed by that instrument generated three major dimensions—*extroversion–introversion*, *emotionality*, and *adventurousness*. In general, relative to control subjects, performing artists tended toward introversion, emotional instability, and caution. There is much variation, however, across the artist subgroups, with actors emerging as extroverted and adventurous, dancers at the emotional extreme, and musicians at the introverted extreme. Complicating these comparisons, however, are sex differences in the composition of the subgroups (e.g., the dancers are predominantly female and the musicians predominantly male).

Interpretation of the array of personality differences among performing artists poses formidable problems. In the case of the Marchant-Haycox and Wilson (1992) data, for example, an hypothesis that a particular personality profile is conducive to the selection of a specific performing arts career receives only partial support. Thus actors' high scores on *expressiveness* is consistent with other data considered earlier, and one can understand how possession of such a trait could contribute to a decision to consider acting as a career. For dancers, on the other hand, the most extreme scores are on the traits *unhappy*, *anxious*, and *hypochondriacal*. One cannot begin to imagine that these characteristics have any bearing on the choice of a dancing career. Ballet careers generally begin in preadolescent childhood, and it truly stretches credibility to believe that the most neurotic children are selected out for ballet training. Rather, such neurotic traits may well be reactive to the kinds of life stresses that a dance career entails. Similarly in the case of classical musicians, the most extreme scores are for the traits *inactive*, *submissive*, and *unambitious*. Again, we cannot quite believe that these traits characterized musicians at the time they embarked on a musical career. Rather, the traits probably reflect the classical musician's realization that he or she is but a part of a large musical ensemble, and that aspirations toward advancement to the status of soloist are unrealizable.

It is evident, in sum, that the personality analysis of performing artists carries with it an array of interpretive difficulties. In the absence of longitudinal studies of performing artists commencing in childhood, we have been left with a set of distinguishing traits, some possibly of genetic origin and some strongly suggestive of a reactive response to the pressures of a performing arts career. Conceivably, the nature of this reactive response is partially attributable to individual differences in susceptibility to stress—a person-by-situation interaction, if you will. Clearly, we have barely scratched the surface of the role of personality in the lives of performing artists. Contradictions abound that call for some resolution. In a survey of dancers contemplating retirement, Ellen Wallach (1988) vividly reported on the emotionally wrenching quality of the separation from dance, and Hamilton and Hamilton (1991) described a high level of suicidal ideation. It is apparent that dancers derive much satisfaction from their careers, and do not relinquish them lightly. How is one to reconcile such information with personality data pointing to heightened levels of dysphoric affect and lessened subjective well-being in dancers?

Where actors are concerned, we might well ask how they manage to maintain their extroverted and adventurous dispositions in the face of the remarkable instability that characterizes acting careers. As we shall soon see, approximately 95% of New York stage actors are not engaged in stage acting at any particular point in time. How do we account for the robust resiliency that actors seem to display in the face of periodic rejection? In the remainder of this chapter, I explore socialization influences—childhood experience that might have contributed to choosing to pursue acting or dance as a career. Then, having chosen a performing arts career, what are the motivational forces at work that lead to persistence in the face of career hardships?

Socialization. In the matter of socialization, consider the 448 actors and dancers sampled in Reciniello's (1987) dissertation. Where parents of these performers are concerned, the data clearly demonstrate substantial involvement in the arts at either the professional or amateur level. For fathers, 21% were professionals, 49% participated in the arts as amateurs. In the case of the mothers, the figures were 22% and 69% for professional and amateur involvements, respectively. In this sample, actors and dancers were basically similar in the pattern of parental artistic involvements.

Consider next the responses of the actors and dancers to Helson's (1965) Childhood Activity Checklist. A factor analysis of these data generated six factors, of which two are especially relevant—an Imaginary Play and a Performing Factor. Of particular interest in the case of Imaginary Play is the degree to which the item content represents apparent childhood analogues of acting at the adult level. In particular, "creating complex imaginary situations," "writing poems and stories," "having an imaginary playmate," and "pretending to be different people" are dramatic by their very nature, and it thus appears that actors almost by direct extension over time have found the perfect field in which to indulge their childhood passions. Of course, dance, too, can have strong dramatic elements, and as we have seen, dancers also score high on the Imaginary Play factor. But it makes eminent sense that actors would score higher than dancers, given the internal kinesthetic focus of dance in comparison to the imaginary role playing that constitutes the essence of drama.

All of these retrospective data suggest that the choice of acting or dancing as a possible profession may be set quite early in childhood, given the observed high level of parental involvement in the arts and the pattern of childhood activity preferences. Those two factors in combination must exert a powerful impact, for it implies that the parents are at least implicitly encouraging the child along pathways close to that child's salient interests.

Motivation. In an effort to understand how actors respond to success and failure, Wilson (1989), in her dissertation research, employed a modified Attribution Style Questionnaire developed by Peterson et al. (1982). Modification took the form of adding items specific to the acting context. For example, respondents are asked to imagine a situation in which they have been unable to find acting work for several months. They are then requested to specify the major cause of that unfortunate situation and to indicate whether that cause would continue to prevail in the future. The foregoing item obviously represents a negative event; other items reflect positive events (e.g., "you get selected out of the cast to assume a larger role.") The cause for such negative or positive events can be attributed internally (i.e., to oneself) or externally (i.e., to other people or circumstances). Furthermore, the cause may be viewed as specific to the particular event described or as likely to prevail when such events occur in the future—in other words, the instability or stability of the cause presumed to account for the event.

It is not too surprising to find that actors' internal attributions for good events are viewed as stable, suggesting that a sense of personal control over good events is accompanied by an expectancy that such control will persist into the future. On the other hand, an internal attribution for a bad event— that one is personally responsible for failing to find acting work, for example, is not necessarily experienced as likely to continue indefinitely. In this respect, actors clearly do not fit the depression pattern (i.e., I am personally responsible for the bad things that are happening to me and that is how it will be into the indefinite future.) Actors obviously do not lend themselves to such despair and hopelessness. Further support for this observation comes from a study of British actors by Phillips (1991). She refers to a group of actors who "survive on perpetual short-term contracts," and describes the group as representative of the "flip-side of stardom." Although these actors occupied a marginal position in the profession, they almost uniformly had a "very deep feeling of being an actor," and "believed that better times were just around the corner."

A Working Model of Career Development in the Performing Arts

Figure 8.1 presents in schematic form a possible working model incorporating the multitude of forces across the life span that are likely to influence the choice and maintenance of a performing arts career. This figure should not be construed as a representation of empirical research outcomes, for as indicated earlier, the performing arts have not been subject to extensive empirical investigation.

Note that Figure 8.1 divides career development into five stages tied to chronological age—birth endowment (not literally a "stage"), early childhood, middle childhood and early adolescence, later adolescence and young adulthood, and career as a performing artist (which can potentially cover a range of several years to the remainder of the life span). The influences on career development are represented in the body of the figure contained within ovals or rectangles, the former signifying intrinsic determinants and the latter, extrinsic determinants.

Arrows connecting the ovals indicate that intrinsic determinants carry over from earlier to later stages. Thus, inherited talent as a birth endowment obviously influences what happens at all subsequent stages. Correspondingly, the emerging aesthetic sensitivity of early childhood activities achieves ever greater refinement and sophistication in the stages that follow chronologically. Arrows connecting the rectangles to the ovals are intended to depict the contribution of the extrinsic influences to the intrinsic factors. It should be understood, of course, that the extrinsic influences contributing to a performing-arts career cannot completely account for the intrinsic forces that motivate such a career. For example, exposure to art forms in the home during early childhood (extrinsic) may well contribute to the child's emerging aesthetic sensitivity (intrinsic), but the latter may also reflect genetic factors that sensitize the child to particular aesthetic domains.

As Figure 8.1 indicates, it is during the middle-childhood to early adolescent period, when the child's cognitive, motor, and expressive skills have become salient, that these skills are put to use in a drive toward competence, whether in music, dance, or drama. The acquisition of competence requires hours of work, and hence the potential for discouragement and eventual dropping-out is likely to be high. Here is where the extrinsic factors play an important role. Arts-relevant school experiences can offer much positive reinforcement (e.g., participating in ensembles for musical, dance, or dramatic performances). Parents who offer emotional support and invest in extracurricular training for their children clearly facilitate movement toward a performing-arts career.

It is not until later adolescence and young adulthood that firm career commitments are made. At this stage, one can begin to talk about genuine expertise and the "flow" experience (i.e., the ease of concentration, absence of boredom, and intrinsic enjoyment associated with the practice of one's craft; see Csikszentmihalyi & Csikszentmihalyi, 1988). Contributing to the acquisition of expertise, of course, is advanced specialized training in the individual's performing arts specialty. Particularly critical at this juncture are performance evaluations that inform the performing-arts aspirant of any weaknesses, for these must be overcome if he or she is to anticipate the possibility of a successful career in a highly competitive field.

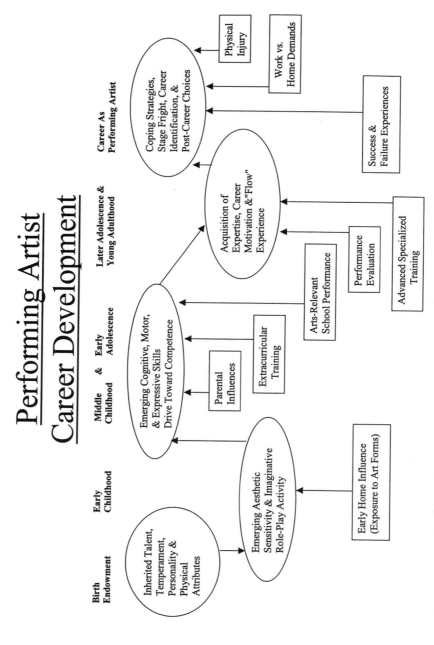

FIG. 8.1. Career development in the performing arts: A generic working model.

By the time young adulthood is reached, one can expect that those aspirants without the requisite talent and motivation would have moved on to other fields. Those few who move on to a career in the performing arts will identify themselves as professional musicians, dancers, singers, actors, and will be subject to all of the rewards and hardships that those fields have to offer. As we have observed in the case of acting, the incidence of failure is so very substantial that adaptive coping strategies are required to maintain one's career identification as an actor. Further, stage fright troubles many performers (see Wilson, 1994, chap. 11), and coping strategies must be developed to deal with it if a performer is to remain in the field.

The figure lists work versus home demands and physical injury as extrinsic factors. For those performers with family attachments whose work requires constant touring, the strain that such travel can have on marital relationships is considerable. Not all performers cope well with such stresses. In the matter of physical injury, ballet dancers are particularly susceptible. If such injury is severe enough, it can seriously disrupt and even end a dance career. It is events such as these along with all of the other exigencies accompanying a performing arts career that accounts for the inclusion of post-career choices under intrinsic factors. For some fields sooner, and for others later, the performer will have to consider post-career options. Such options, of course, are strikingly different for the dancer giving up dancing at age 35, and the musician retiring from a symphony orchestra at age 70.

Figure 8.1 is intended as a generic working model for the career development of performing artists. No doubt, models constructed for the different performing arts would reveal some variation from the generic model as well as greater precision regarding the forces at work in each field. It is common knowledge, for example, that ballet careers begin with children as young as 7 to 8 years of age. Musical careers may begin even earlier. For these performing arts, a direct trajectory can be traced from the child's to the mature performer's activities. In contrast, it is dubious whether acting careers (apart from a small minority of child actors) formally begin at such young ages, and the trajectory from childhood activities to the profession of acting is likely to display numerous twists and turns.

In sum, the working model displayed in the figure is intended as a heuristic device to promote future research on the forces that contribute to the development of performing artists. For investigators seeking a relatively uncultivated field, the study of performing artists offers an inviting target.

REFERENCES

Allard, F., & Starkes, J. L. (1991). Motor skill experts in sports, dance, and other domains. In K. A. Ericsson & J. Smith (Eds.), *Toward a general theory of expertise* (pp. 126–152). New York: Cambridge Univ. Press.

Allen, J. S. (1992). Educating performers. *American Scholar, 61,* 197–212.

Bakker, F. C. (1988). Personality differences between young dancers and non-dancers. *Personality and Individual Differences, 9,* 121–131.

Cantor, N., & Kihlstrom, J. F. (1987). *Personality and social intelligence.* Englewood Cliffs, NJ: Prentice-Hall.

Csikszentmihalyi, M., & Csikszentmihalyi, I. S. (Eds.) (1988). *Optimal experience: psychological studies of flow in consciousness.* New York: Cambridge University Press.

Csikszentmihalyi, M., Rathunde, K., & Whalen, S. (1993*). Talented teen-agers: The roots of success and failure.* New York: Cambridge University Press.

Ericsson, K. A. (1996). The acquisition of expert performance: an introduction to some of the issues. In K. A. Ericsson (Ed.), *The road to excellence* (pp. 1–50). Mahwah, NJ: Lawrence Erlbaum Associates.

Friedman, H. S., Prince, L. M., Riggio, R. E., & DiMatteo, M. R (1980). Understanding and assessing nonverbal expressiveness: The affective communication test. *Journal of Personality and Social Psychology, 39,* 333–351.

Goffman, E. (1959). *The presentation of self in everyday life.* Garden City, NY: Doubleday Anchor.

Hamilton, L. H., & Hamilton, W. G. (1991). Classical ballet: Balancing the costs of artistry and athleticism. In *Medical problems of performing artists* (pp. 39–44) Philadelphia: Hanley and Belfus.

Helson, R. (1965). Childhood interest clusters related to creativity in women. *Journal of Consulting Psychology, 29,* 352–361.

Kogan, N. (1989). A stylistic perspective on metaphor and aesthetic sensitivity in children. In T. Globerson & T. Zelniker (Eds.), *Cognitive style and cognitive development,* (pp. 192–213). Norwood, NJ: Ablex.

Kogan, N. (1994). Cognitive styles. In R. Sternberg (Ed.), *Encyclopedia of human intelligence* (pp. 266–273). New York: Macmillan.

Kogan, N. (2000). On becoming more general with age. In J.E. Birren & J.J.F. Schroots (eds.). *The history of geropsychology in autobiography* (pp.157–171). Washington, DC: APA Publications.

Kogan, N., Connor, K., Gross, A., & Fava, D. (1980). Understanding visual metaphor: developmental and individual differences. *Monographs of the Society for Research in Child Development, 45* (1, Serial No. 183).

Noice, T., & Noice, H. (1997). *The nature of expertise in professional acting: A cognitive view.* Mahwah, NJ: Lawrence Erlbaum Associates.

Peterson, C., Semmel, A., von Bayer, C., Abramson, L. Y., Metalsky, G. I., & Seligman, M. E .P. (1982). The attribution style questionnaire. *Cognitive Therapy and Research, 6,* 287– 299.

Phillips, E. (1991). Acting as an insecure occupation: The flipside of stardom. In G. D. Wilson (Ed.), *Psychology and performing arts.* (pp. 133–142). Amsterdam: Swets and Zeitlinger.

Reciniello, S. (1987). *Toward an understanding of the performing artist.* Unpublished doctoral dissertation, Graduate Faculty, New School for Social Research.

Sloboda, J. (1991). Musical expertise. In K. A. Ericsson & J. Smith (Eds.) *Toward a general theory of expertise*. (pp. 153–171). New York: Cambridge University Press.

Sloboda, J. (1996). The acquisition of musical performance expertise: Deconstructing the "talent" account of individual differences in musical expressivity. In K. A. Ericsson (Ed.), *The road to excellence* (pp. 107–126). Mahwah, NJ: Lawrence Erlbaum Associates.

Snyder, M. (1987). *Public appearances, private realities*. New York: Freeman.

Starkes, J. L., Deakin, J. M., Lindley, S., & Crisp, F. (1987). Motor versus verbal recall of ballet sequences by young expert dancers. *Journal of Sport Psychology, 9,* 222–230.

Sternberg, R. (1997). *Thinking Styles*. New York: Cambridge University Press.

Wagner, R., Winner, E., Cicchetti, D., & Gardner, H. (1981). "Metaphorical" mapping in human infants. *Child Development, 52,* 728–731.

Wallach, E. (1988). *Life after performing: Career transitions for dancers*. Boston: Life After Performing Project.

Welsh, G. S. (1980). *Welsh figure preference test*. Palo Alto, CA: Consulting Psychologists Press.

Werner, H., & Kaplan, B. (1963). *Symbol formation*. New York: Wiley.

Wilson, G. D. (1994). *Psychology for performing artists*. London: Jessica Kingsley Publishers.

Wilson, M. J. (1989). *An attributional analysis of career productivity in the field of professional acting*. Unpublished doctoral dissertation, Graduate Faculty, New School for Social Research.

Winner, E. (1996). The rage to master: The decisive role of talent in the visual arts. In K. A. Ericsson (Ed.), *The road to excellence* (pp. 271–301). Mahwah, NJ: Lawrence Erlbaum Associates.

III

VALIDITY AND VALUES IN PSYCHOLOGICAL AND EDUCATIONAL MEASUREMENT

9

Validity for What?

Donald W. Fiske
University of Chicago

The title of my chapter, as some readers may recall, is that of a paper published in 1946 by Jack Jenkins. He was my first mentor on the topic of validity. I served under him in the Aviation Psychology section of the Navy's Bureau of Medicine and Surgery during part of World War II. I use his title as a way of remembering and honoring him, and also for its pithiness and relevance.

I started writing this chapter with a sentence that read: "Validity is an integrated evaluative judgment of the degree to which empirical evidence and theoretical rationales support the *adequacy* and *appropriateness* of *inferences* and *actions* based on test scores or other modes of assessment."

Then I stopped. There was something familiar about that sentence. Oh, yes! I suddenly recalled that these were the opening words in Sam Messick's chapter in the *Educational Measurement* book (1989). That is a top-notch chapter extending our ideas about validity. Particularly noteworthy was his invocation of current discussions of relevant philosophy of science.

I had a passing thought that a chapter summarizing Sam's chapter might be the most useful thing for me to prepare, but there might be copyright problems.

So instead, let's look at validity as the concept has developed from the 1930s to today. It is an interesting record. I do this by noting some of the major papers published in this period. This is a personal sample. Others would generate a different list.

Before World War II, validity was seriously neglected. A reasonable correlation with a conveniently available and acceptably relevant criterion was considered enough. If anyone started impudently to ask about the reliability and validity of that criterion measure, someone would change the subject of the conversation. After all, one could ask about the adequacy of the criterion for the criterion, and so on.

I think it was World War II that forced psychologists to rethink the problem of validity. We could no longer just ask: "Does this test predict the outcome of training?" We had to ask: "Does this test predict performance on the job, such as skill in combat?" and "How does one assess that?" Does anyone want to volunteer as observer-rater for studying personnel in combat?

In his paper, *Validity for what?* (1946), Jenkins reflected on the professional lessons learned during the war by psychologists working in the Armed Services. He pointed out that, before World War II, the major emphasis was on the predictor test, with any old criterion being hauled in, as needed. In that war, the psychologists working on personnel selection and classification quickly saw the need to pick and study each criterion carefully. The criteria must be valid. But what do you do if scores from two immediately successive flight checks (work sample tests, each conducted by an experienced instructor), correlated with each other around .00 (yes, zero!)? You can fire the instructor you like least, but that won't fix things up. The problem was not just due to subjectivity in instructor ratings.

Psychologists were also disturbed to discover that there was an essentially zero correlation between the test and the retest the next day of graduates from bombardier school. A moment's thought about the situation makes one realize the multiple determinants of the nice, neat measure of the distance between where the dummy bomb landed and the target: How well did the pilot line up the bomber before turning it over to the bombardier? Did wind and weather affect the accuracy? So even an objective measure—distance—may have its limitations.

From these results, psychologists saw that they had to be concerned about the validity for criteria, and that they should be cautious about criteria that a priori seemed quite adequate. And as a staff officer, what would your recommendation be to your C. O. if you obtained results like these? (I am afraid I do not recall what the military officers did to resolve these serious problems, but we won the war anyway.)

After the war, some psychologists continued to work in their ivory towers, concerned primarily with the tests themselves, with only passing attention to relationships between tests and the real world. Harold Gulliksen's *Theory of Mental Tests* is an excellent presentation of that approach as of 1950. In that book, he was more concerned with true scores than with test validity as obtained in the real world. That same year, however, he published a paper in the *American Psychologist* on intrinsic validity, arguing that psychologists must assess the intrinsic validity of the criterion. By its correlations with other measures, we can learn about the criterion. He distinguished between intrinsic content validity for achievement tests and intrinsic correlational validity for ability tests.

Guilford was more practical. By the second edition of his *Psychometric Methods* (1954), he offers not only a careful statement of the classical work on validity but also hints of things to come, with references to subjects' motivations and to response sets. Regrettably, this edition omitted his citation (found in the first edition) of Clark Hull's 1928 book on *Aptitude Testing.* (That date is not an error. It was before Hull got into how rats learn.) Hull identified three classes of aptitude criteria: product criteria, such as amount of work done; action criteria where one measures what occurs, such as the speed of a runner or the height of the bar in pole-vaulting; and finally subjective judgments, if nothing else is available.

A major shift in our thinking about validity, and a major advance, came with the work leading to the first *Technical Recommendations for Psychological Tests and Diagnostic Techniques* published by the American Psychological Association in 1954. The authors' basic distinctions between content, concurrent, and predictive validity helped to structure our thinking. This committee report was followed by the Cronbach-Meehl paper on construct validity (1955). Those authors pointed out that the basic notion of construct validity cannot be expressed by a single coefficient. It is a pattern of results consistent with the pattern specified by the conceptualization of the construct. One basic statement in that paper deserves our attention and careful thought: "The investigation of a test's construct validity is not essentially different from the general scientific procedures for developing and confirming theories" (p. 300).

That paper and the *Technical Recommendations* document started a concern with validity of constructs and not just with the validity of a single test. But the spread of concern with validity did not stop there. It went over to validity of the whole research plan: To be more specific, "validity for what" became questions about the validity of conclusions, of interpretations, and of generalizations. It was almost as if we began to ask about the validity of each piece of information in our whole research enterprise. We'll turn to that development later in this chapter.

Concern with classical problems continued alongside concern with construct validity. In 1957, Loevinger published a monograph, *Objective tests as instruments of psychological theory.* A large part of the text is concerned with construct validity. As a part of validity, she designated structural validity, which includes the fidelity of the structural model to the structural characteristics of the nontest manifestations of the trait. She comments on many topics, but does not have as clear a message as the Cronbach-Meehl paper on construct validity.

Staying pretty much with the old question of the validity of a test, Don Campbell and I, in 1959, published *Convergent and Discriminant Validation by the Multitrait-Multimethod Matrix*. (I give the whole title because it gets misquoted occasionally, even by top university presses.) This paper asked the field: "What are you going to do about the fact that there is a lot of method variance in our measurements, perhaps even more method variance than concept-relevant variance?" For the last 41 years, we have waited for an answer, while papers continue to report much the same kinds of depressing multitrait-multimethd matrices as the ones we included in our paper, with large amounts of method variance and low values in the between-method validity diagonal.

Yet that paper continues its phenomenal citation rate, still running around a hundred per year. That rate still puzzles me. Lee Cronbach (1989, p. 153) thought it was because we offered a recipe for investigating construct validity, in spite of our statements about the difference between construct validity and convergent and discriminant validation (p. 100). Perhaps so. But the citations indicate to me that the ideas and procedures in that paper are still spreading. (I am tempted to say, spreading like a weed). Many of the current citations are in journals that are fairly far outside psychology and that I, and I would guess you too, do not recognize.

A few of the contemporary papers deal with proposals for analyzing those matrices. Regrettably, there seems to be no consensus yet on how to do it. Is the problem here that we don't know how to handle the matter of method variance conceptually? Is the notion of method variance too comprehensive, covering up too many diverse kinds of variance? We seem to be up against a brick wall there.

A few years later, but still several decades ago, the issue of validity began to appear in a variety of contexts. The question "validity for what?" had an increasing number of answers. In 1963, Campbell and Stanley came out with a chapter that became a book that started a line of theoretical controversy. Given a particular experimental design, what inferences could be made from the obtained results? And if the design was quasi-experimental, how much did that restrict the investigator?

The sequel to that monograph, Cook and Campbell (1979), introduced some new labels for particular aspects of validity, such as statistical conclusion validity and construct validity of putative causes and effects. For each type of validity, they list a number of threats. They are really very helpful to the student, although their list probably also increases student anxiety, supporting that basic oracular warning, from Murphy, about research plans: "If anything can go wrong, it will" and its partner, "If you fix things up so that nothing can possibly go wrong, it still will."

The almost sudden flare-up of program evaluation, a much-needed body of effort fostered by legal requirements for social plans in government-supported research on social programs, did much to stimulate thoughtful analyses of the problem. One group working together on this endeavor was the Stanford Evaluation Consortium. It generated two major works: *Toward Reform of Program Evaluation* (Cronbach, L. J., et al., 1980) and *Designing Evaluations of Educational and Social Programs* (Cronbach, L.J., 1982). His UTOS notational and analytic system provides an excellent basis for thinking about many fundamental validity issues. (In UTOS, U stands for the unit studied, T for the treatment, O for the Observing operation, and S for the setting.)

Cronbach's 1989 picture of *Construct Validity after Thirty Years* came out a few years later. He noted the great transformation from construct validation as an approach developed for applications where other forms of test validity cannot be applied (for example, the validation of projective tests) to construct validation as the base on which all other forms of validity rest. Alternatively we can look at the other forms of validity as contributing to construct validity.

Meanwhile, Boruch, Cordray, and others at Northwestern were working on their own agenda, which included secondary analysis, the desirability of having a body of evaluation data reexamined by an independent group, using different analytic methods. After all, what you get out of data depends on how you analyze them.

The increasing significance of construct validity is reflected in Sam Messick's analysis of the concept. He distinguishes six aspects: *Content, Structural, Generalizability, External, Consequential,* and *Substantive* and goes on to say that these "function as general validity criteria or standards for all educational and psychological measurement" (Messick, 1995, p.744. (The original statement of the analysis was made at least 6 years earlier.) In other words, these are matters that all of us who are concerned with measuring should worry about.

The *Content* aspect is concerned with the construct domain: What is in that domain and what is outside it? In particular, does the assessment of the construct include tasks that provide a representation of all parts of the domain?

The *Structural* aspect of construct validity addresses the consistency between the internal structure of the assessment and what is known about the internal structure of the construct domain. The theory of the construct domain should guide the rational development of the construct-based scoring criteria.

Messick's *Generalizability* aspect of construct validity "examines the extent to which score properties and interpretations generalize to and across groups, settings, and tasks, including generalizability of test-criterion relationships across settings and time periods" (Messick, 1996, p.9). In his later discussion, he included in this aspect the consistency of performance across tasks. Couldn't the degree of such consistency be expected to vary with the delineation of the construct? A heterogeneous construct should, quite appropriately, have low mean intertask correlations, assuming that different tasks are aimed at different parts of the construct domain.

The *External* aspect of validity refers to the pattern of relationships between assessment scores and criterion measures in applied situations and also the relationships among the assessment scores.

The *Consequential* aspect "appraises the value implications of score interpretation as a basis for action as well as the actual and potential consequences of test use, especially in regard to sources of invalidity related to issues of bias, fairness, and distributive justice" (Messick, 1996, pp.9–10).

The *Substantive* aspect of construct validity is focused on the processes used by respondents: Are they the ones that were intended on the basis of the domain processes?

Should we try to maximize the similarity between the processes required for successful answering of a test item and those embedded in the construct as delineated? At one time, I was convinced that close agreement between these was necessary for good measurement. But as I thought more about it, I realized that rarely could the two processes be expected to be similar. To be sure, one can measure achievement in multiplication by asking the subject to multiply some pairs of numbers, or measure competence in spelling by asking the subject to spell some words. But that is about as far as one can go.

In *Measuring the Concepts of Personality*, I suggested three test designs: simulated stimuli, a priori related process, and empirically related process. A test of field independence illustrates the simulated stimuli type of design, subject reports of prior behaviors illustrates the a priori related process, and the MMPI the empirically related process. We use whichever is possible and promising for the task at hand.

After studying Messick's comprehensive analysis of construct validity, one would hesitate to undertake the determination of the construct validity of any assessment operation. One sees why construct validation is seen as a never-ending procedure. One also speculates (or dreams) about the possibility of going back to nontest behavior, to opportunities for appraising actual manifestations of the construct under naturalistic conditions: forget the ethical problems, forget the difficulties in obtaining samples that cover the construct domain, forget the difficulties in obtaining reliable judgments of the construct from recordings.

No, let's forget that daydream and get back to measuring procedures where we, the authorities, can tell our subjects as subjects what they have to do.

Back to reality. With a bit of luck, our work on construct validity of measurements and of forms of validity in research designs will complement each other, so that we can fit the various pieces into one big picture.

As Cronbach and Meehl said at the end of their 1955 paper (and as I have quoted earlier), construct validation is essentially the general scientific approach for testing theories. In pursuing it, we are doing what colleagues in other sciences have been doing all along. But our thinking about it may help us to understand better what we are doing.

Anastasi wrote in 1986 that construct validation is a never-ending process. It is however, not a task for Sisyphus, doing the same thing over and over. And we are moving ahead. We have identified a major problem in psychology, and that is the first step toward solving it.

Construct validity refers to a goal. It may be a will-o'-the-wisp, leading us farther and farther down a road. I say that because rarely if ever have I seen a completely executed program for establishing the construct validity of anything, an assessment procedure or a construct. Yes, construct validation is a never-ending process, partly because the construct validation of one assessment procedure depends to some extent on the construct validation of other constructs and assessment procedures.

To summarize what this chapter has argued up to this point, there has been a development from one loose concept of validity to multiple meanings. Validity is a constantly expanding problem. Even by 1980, Messick counted 17 usages and labels for kinds of validity. Those working on a single test seek to increase its reliability and hence its validity, a reasonable assumption if one has some validity to begin with. But others are concerned with the validity of the criteria. More broadly, we are concerned with the validity of everything we use, and not just the validity of all the measurement procedures used, but also the validity of the research design, the validity of the experimental methods (including the validity of the stimuli themselves), and the validity of our conclusions and inferences. Fundamentally, construct validity underlies all of these aspects of research. So "Validity for What?" Validity for predictor tests and for criteria. Validity for everything we use and do in research.

On the validity matter, does anyone feel completely comfortable with where we are today? I am impressed by the progress we have made on the topic, and particularly with the extending of our validity concerns to components of the research process other than the test or measuring instrument. Because I have retired from the fray, I am a bit reluctant to point out scholarly research tasks still not done. But let's go back to consider the basic question: What are we trying to understand?

I will put aside, for now, the question whether our units, the things to which we assign numbers, are the right size. The units we now use have led us to fruitful research, but I am uncertain whether we have used units of optimal size. We seem to have settled on units about which we can communicate readily and yet which are not too broad. For example, we don't feel that measuring Spearman's g would tell us much. At the other extreme, Newtson's evidence (e.g., 1976) that we can identify rather short units of behavior has not persuaded many people to follow his lead. In general, outside of biological psychology, the units used by psychologists have remained pretty much the same over many decades.

In my *Measuring the Concepts of Personality* book (1971), there is a chapter on "The Specification of Constructs," running about 30 pages. Please don't ask me the embarrassing question, have I ever fully specified a construct, following the prescriptions given in that chapter? I have done so only partially, not completely.

Some investigators are not concerned with having a detailed preliminary statement of their construct at the outset of their research: They feel that it will gradually evolve as their research results come in. I differ with that approach. If we don't spend some time and energy trying to speculate about our construct, a priori, we will never get around to doing it until we try to write our next grant proposal, and that may be too late.

Each of us has his or her own definition of each commonly used concept (see my *Strategies for Personality Research*, pp. 7–8). That is evident in the personality field, and I suspect it is to some extent true for the concepts in the aptitudes and abilities domain. If each of us specified more explicitly the constructs we used in our research, we could begin to see how much the individuality of our construing contributed to our findings and especially to differences between our findings and those of other researchers.

But consider what these differences in findings do to the notion of construct validity. In your research, are you validating my construct or yours? Note that you and I have often used the same label for our two constructs.

What implications does this discussion of what do we want to understand have for validity? In a sense, it precedes validity. We have to settle the question of what we are trying to understand, at least to some degree, in order that the validity issue can have some meaning.

We feel we know our construct, we believe firmly that we know what we are trying to measure, so we don't need to specify it in elaborate detail. Or do we? We believe we know what hunger and thirst are, because we have experienced them. But a physiological psychologist finds them to be fairly complicated. I'd put love in that category of things we all know about, but Sternberg and Barnes (1988) found it necessary to produce a whole book on the subject.

Given all the theoretical and practical considerations mentioned above, is it possible to create a fully valid test or performance assessment? Will we ever approach the degree of validation obtained in the natural sciences? Not until we have better units. Not until we have better constructs. Not until we have a better idea of what we are doing, and where the behavior itself fits in.

REFERENCES

Anastasi, A. (1986). Evolving concepts of test validation. *Annual Review of Psychology, 37*, 1–15.

Campbell, D. T., & Fiske, D. W. (1959). Convergent and discriminant validation by the multitrait-multimethod matrix. *Psychological Bulletin, 56*, 81–105.

Campbell, D. T., & Stanley, J. C. (1963). Experimental and quasi-experimental designs for research on teaching, in N. L. Gage, (Ed.), *Handbook of research on teaching*, 171–246. Chicago: Rand McNally.

Cook, T. D., & Campbell, D. T. (1979). *Quasi-experimentation: Design and analysis issues for field settings*. Chicago: Rand McNally.

Cronbach, L. J. (1982). *Designing evaluations of educational and social programs*. San Francisco: Jossey-Bass.

Cronbach, L. J. (1989). Construct validation after thirty years. In R. L. Linn (Ed.),*Intelligence, measurement, theory, and public policy*, 147–177. Urbana: University of Illinois Press.

Cronbach, L. J., & Meehl, P. E. (1955). Construct validity in psychological tests. *Psychological Bulletin, 52*, 281–302.

Cronbach, L. J., Ambron. S. R., Dornbusch, S. M., Hess, R. .D., Harnik, R. C., Phillips, D. C., Walker, D. F., & Weiner, S. S. (1980). *Toward reform in program evaluation: Aims, methods and institutional arrangements.* San Francisco: Jossey-Bass.

Fiske,.D. W. (1971). *Measuring the concepts of personality.* Chicago: Aldine.

Fiske, D. W. (1978). *Strategies for personality research.* San Francisco: Jossey-Bass.

Guilford, J. P. (1954). *Psychometric methods* (2nd ed.). New York: McGraw-Hill.

Gulliksen, H. (1950). Intrinsic validity. *American Psychologist, 5*, 511–517.

Gulliksen, H. (1950). *Theory of mental tests.* New York: Wiley.

Hull, C. L. (1928). *Aptitude testing.* Yonkers on Hudson: World Book.

Jenkins, J. G. (1946). Validity for what? *Journal of Consulting Psychology, 10*, 93–98.

Loevinger, J. (1957). Objective tests as instruments of psychological theory. *Psychological Reports, 3*, 635–694.

Messick, S. (1975). The standard problem: Meaning and values in measurement and evaluation. *American Psychologist, 30*, 955–966.

Messick, S. (1980). Test validity and the ethics of assessment. *American Psychologist, 35*, 1012–1027.

Messick, S. (1989). Validity. In R. L. Linn (Ed.), *Educational Measurement* (3rd ed.), pp.13–103. New York: American Council on Education/Macmillan Publishing Co.

Messick, S. (1995). Validation of psychological assessment: Validation of inferences from persons' responses and performances as scientific inquiry into score meanings. *American Psychologist, 50*, 741–749.

Messick, S. (1996). *Validity and washback in language testing.* Educational Testing Service, Research Report No. 96–17.

Newtson, D. (1976). Foundations of attribution: The unit of perception of ongoing behavior. In J. Harvey, W. Ickes, & R. Kidd (Eds.) *New Directions in Attribution research*, (pp. 223–247). Hillsdale, NJ: Lawrence Erlbaum Associates.

Sternberg, R. J., & Barnes, M. L. (Eds.) (1988). *The psychology of love.* New Haven: Yale University Press.

Technical recommendations for psychological tests and diagnostic techniques. (1954). *Psychological Bulletin Supplement, 51* (2), 1–38.

10

Cognition and Construct Validity: Evidence for the Nature of Cognitive Performance in Assessment Situations

Robert Glaser
University of Pittsburgh

Gail P. Baxter
Educational Testing Service

The study of human cognition and the measurement of educational achievement are beginning to cross intellectual and empirical paths. Current efforts to define the conditions of educational attainment with the integral use of assessments demand an explicit alliance of these disciplines. Cognitive research has described processes, strategies, and structures of knowledge that contribute to competent performance and identified the characteristics of performance change as subject-matter competence develops. This work is contributing to a better understanding of what learning involves, to a theoretical and empirical base for measuring what has been learned, and to the formulation of methods for addressing certain aspects of the construct validity of performance assessments.

Construct validity in a modern context of cognitive process interpretation would imply that assessment situations be evaluated in terms of the coordination of knowledge and skills in a particular domain and the associated cognitive activities that underlie competent performance (Glaser 1981; Linn, Baker, & Dunbar, 1991; Messick, 1994, 1995). Of critical importance is that " . . . the level and sources of task complexity should match those of the construct being measured and be attuned to the level of developing expertise of the students assessed" (Messick, 1994, p. 21). In this regard, two aspects of the assessment situation merit attention: (a) the relationship between the goals of the task and the performance elicited by the assessment situation (i.e., substantive aspect) and (b) the relationship between elicited performance and assigned performance score (i.e., structural aspect). These two aspects of construct validity, the nature of the performance elicited and the quality of the performance scored, are a focus of this chapter.

A basis for analyses that bear directly on these issues derives from cognitive studies of human performance in various domains. It is now possible to describe the characteristics of learning and developing knowledge (Anderson, 1985; Glaser, 1984; Resnick, 1989), and the key distinguishing performance features of those who have attained more or less competence in a domain of knowledge (Chi, Glaser, & Farr, 1988; Ericsson & Smith, 1991). Levels of achievement or performance can now be described in ways that make salient the cognitive activities involved so they can be observed and measured.

In our own work we have focused attention on the cognitive activities that are elicited and scored in science assessment situations. Central to our approach is the conceptualization of subject-matter achievement or task performance with respect to the quality of cognition that develops with learning and experience. To capture the specific properties of science assessment tasks, we introduce a content-process space that depicts the relative demands for content knowledge and science process skills requisite for successful task completion. Consideration of cognitive activity in the context of the subject matter demands for content and process skills provides a framework for evaluating some aspects of the construct validity of performance assessments (Baxter & Glaser, 1998).

In what follows, the features and application of this evaluative framework are described. Examples from an analysis of the task and scoring features of science assessments illustrate: (a) ways in which variation in the relative content and process demands of the task influence the type or nature of cognitive activity that is observed, and (b) ways in which variation in the quality of cognitive activity (i.e., novice to expert) are reflected in differential performance scores.

ANALYTIC FRAMEWORK

The framework described here considers both performance and context—performance in terms of the cognitive activities involved in problem solving, and context in terms of the content and process task demands of the assessment situation. This structure anticipates the nature and extent of cognitive activity likely to be observed in particular assessment situations and provides a structure for evaluating: (a) the relationship between the subject matter and cognitive characteristics of assessment situations and (b) the extent to which developers' intentions are realized in performance assessments that purport to measure reasoning, understanding, and complex problem solving.

Cognitive Components of Competence

Numerous studies comparing competent or practiced problem solvers with new learners provide a strong empirical and conceptual basis for placing primary emphasis on quality of student cognition when designing and evaluating assessments. Three fundamental notions are relevant here. First, learning is best characterized as a change in the nature and use of knowledge. This change in the quality and structure of acquired knowledge enables certain cognitive processes. Consequently, awareness of and attention to these knowledge-generated processes represents possibilities for assessment design that might improve learning. Second, these cognitive changes are indicative of effective learning and experience with a body of knowledge. As such they provide signposts of increasing competence that can be used to evaluate the outcomes of educational efforts. Third, how knowledge is acquired determines how it is used. Indeed, it is possible to acquire knowledge in such a way as to preclude thinking. Likewise, it may be possible to design assessment situations in such a way that the demands for cognitive activity are minimal.

The nature and quality of cognitive activity underlying an individual's performance reflects the experience, degree of learning, and state of knowledge of the problem solver (see Table 10.1). Succinctly put, integrated knowledge structures, characteristic of competent students, are displayed in the ability to represent a problem accurately with respect to underlying principles; to select and execute goal-directed solution strategies based on an understanding of the task; to monitor and adjust performance when appropriate; and to offer complete, coherent explanations and justifications for problem-solving strategies and adjustments in performance. In contrast, less competent students are characterized by fragmented knowledge, knowledge that remains isolated from an understanding of the conditions or situations in which particular conceptual or procedural skills would be appropriately used. These students generate surface-level representations of

TABLE 10.1
Cognitive Activity and Structure of Knowledge

Cognitive Activity	Structure of Knowledge ------------>	
	Fragmented	Meaningfully Organized
Problem Representation	Surface features and shallow understanding	Underlying principles and relevant concepts
Strategy Use	Undirected trial-and-error problem solving	Efficient, informative, and goal oriented
Self-Monitoring	Minimal and sporadic	Ongoing and flexible
Explanation	Single statement of fact or description of superficial factors	Principled and coherent

the task, engage in trial-and-error solution strategies, monitor sporadically and ineffectively, and offer fragmented explanations of task-related concepts.

This list of cognitive activities should not be interpreted as the necessary requirements for all performance assessments. Rather, the intent is to focus attention on certain observable features of differential competence and subject-matter achievement. The realization of particular cognitive performance objectives in science assessment situations stems, in part, from the content and process demands of the task involved. Developers can manipulate task features to engage students in some cognitive activities (e.g., explanation) but de-emphasize others (e.g., self-monitoring).

Content-Process Space

One can conceptualize the task demands for content knowledge on a continuum from rich to lean. Similarly, the task demands for process skills can be conceived along a continuum from open to constrained (see Figure 10.1). The location of an assessment task within this content-process space is related to the nature and extent of cognitive activity underlying performance, and as such, provides a useful schema for describing cognitive task demands—those intended by the test developer and those realized in the assessment situation. It is important to note here that the position of a task in a particular quadrant prior to analysis specifies task features that may influence performance but does not imply the relative merit of that task form. In what follows, four examples of current assessment practice illustrate the correspondence between the content and process demands of the task and the kinds of cognitive activity that are observed.

Content Rich-Process Open. "Exploring the Maplecopter" is a good example of a content rich-process open task. High school physics students are asked to design and carry out experiments with a maple seed to explain its "flight to a friend who has not studied physics" (Baron, Carlyon, Greig, & Lomask, 1992). For this task, identification of the causal variables involved requires knowledge of physics concepts of force, motion, and aerodynamic effects; the ability to design and carry out controlled experimentation; and the effective employment of model-based reasoning skills.

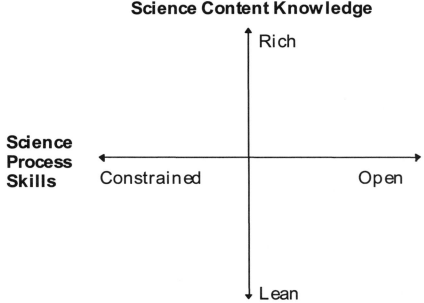

FIG. 10.1. Content-process space of science assessments.

Given that the problem does not have a clean simple solution, it is rich with opportunities for students to apply their subject-matter knowledge and in-school experience to · develop an understanding of an everyday phenomenon—the flight of the maple seed. In this situation, successful performance is dependent on an adequate representation of the problem, sustained and systematic exploration strategies (observation and experimentation), monitored progress toward describing the flight of the maple seed, and explanation of the causal relationships observed and tested.

Content Lean-Process Constrained. In contrast to the maplecopter task, tasks that are knowledge lean-process constrained require minimal prior knowledge and limited school experiences with subject-specific concepts and process skills for successful completion. Rather, students are guided to carry out a set of procedures and then asked to respond to questions about the results of these activities. For example, consider a task that asks 8th-grade students to study the effects of a train derailment and the resulting chemical spill on the surrounding environment (California Department of Education, 1993).

As part of their investigation, students replicate potential chemical reactions from that situation. They are explicitly directed to add measured amounts of the relevant substances in a predetermined sequence to set up three chemical reactions. Following this, they are prompted to observe each of these reactions for temperature, color change, and "other changes observed." A table is provided to guide recording of the specified observations. Students are then posed a series of questions that, for the most part, can be answered by rereading data from the table of observations or other information provided. For tasks of this type, generative opportunities for problem representation, strategy use, and monitoring are precluded by the step-by-step procedures. Furthermore, the knowledge requirements are given in the task so that student responses are independent of the kinds of formal instructional experiences they bring to the situation.

Content Lean-Process Open. Assessment tasks of this type require students to coordinate a sequence of process skills with minimal demands for content knowledge. For example, the "Mystery Powders" assessment asks 5th-grade students to identify the substances in each of six bags from a list of five possible alternatives (Baxter, Elder, & Shavelson, 1997). Students are presented with relevant indicators and tools and told they can use this equipment in any way they wish to solve the problem.

With these instructions, students represent the problem in terms of actions that follow from what they know about the properties of substances and ways to identify them (i.e., tests and relevant observations). They then implement a strategy, such as adding vinegar to a substance, and revise that strategy, if necessary, based on task-feedback (no fizz, try iodine to test for cornstarch). As they monitor their progress toward problem solution, students attend to and coordinate multiple pieces of information including knowledge of task constraints, knowledge of critical aspects of their previous investigations, and interpretations of current trials.

In this situation, processes are open in terms of test selection (number and type of test) and test sequence that can be carried out more, or less, efficiently as a function of effective monitoring and students' knowledge of the relationship between substances and their identifying tests. The content knowledge requirements are lean; students need to know how to replicate previous investigations and how to match current trials with records of in-class observations of test-substance outcomes. Although tasks of this type require student-generated process skills, their use may become routinized in situations where the demands for content knowledge are minimal.

Content Rich-Process Constrained. Tasks that are content rich-process constrained emphasize knowledge generation or recall. For example, high school students were asked to "describe the possible forms of energies and types of materials involved in growing a plant and explain fully how they are related" (Lomask, Baron, Greig, & Harrison, 1992). A comprehensive, coherent explanation revolves around a discussion of inputs, processes, and products such as the plant takes in water, light, and carbon dioxide. Through the process of photosynthesis, light energy is converted into chemical energy used to produce new materials such as sugar needed for plant growth; in addition oxygen is given off (e.g., Gregory, 1989; Solomon, Berg, Martin, & Villee, 1993). In developing their explanations, students make decisions about which concepts are important and how these concepts are related, thereby reflecting their conceptual understanding of the topic. Although the opportunities for explanation are apparent, opportunities for other activities such as planning, selecting, and implementing appropriate strategies or monitoring problem-solving procedures are less so.

In summary, specifying cognitive activities in the context of the subject-matter demands (i.e., content and process) provides a framework for anticipating the impact of assessment features on student performance. Tasks can be designed with specific cognitive goals in mind, and task quality can be judged in terms of an alignment with the goals and purposes of the developers. Furthermore, scoring systems can be designed to attend to the quality of cognitive activity rather than the easily quantifiable aspects of performance. Examination of the alignment of tasks and scoring systems in a sample of assessment efforts is now described.

INVESTIGATING ASSESSMENT PRACTICE

The properties and objectives of assessments and scoring systems visible in model testing programs across the country were examined (Baxter & Glaser, 1998). In each of the assessment situations, we analyzed verbal protocols, observed student performance, examined student written work, and reviewed task instructions and scoring criteria. The goal was to ascertain whether and how these assessments are measuring cognitive capabilities that distinguish various levels of student achievement. Two questions focused our analyses. First, to what extent are the intentions of test developers reflected in the cognitive activities requisite for successful task completion? A correspondence between the performance goals as described by the test developer and the performance elicited in the assessment situation provides some evidence for the substantive aspect of construct validity (Messick, 1994, 1995). Second, to what extent are students' scores reflective of the quality of observed cognition? A strong, positive relationship between the quality of the elicited performance (i.e., novice to expert) and performance score (low to high) provides some evidence for the structural aspect of construct validity (Messick, 1994, 1995).

We describe here four categories of assessments illustrative of the kinds of hits and misses experienced by test developers in their efforts to design cognitively complex science performance assessments. Two categories— Uniform Performance and Goals Misinterpreted—exemplify the difficulty in translating task goals into assessment situations, and two categories— Understanding Overestimated and Cognitive Consistency—illustrate the necessity of developing scoring criteria that reflect the complexity of the task. Each of these is described in turn.

Uniform Performance. In some performance assessment situations, a potentially knowledge rich-process open activity was configured to elicit only uniform performance with little opportunity for differentiation. For example, consider a plate tectonics task designed to measure 8th-grade students' understanding "of the process that causes rock layers to fold and twist" (California Department of Education, 1993b). Students were provided with a cardboard model and guided through a sequence of procedures for manipulating it. They then were asked to respond to questions based on the results of these procedures. Student responses required description of their observations, and for this purpose, a list of relevant conceptual terms was provided. However, in responding to the task (and scoring performance), there was no requirement for the use of these technical terms or for students to recognize the cardboard model as a representation of the movement of the earth's plates and the resulting changes of that movement. Rather, performance could be independent of an understanding of how geological and geomorphic processes have shaped the earth, understandings that the task was designed to measure.

Goals Misinterpreted. We observed other situations whose design made it too easy for students to interpret the problem at a level that was inconsistent with the goals of the developers. For example, in describing the possible forms of energy and types of materials involved in the digestion of a piece of bread, high school students were expected to explain how carbohydrates in bread are converted into usable energy and other byproducts through cellular respiration (Lomask et al., 1992). A typical response was: "The food must first be broken down with the help of your teeth. Then once in the stomach the acids break it down even more. After the stomach it enters the intestines and there are more chemicals that break down the food that is to be digested." Contrary to the specific objectives of the developers, students' responses did not reflect their understanding of cell respiration; they could interpret the problem in ways that bypassed the knowledge they may have acquired in classroom instruction.

Understanding Overestimated. We also observed situations where everyday knowledge or simplified interpretations of complex concepts were recognized as adequate for successful task completion. One example is the bugs classification task. Fifth-grade students were given a collection of plastic replicas of bugs and asked to organize them for a museum display (California Department of Education, 1993a). In scoring student performance, distinctions were not made between arbitrary and scientific classification systems (Mayr, 1976). Arbitrary and utilitarian classification systems, such as sorting buttons or cataloguing books in the library, are undertaken with a goal to reduce the heterogeneity of the objects into manageable categories; one scheme is not necessarily any better than another. In contrast, a biological classification is explanatory (i.e., shows evolution of insect or plant) and predictive (i.e., new discoveries are incorporated with little modification to the overall system). In this situation, students were essentially permitted to sort on any basis; high scorers could not be distinguished from low scorers in terms of their knowledge of the morphological features of insects or an understanding of the evolutionary basis of shared characteristics. Lack of attention to knowledge-based distinctions underlying students' performance reduced this potentially knowledge rich-process open classification task to a simple sorting task, rendering scores uninterpretable.

Cognitive Consistency. We did identify tasks that elicited cognitive activity consistent with the intended goals for a problem-solving task. A good example is the "Electric Mysteries" task where 5th-grade students are asked to identify the circuit components enclosed in each of six black boxes by constructing test circuits with relevant equipment. Students' plans for solving the problem, solution strategies, monitoring activities, and explanations were reflective of their knowledge of the effects of changing various components in a circuit. The nature and quality of these activities were related to their performance score (Baxter, Elder, & Glaser, 1996). Students with high scores described a plan consisting of procedures and interpretation of possible outcomes, they expressed through their explanations an understanding of the conceptual knowledge of circuits; they demonstrated an efficient, principled approach to solving the problem; and they engaged in frequent and flexible monitoring. In contrast, students with low scores offered a hypothesis when asked for a plan, provided a factual statement when asked for an explanation, invoked a trial-and-error strategy of "hook something up and see what happens" to guide their problem solving, and monitored sporadically while carrying out the Electric Mysteries assessment.

These examples, taken from our analyses of a number of prominent science assessments: (a) highlight the consistencies and inconsistencies between the intentions of test developers and the kinds of performances realized in assessment situations, (b) underscore the need to define task performance (i.e., scoring) in terms of the nature and quality of cognitive activity, and (c) call attention to the difficulty in translating test objectives into assessment situations without the benefit of well-defined structures or rules for the design of performance measures.

What is readily apparent from these results is the need for empirical justification for inferential bridges from performance scores to the nature and extent of student learning. Equally important is the need to sensitize test developers to ways in which students' thinking and reasoning can be elicited and scored—an important step toward progress in the development of assessments commensurate with educational goals. As Anastasi pointed out some 30 years ago, "Increasing specialization has led to a concentration upon techniques for test construction without sufficient consideration of psychological research for the interpretation of test scores" (1967, p. 305). It is now necessary to use knowledge of modern cognition as the foundation for the design and use of assessments in education.

CONCLUDING COMMENTS

Messick has expressed continuing concern for the evidential basis for construct validity. It is useful to think of the facts and evidence in terms of a theory of human performance for the purposes of test design and the interpretation of measurement procedures. As described in this chapter, mapping cognitive activity onto the relative demands for science content knowledge and process skills forces coherent articulation of assessment concepts and practices that are informed by knowledge of human cognition and learning. Essential in this regard is recognition of the qualitative differences in performance that signal degrees of learning and experience with a subject matter. Explicit attention to these differences will: (a) enhance the quality of current practice for the design and interpretation of achievement measures, (b) enable the definition and analysis of consistency and errors in performance interpretation, and (c) suggest key considerations for eliciting and scoring performance. In this chapter, we offered a beginning framework for these purposes.

Progress in the development of structures to guide the design and evaluation of performance assessments will require refinement of the framework described here. Consideration also needs to be given to specific understanding of the course of learning and growth of knowledge in other content domains, and the elaboration of the particular characteristics of developing competence appropriate to these subject matters. An important endeavor to be undertaken for improved assessment is empirical research that demonstrates the impact of changes in design features on the quality of cognition observed in assessment situations. Our work also has indicated that the kind of analysis we propose is particularly useful for evaluating scoring procedures and judgments of performance. We pointed to cases where performances have been overestimated or where students scored highly but essentially missed the concept involved. As Linn (1982) noted ". . . providing the evidence and logical analysis that supports the uses and interpretations of test scores is the fundamental psychometric problem" (p. 13). The message of this chapter has been that such evidence can be derived from consideration of cognitive activity in relation to the content and process skills of the subject matter. Still to be considered is the use of theories of human performance as a basis for the systematic design of performance assessment.

ACKNOWLEDGMENTS

This work was supported by a grant from the National Center for Research on Evaluation, Standards, and Student Testing (CRESST) through U. S. Department of Education Office of Educational Research and Improvement Award #R305B60002. Opinions expressed are those of the authors and not necessarily the supporting agencies.

REFERENCES

Anastasi, A. (1967). Psychology, psychologists, and psychological testing. *American Psychologist, 22*, 297–306.

Anderson, J. R. (1985). *Cognitive psychology and its implications* (2nd ed.). New York: W. H. Freeman and Company.

Baron, J. B., Carlyon, E., Greig, J., & Lomask, M. (1992, March). *What do our students know? Assessing students' ability to think and act like scientists through performance assessment.* Paper presented at the Annual Meeting of the National Science Teachers Association, Boston.

Baxter, G. P., Elder, A. D., & Glaser, R. (1996). Knowledge-based cognition and performance assessment in the science classroom. *Educational Psychologist, 31*(2), 133–140.

Baxter, G. P., Elder, A. D., & Shavelson, R. J. (1997). *Effect of embedded assessments on performance in elementary science classrooms.* Unpublished manuscript, University of Michigan.

Baxter, G. P., & Glaser, R. (1998). Investigating the cognitive complexity of science assessments. *Educational Measurement: Issues and Practice, 17*(3), 37–45.

California Department of Education (1993a). *Science grade 5 administration manual.* Sacramento, CA: Author.

California Department of Education. (1993b). *Science grade 8 administration manual.* Sacramento, CA: Author.

Chi, M. T. H., Glaser, R., & Farr, M. (Eds.). (1988). *The nature of expertise.* Hillsdale, NJ: Lawrence Erlbaum Associates.

Ericsson, K. A., & Smith, J. (Eds.). (1991). *Toward a general theory of expertise: Prospects and limits.* New York: Cambridge Press.

Glaser, R. (1981). The future of testing: A research agenda for cognitive psychology and psychometrics. *American Psychologist, 36*, 923–936.

Glaser, R. (1984). Education and thinking: The role of knowledge. *American Psychologist, 39*(2), 93–104.

Gregory, R. P. F. (1989). *Photosynthesis.* New York: Chapman and Hall.

Linn, R. L. (1982). Two weak spots in the practice of criterion-referenced measurement. *Educational Measurement: Issues and Practice, 1*(1), 12–13, 25.

Linn, R. L., Baker, E. L., & Dunbar, S. B. (1991). Complex, performance-based assessment: Expectations and validation criteria. *Educational Researcher, 20*(8), 5–21.

Lomask, M., Baron, J., Greig, J., & Harrison, C. (1992, March). *ConnMap: Connecticut's use of concept mapping to assess the structure of students' knowledge of science.* A symposium presented at the Annual Meeting of the National Association of Research in Science Teaching, Cambridge.

Mayr, E. (1976). *Evolution and the diversity of life: Selected essays.* Cambridge, MA: Belknap Press of Harvard University.

Messick, S. (1989). Validity. In R. L. Linn (Ed.), *Educational Measurement* (3rd ed., pp. 13–104). New York: Macmillan.

Messick, S. (1994). The interplay of evidence and consequences in the validation of performance assessments. *Educational Researcher, 23*(2), 13–23.

Messick, S. (1995). Validity of psychological assessment: Validation of inferences from person's responses and performance as scientific inquiry into score meaning. *American Psychologist, 50*(9), 741–749.

Resnick, L. B. (Ed.). (1989). *Knowing, learning, and instruction. Essays in honor of Robert Glaser.* Hillsdale, NJ: Lawrence Earlbaum Associates.

Solomon, E. P., Berg, L. R., Martin, D. W., & Villee, C. (1993). *Biology* (3rd ed.). Orlando, FL: Harcourt Brace Jovanovich.

11

Seeking Fair Alternatives in Construct Design

Warren W. Willingham
Educational Testing Service

It is a personal pleasure to recognize the many contributions of a friend and colleague who has had such beneficial influence on educational and psychological measurement. Sam has been a leader in molding the way we think and in creating the structures on which we hang our better ideas. Such accomplishment deserves high honor.

In this chapter I want to discuss an important issue concerning fairness in test design—a consequential issue that is too little appreciated. My comments originate in a project in which I was involved with Nancy Cole and others in the 1990s—a study of Gender and Fair Assessment (Willingham & Cole, 1997). Cole deserves equal credit for the concern about fairness in test design, but she is not responsible for liberties I may take here in extending the topic. A brief overview of the ETS Gender Study will provide useful context for my remarks.

A group of ETS researchers undertook this study for three reasons. We hoped to help clarify some confusing findings regarding gender differences; we realized that testing organizations need to know more about fairness issues in order to cope with new forms of assessment; and we believed that a careful study of gender difference and similarity would provide a useful template for studying fairness issues generally.

This was a 4-year study involving extensive review of previous work and quite substantial data assembly—about 1500 data sets involving some 400 tests and related measures of experience, attainment, and proficiency. Our review of previous research convinced us that observed patterns of gender difference are distorted by three confounded effects: construct differences, sample differences, and cohort differences (i.e., differences by grade and year). We focused especially on large, nationally representative samples in order to better disentangle the construct, sample, and cohort effects.

Our analysis showed almost no overall gender difference in test results for representative samples of 12th graders. But we did find important differences on particular constructs: for example, sizable differences favoring men on mechanical tests, and sizable differences favoring women in writing. We also found sample differences—especially differences in selected samples, associated with the typically greater spread of male scores. And we found some important cohort differences. The male advantage in math and science scores at grade 12 has dropped dramatically, to roughly one fourth of what it was in the early 1960s (see Flanagan, et al., 1964; Willingham & Cole, 1997, p. 113). As we know, young women are now much more engaged with those subjects than was true a generation ago.

In the course of this work, Nancy Cole and I became much impressed with the extent to which gender differences on different test constructs correspond with patterns in the preferences and activities of young women and men outside of school, as well as their educational choices (Cole, 1997). Such differential interests and experience can have important fairness implications for what we decide to measure—and also, how we measure it.

How we measure refers to content specifications as well as format. Within broad areas—such as verbal or quantitative skills—a different test purpose may require different test content. We found that the choice can impact gender differences in important ways. We also found that test format can have an important effect on gender differences. These format effects seem more due to the latent cognitive skills invoked by different formats than to aspects of the format per se. By the latter, I mean such issues as guessing on multiple-choice tests or familiarity with computers (Bridgeman & Schmitt, 1997; Willingham & Cole, 1997, p. 244–78). I come back to the latent cognitive skills later in this chapter.

Notice that both aspects of how we assess—content specifications and format choice—concern how a test is designed, not its actual construction or administration. In my view, a major implication of the ETS Gender Study is the strong suggestion that test design has more potential as a source of fairness issues than do the technical details of construction and administration—issues to which testing organizations devote a great deal of attention in research and in the day-to-day operation of testing programs. It is this aspect of test design that forms my thesis and leads me to direct some practical comments to one corner of psychometric theory, deposited there by Sam Messick in 1980, waiting patiently for us to catch up with it.

The Thesis. In any given situation involving the use of educational tests, there is always the possibility of different tests; that is, alternate constructs or alternate ways of representing a construct. Typically, there are competing arguments on the various validity considerations that influence choices among the alternatives—also practical considerations like how much time it will take to administer the test and how much it will cost the examinees. We are used to dealing with such judgments.

It is less common to recognize that plausible alternatives with otherwise comparable validity can result in nontrivial differences in the patterns of subgroup performance. That situation poses problems—ethical, technical, and practical. My thesis is simply stated: I believe that we can materially advance test fairness with better procedures for weighing the consequences of alternate construct designs. I note briefly these lines of argument: social, psychometric, and empirical examples.

The Social Context

Our younger colleagues in measurement are doomed to live in exciting times. Since the 1960's, testing has consistently attracted devotion as well as criticism. But we have never seen such abuse as in the past decade— challenges to the form, the relevance, and the fairness of testing.

Figure 11.1 shows Sam Messick's (1980) familiar representation of construct validity. The matrix distinguishes four accumulating facets of validity. The last is "social consequences." That facet adds much to our perception of the topic: the social benefit that results from a valid test serving its purpose, the social tensions that result from different values and different perceptions of purpose and outcome, and the so-called side effects of using the test.

During the 1990's, two social consequences of testing assumed such proportions as to create major new themes and to transform priorities in testing practice. One is the group differences observed in test performance; the other is the presumed negative or hoped-for positive impact of tests on the educational process.

These concerns are not going away. It is important that we deal with them more effectively than we have. Otherwise, valid uses of tests may be sacrificed, regardless of the quality of our constructs. In earlier days, test users were mainly concerned about validity narrowly conceived; namely, utility for the immediate purpose. Today, the validity of a test is increasingly judged on the proving ground of social consequences.

	Test Interpretation	Test Use
Evidential Basis	Construct validity	Construct validity + Relevance/utility
Consequential Basis	Value implications	Social consequences

Source: Messick, 1980

FIG. 11.1. Facets of Validity

As we know, enthusiasm for and worries about the educational impact of tests has spawned large initiatives: standards-based assessment, the national test, and so on. Test fairness has important ties to these concerns. Group impact and educational impact are the quintessence of social consequence. They drag measurement practice into that fourth quadrant.

Measurement Considerations

Test Design is Critical. In Figure 11.1, social consequences are the outcome of test use. That does not necessarily mean that test use is the stage of the assessment process where decisions are most likely to affect group differences. If there are limited test options to consider, then the decisions most likely to bear on test fairness must come earlier. Test design is a natural place to look, because we design tests with a use in mind.

There was a time when the user typically decided whether to test, which test to use, and whether it was valid for the purpose. That is still true for some types of tests, but for the most important present-day educational tests, the options as to construct choice lie mostly in the design stage. We do not usually build several different high-stakes tests and then expect users to consider carefully the utility and consequences of each test, and decide—as independent practitioners—which test to use. We design high-stakes tests with an intended purpose and population in mind. We build the test in consultation with users, verify its validity and quality, and then the test is put to use—more or less as intended. This is the typical scenario with admissions tests, scholarship tests, major placement tests, and to a considerable degree, the most frequently used commercial achievement tests. Thus, much hangs on test design.

There are Options in Test Design. Constructs are not provided by some higher power. In large measure, we still use old-fashioned expert judgment in writing sensible items, and then apply quite modern statistical techniques to assemble tests and to see what we have. In educational testing certainly, constructs are complex. Even in relatively homogeneous tests, the tested construct is layered with latent skills and knowledge bundles.

We try to design test constructs by deciding what should be part of the construct and what should not, but these decisions are certainly not based on sure knowledge of the cognitive skills involved or what threats to construct irrelevance may lurk in the assessment format. Describing this process as construct design is perhaps more flattering than factual. Nevertheless, my point is, we make choices—deliberate or unknowing.

There are Consequences to the Options. It is understandable that individuals and groups of examinees might perform better on one construct than another, but why are there choices that affect fairness? We always shoot for the most valid test. Isn't the most valid test the fairest test? That is generally true, but not always by any means. For example, adding verbal to math gives an admissions test greater predictive validity overall, but worsens the underprediction of grades for language minority students (Ramist, Lewis, & McCamley-Jenkins, 1994, Tables 5 & 8).

There may be good reasons—educational or social—for favoring different representations of a construct. As a result, inconspicuous latent skills embedded in the construct may enhance its relevance for some purposes, but also alter the pattern of group differences. And most important, tests invite different interpretations of validity because tests often have multiple uses, and some argue, major side effects.

What if two test designs that are otherwise equally valid favor different groups? How does one resolve that choice? What fairness principle is involved here? Definitions of test bias have always been based on the notion of differential validity. Increasingly, we have come to regard test fairness as the generalization of that idea; that is, comparable validity across groups (Cole & Moss, 1989; Moss, 1995). One can think of test fairness as the absence of invalid group differences, but that principle is manifested differently in different aspects of the assessment process (Willingham, 1998).

Nancy Cole and I have argued that fair test design means providing comparable opportunity for examinees to demonstrate knowledge and skills they have acquired that are relevant to the purpose of the test. In the language of construct validity, this comparability means adequate construct representation. Therefore, if alternate constructs show different patterns of group means, the critical question is which pattern best reflects comparable opportunity for different groups to demonstrate their relevant knowledge and skills? From this perspective, the goal is not to balance the mean scores of different groups, but to design valid assessments that yield outcomes consistent, overall, with other information that is pertinent to the purpose of the test.

Some Examples

The most important decisions in test design are not easily changed, once a test is introduced. Three design decisions can be critical: the choice of construct, how the construct is represented, and the choice of assessment format. The following five examples from the ETS Gender Study illustrate how such decisions can impact group differences and the fairness of a test. These examples concern the use of high-stakes educational tests. Fairness is an ethical concern about the effects of test use, and it is especially the scores of high stakes tests that can have a direct and consequential impact on individual examinees.

1. *Rational design*—an illustration involving construct choice. In many testing situations, construct choices are based more on judgment and values than empirical evidence. Willingham and Cole illustrated a common fairness issue by showing what can happen when a school board chooses one combination of tests over another for a school-leaving exam (Willingham & Cole, 1999, p. 241–243). They used NELS and NAEP data to compare four pairs of tests with respect to the number of females and males who would fail to earn a diploma. The four pairs were based on different values or utility arguments, in each case a quite plausible rationale involving community or national interests. It's easy to imagine a school board choosing any of the four. The results are shown in Table 11.1.

    Applying the same passing criteria to each leaving exam, resulted in a gender difference in the outcome that varied from about a third more female failures for Pair 1 (Math & Science), to three times as many male failures for Pair 4 (Reading & Writing). All of these outcomes can't be right. Which outcome best fits other facts in the situation? How important are the

TABLE 11.1
Four Hypothetical Choices for a
Two-Test School Leaving Exam: Who Fails?

Pair of Tests in Leaving Exam	Ratio of Female to Male Failures*
1. Math & Science	1.31
2. History & Science	1.04
3. Reading & Math	.78
4. Reading & Writing	.34

* "Failures" scored in the bottom 10% on both tests.
Source: Willingham & Cole, 1997, p. 243

failure rates compared to the utility arguments? How important are the practical arguments that held the School Board initially to only two subtests? Such questions of construct choice need to be raised when the examination is first designed, not after it is administered.

2. *Writing as writing*—another illustration involving construct choice. A strong argument for the direct assessment of writing proficiency is the wide applicability and significance of writing skill in academic work and in adult life. We often elect not to assess writing because of the practical problems of scoring essays. But choosing not to assess writing raises a fairness problem for women. Of all the strictly academic tests routinely administered, writing shows the largest gender difference, and it favors women (Willingham & Cole, 1997, p. 260).

Two recent analyses illustrate the obvious fact that adding writing will moderate the gender difference that tends to favor males in test batteries at higher age levels. One concerned an admissions test (Bridgeman & McHale, 1996), the other involved a placement test (Willingham & Cole, 1997, p. 284–85). In each of these analyses, the addition of writing brought test performance more in line with criterion performance. There is no indication that writing will add to the prediction of GPA (Bridgeman, 1991), but it is widely argued that including writing makes for a more valid test battery because assessing writing has a beneficial washback effect on the educational process. Thus, the choice on whether to include writing is likely to pit fairness and positive educational consequences against practical difficulties, like cost to the examinee.

3. *Writing as a latent skill*—an illustration involving format choice. There have been a number of reports suggesting that men do better on the multiple-choice format and women do better on the essay format. There is much data to confirm that tendency, but the issue is more complicated. Table 11.2 shows average gender differences on the multiple-choice and essay sections of Advanced Placement examinations in four areas. The first two subject areas—language and literature and mathematics—show no format effect; that is, the amount of gender difference is the same in the two formats. The other two areas—natural science and history and government—show a gender difference favoring males, larger on the multiple-choice section than on the essay section. This differential format effect across subjects is consistent in AP exams from year to year (Willingham & Cole, 1997, p. 260–62). Much the same subject pattern has been described in the GCE exams in England (Murphy, 1982).

Why the subject difference? The work of Breland, Danos, Kahn, Kubota, & Bonner, (1994) clearly implicates writing as a major source of the format effect on the AP History exams. In this analysis, writing skill appears to interact with content knowledge, which strengthens the supposition that writing is important to proficiency in history (Willingham & Cole, 1997, p. 264). Such results suggest a reasonable question in the design of any educational test. Namely, "How important is writing to the intended construct?"

4. *Spatial as a latent skill*—another illustration involving format choice. In 27 AP examinations, Willingham and Cole found that wherever there was a format effect—in about half of the examinations—free-response favored women and multiple-choice favored men (Willingham & Cole, 1997, p. 261). Is that a generalizable result? No, it depends what one means by free-response. The 1990 NAEP Science Assessment showed a small difference favoring males on a multiple-choice section, and a larger difference favoring males on a figural-response section (Jones, Mullis, Raizen, Weiss, & Weston, 1992). It was the men who did better on free-response, not the women.

The items in this section appear to call on spatial visualization—a skill on which males tend to perform well. In another analysis, a NELS

TABLE 11.2
Standard Gender Difference on the Multiple-Choice and
Free-Response Sections of AP Examinations in Four Subject Areas

	Mean Gender Difference	
	M-C Section	F-R Section
Language & Literature	.01	.04
Mathematics	-.27	-.28
Natural Science	-.42	-.21
History & Government	-.31	.00

Source: Willingham & Cole, 1997, p. 262 (Jones, Mullis, Raizen, Weiss, & Weston, 1992).

performance test involving figural material yielded a similar result (Pollack & Rock, 1997). In these two assessments free-response apparently meant spatial visualization. But in Advanced Placement, free-response usually means writing—a quite different cognitive implication and a quite different gender result.

There is a lesson here. We are prone to think of bias and fairness issues as construct irrelevance—something quirky about the test. But this fairness issue is not construct irrelevance. Both writing and spatial skills are relevant to science. The question is whether the balance of writing and spatial skills in the test accurately reflects the criterion domain.

5. *Achievement in mathematics*—an illustration involving construct representation. Educational test batteries normally include a mathematics test because mathematical skills are critical to many areas of study and a number of career lines. Gender differences follow a dissimilar pattern in different aspects of math proficiency(i.e., different construct components). Many studies have shown the same general result. Females tend to do better on basic facts and computation. Males tend to do better on math reasoning, particularly at higher age levels (Willingham & Cole, 1997, p. 286–89).

Mathematics illustrates why choosing how to represent a construct can create a disjunction between utility and fairness. Test function is the mediating consideration. If a math test is designed for course placement, basic facts and computation may be the most appropriate content. If the test is designed for selection, reasoning is usually considered more appropriate. If an important effect of the test score is to signal general proficiency in mathematics and readiness for a range of careers that require some math, some of both construct components may be appropriate. Controversy about the fairness of a mathematics test tends to arise when the test has an ambiguous blend of purposes.

What Steps to Take?

Before considering practical implications, a few caveats should be noted. The foregoing examples focus only on gender. There are other groups that must be considered. Furthermore, fairness pertains equally to individuals. Fairness is not served by making a test less valid for individuals in order to favor particular groups.

Nor is fairness served by attending only to the construct of interest. Recall Cronbach's dictum (1980, p. 103), "The whole selection system is to be justified, not the test alone." It is essential to take account of other measures used with the test. Will the overall pattern of information yield valid and fair results?

Performance assessment and computer-based testing are major cross-cutting themes that aggravate the format problem. Both of these trends enlarge the possible domain of skills for more effective measurement. Both also open a Pandora's box of latent skills, construct relevant and construct irrelevant, with great potential for adding validity as well as challenging fairness. Indeed, it is an exciting time.

The decisions we make in designing test constructs clearly have the potential for sizable group impact. By contrast, a decade of research and experience with DIF analysis has yielded modest effects (Bridgeman & Schmitt, 1997; O'Neill, Wild, & McPeek, 1998). In my view, it's no contest; there are more consequential fairness issues in test design than in test construction—more potential for differential action in constructs than in items. Furthermore, fair test design may often be the best influence we have on fair test use.

It is important to be able to study and to debate publicly the rationale and the consequences of the choices we make in creating assessment devices. For theoretical as well as practical reasons, such study and debate is possible with construct choices in test design, problematic with item choices in test assembly. As I proposed at the outset, we need better procedures for weighing the fairness consequences of alternate test designs. What steps might help to achieve that end? I suggest four.

First, Formalize the Fairness Objective. An evaluation of possible fairness consequences of design alternatives should be a more explicit part of the development of any test—a more formal step in the process. This step might include several considerations: a) the possibilities for alternate construct designs; b) the effects of such alternatives on patterns of group performance and different interpretations of validity; c) other measures that will be or could be used to help insure a valid use of the test; and d) more systematic collection of representative judgments on fairness issues suggested by different construct designs.

Second, Take Construct Analysis More Seriously. A powerful method for weighing the validity and fairness implications of alternate test designs is multivariate analysis that includes construct components, criterion alternatives, markers for key latent skills, and important subgroups. Such work offers an improved basis for evaluating possible design tradeoffs between educational consequences and subgroup impact. The classic study of the Formulating-Hypotheses test by Ward, Frederiksen, and Carlson (1980) is a good model. This type of developmental research is costly, but would be justified in the case of major tests. If such studies were done more regularly, findings would accumulate for the benefit of all tests.

Third, Study Format Effects. Complex proficiencies require diverse skills. Using diverse assessment formats can improve the validity and fairness of testing because different formats may be needed to assess diverse skills. New types of assessment such as computer-based testing and performance assessment are intended to do just that. Insuring the fairness of new assessments will depend, in part, on extending what we know about the relationship between the test format employed and latent skills in the construct tested. In fact, weighing the fairness consequences of alternate test designs may be problematic without more informative studies of format effects.

And finally, I propose we start at the end. The final suggestion is to focus test design first on the educational consequences of using the test— the immediate and the distal effects, the consequences for individuals as well as the educational system. If the proposed test succeeds in serving its intended purpose, will that be a good thing? Starting with the possible consequences of assessment raises timely, tough questions in the imagined context of actual use.

It is in the last quadrant of Sam Messick's matrix that we best perceive the multiple interpretations of validity, the side effects that may be main effects, and the conflicting values that create divergent impressions of a fair or unfair test. We measurement specialists correctly maintain that it is the user who must make the final judgment on whether to use a test. But it is the measurement specialist who is often the best-informed and has the heaviest hand in designing the test that will probably be used.

REFERENCES

Breland, H. M., Danos, D. O., Kahn, H. D., Kubota, M. Y., & Bonner, M. W. (1994). Performance versus objective testing and gender: An exploratory study of an Advanced Placement history examination. *Journal of Educational Measurement, 31*, 275–293.

Bridgeman, B. (1991). *Essays and multiple-choice tests as predictors of college freshman GPA* (ETS RR-91-3). Princeton, NJ: Educational Testing Service.

Bridgeman, B., & McHale, F. (1996). *Gender and ethnic group differences on the GMAT analytical writing assessment* (ETS RR-96-2). Princeton, NJ: Educational Testing Service.

Bridgeman, B., & Schmitt, A. (1997). Fairness issues in test development and administration. In W. W. Willingham & N. S. Cole (Eds.), *Gender and fair assessment* (pp. 185–226). Mahwah, NJ: Lawrence Erlbaum Associates.

Cole, N. S. (1997). Understanding gender differences and fair assessment in context. In W. W. Willingham & N. S. Cole, *Gender and fair assessment* (pp. 157–183). Mahwah, NJ: Lawrence Erlbaum Associates.

Cole, N. S., & Moss, P. A. (1989). Bias in test use. In R. L. Linn (Ed.), *Educational measurement* (3rd ed., pp. 201–219). New York: American Council on Education & Macmillan.

Cronbach, L. J. (1980). Validity on parole: How can we go straight? In W. B. Schrader (Ed.), *New directions for testing and measurement, 5. Measuring achievement over a decade. Proceedings of the 1979 ETS Invitational Conference* (pp. 99–108). San Francisco: Jossey-Bass.

Flanagan, J. C., Davis, F. B., Dailey, J. T., Shaycoft, M. F., Orr, D. V., Goldberg, I., & Neyman, C. A., Jr. (1964). *Project TALENT: The American high-school student* (Final Report for Cooperative Research Project No. 635, U.S. Office of Education). Pittsburgh, PA: University of Pittsburgh.

Jones, L. R., Mullis, I. V., Raizen, S. A., Weiss, I. R., & Weston, E. A. (1992). *The 1990 science report card: NAEP'S assessment of fourth, eighth, and twelfth graders.* Princeton, NJ: Educational Testing Service, National Assessment of Educational Progress.

Messick, S. (1980). Test validity and the ethics of assessment. American *Psychologist, 35*, 1012–1027.

Moss, P. A. (1995). Themes and variations in validity theory. *Educational Measurement: Issues and Practice, 14*, 5–13.

Murphy, R. J. (1982). Sex differences in objective test performance. *British Journal of Educational Psychology, 52*, 213–219.

O'Neill, K. A., Wild, C. L., & McPeek, W. M. (1998). *Identifying differentially functioning items on the Graduate Record Examination General Test.* Manuscript submitted for publication.

Pollack, J. M., & Rock, D. A. (1997). *Constructed response tests in the NELS: 88 high school effectiveness study.* Washington, DC: National Center for Education Statistics.

Ramist, L., Lewis, C., & McCamley-Jenkins, L. (1994). *Student group differences in predicting college grades: Sex, language, and ethnic group* (CB Rep. No. 93-1; ETS RR-94-27). New York: College Entrance Examination Board.

Ward, W. C., Frederiksen, N., & Carlson, S. B. (1980). Construct validity of free-response and machine-scorable forms of a test. *Journal of Educational Measurement, 17,* 11–29.

Willingham, W. W. (1999). A systemic view of test fairness. In S. Messick (Ed.), *Assessment in higher education*. Mahwah, NJ: Lawrence Erlbaum Associates.

Willingham, W. W., & Cole, N. S. (1997). *Gender and fair assessment*. Mahwah, NJ: Lawrence Erlbaum Associates

12

Validity of Constructs Versus Construct Validity of Scores

David E. Wiley
Northwestern University

This chapter has a twofold origin. First in *Test validity and invalidity reconsidered* (Wiley, 1991), I expressed a preference for separating validity questions about test use and consequences form those concerning the relations between test scores and constructs. My rationale, at the time, was that investigations concerning test use and its consequences involved, at base, issues about the social organization of human activity, whereas investigations concerning relations between test scores and construct primarily involved the psychology of individuals. As I discuss later in this chapter, I now find it less useful to sharply separate these perspectives.

Part of the reason for this change in view has to do with my recent (mostly collaborative) work on standards-based assessment (Kopriva, Wiley, & Schmidt, 1997; Wiley, Kopriva, & Shannon, 1997; Young, Resnick, & Wiley, 1997; Kopriva & Wiley, 1996). This work was strongly influenced by participation in the New Standards Project and by my long–standing collaboration with Rebecca Kopriva. The social and political context within which standards-based assessment has arisen makes it clear that although many questions about construct validity can be profitably narrowed to focus on individuals, central issues such as how constructs are selected for measurement can only be adequately addressed by understanding the social context within which these determinations are made.

Although the context for these activities is socially and politically complex, most of this recent work in which I have participated has been productively focused more specifically, (i.e., on construct validity in the narrow sense). The work has been organized around four questions:

1. What is a construct domain (i.e., how should domains be defined, organized, and structured)?
2. How should constructs be selected and specified in domain terms?
3. How should tests be developed to measure these specified constructs?
4. How should domain-based specifications of constructs be utilized in the validation of test scores developed from them

Most progress has been made toward answering questions 3 and 4. However, important beginnings have been made on question 1 and 2 as well. Some of this is sketched further in the chapter.

A second part of the chapter focuses on approaches to questions of test use and consequential aspects of validity? Three questions structure this discussions:

1. What conceptual schema can be profitably used to frame questions about test use and the consequences of such use?
2. What role should constructs play in this schema?
3. How should such a schema be utilized in construct validation?

CONSTRUCT VALIDATION

Preliminaries

Constructs, Tasks, and Scores.

Constructs and Tasks. In this chapter, the term construct encompasses characteristics that are commonly classified as cognitive, focusing more specifically on educational achievement. A construct, here, is an ability (i.e., is a human characteristic required for successful task performance). At the simplest level, these constructs can be identified with capacities to perform classes of tasks defined by task specifications. Because they must enable more than a single task performance, the concept implicitly follows from the formulation of an equivalence class of task implementations or realizations, all of which require possession of the same *ability* construct for successful performance. However, in order to be an ability, a human characteristic must not only differentiate successful from unsuccessful task performance, but must also apply to some tasks and not to others. That is, every ability must be defined so that it subdivides tasks into two groups: those to which that ability applies and those to which it does not.

Learning Goals and Task Performances. In order to comprehend achievement constructs, we must link task performances to the learning goals they instantiate. To do this we must distinguish learning goals from teaching specifications. Curriculum is usually defined in terms of the goals that are to be addressed by a learning system. Such goals refer to what is desired or intended to be learned by students (i.e., what students should become capable of doing after completing instruction). In contrast, teaching specifications, whether phrased in terms of syllabi, lesson plans, or specifications for learning activities, address what instruction must, should, or may take place. These specifications are often phrased as guidelines and linked to goals, but they usually take the form of examples of relevant instruction that are not explicitly analyzed in terms of the total set of goals. In short, we frame educational goals in terms of abilities to be acquired, but we frame instruction in terms of activities (tasks) to be carried out.

During this century, student learning goals have increasingly been phrased in psychological terms. That is, *doing* has been defined in terms of task performance and *capability* has become terminologized as knowledge, skill, or ability. Teaching specifications, on the other hand, are usually phrased in social organizational terms. They focus on activities, mostly defined in terms of what teachers should do with students; less frequently, in terms of student participation in instruction.

Thus, although goals refer most directly to the attributes successful students should come to possess, the operational focus of goals is actually the activities in which the students participate. Obviously, these activities should be selected or created with the goals in view. It is these activities (lessons, tasks) that are intended to promote or assess the learning of the intended capabilities. The *unit* or entity for which goals are established is therefore some kind of learning activity (or part or one, or an aggregate of several). These units range from an entire school system's full instructional program through those mounted within it for a school, a class, a course, a lesson, a test, or a single task.

Thus, goals are abilities or capabilities, which students are intended to acquire. The structure of interrelations among goals is complex. First, some capabilities are prerequisite to others. That is, some specific learnings must take place before others can occur. (This is not to say that in any curriculum there are not arbitrary orderings of the skills to be acquired, only that there exist some abilities that cannot be acquired before certain others.) Second, capabilities are usually thought of as groupable, that is clusters of capabilities are conceived as (broader) capabilities themselves, for example, both *decoding* and *reading* are skills or abilities, as are *linear equation solving* and *algebra*.

As set forth in Haertel and Wiley (1993), a *task performance* is a human activity that has a performance goal; a beginning, an end, and therefore, a (possible variable) duration; and that can be evaluated with respect to success in attaining its goal. The *performance goal* is the goal toward which the task performance is directed (the goal set for the test taker), as opposed to the learning or assessment goal that task formulator might have in using the task to further learning or make inferences about ability. This performance goal is not an intended ability; it is a desired end state. The process and the products of the performance must be characterizable in relation to the performance goal. This might only mean that performance is judged to be either satisfactory or not, or it might imply an elaborate multicriterial evaluation.

A *task specification* is a setting of the conditions under which a task performance can take place. It allows a task to be defined in such a way that it can be performed more than one time by more than one person or group. For example, an open and a closed book examination might have the same goals of successful performance for the individuals taking the examinations, but the specification of conditions is sufficiently different that the two would commonly be judged as distinct tasks. The task context dealt with in this section is performance or extended response tasks. Multiple choice tasks will be addressed as special cases when appropriate.

Typically such a specification would address:

1. The environment or circumstances within which the task performance will take place:

   - physical environment
   - timing
   - tools, equipment, physical resources, etc., to be made available
   - information to be made available

2. Any communications directed to the person performing the task, which might include:

   - delineation of its performance goal, including the evaluation criteria
   - performance constraints (i.e., the circumstances within which it is to be performed)

- the tools that could be used to perform it.

A task specification sets up an equivalence class of task implementations or realizations, such that a realization belongs to a specification's equivalence class if and only if its conditions match those of the specification. It is this framework that allows two different individuals to perform the same task, or more than one performance of the same task by a single individual. *A full task definition* includes both the task goal and the task specification, thereby providing the context for both the performance and its evaluation. A task performance ensues from implementing the definition.

Structures. Both tasks and abilities may be structured. Structure, for our purposes here, consists of subdivisions of a group of entities such that those entities within the same subdivision are considered more similar than those in different subdivisions. Structures can be complex in that subdivisions may be partial, may be further divided, may be overlapping, or may be recombined. That is, structures need not be simple partitions or hierarchies.

Much current educational work, especially that linked to testing, is premised on the direct correspondence of abilities and tasks. Thus, tasks often are hierarchically organized into content domains and skills. These are usually defined by identifying them with a class of task–ability pairs without explicitly distinguishing whether the skill category system applies to the tasks or to the abilities. The issue here is not whether goal or ability distinctions can be unlinked from task distinctions. They clearly cannot, as skills are abilities to perform tasks (i.e., they are linked by definition). The main point is that (potentially complex) joint structures of abilities and tasks do not consist of simple one-to-one correspondences of task and ability.

In the instructional context, there is no essential difference between learning and test tasks. All are classroom activities or components of such activities. They only differ in the intent of their use. Learning tasks require particular clusters of abilities for their successful performance. The instructional intent is to select learning tasks that require both the abilities to be learned (targets) and abilities during task performance. Test tasks traditionally do not have learning goals, but they do require particular clusters of abilities. Their primary function is to assess whether abilities necessary for successful performance have been acquired.

Two Uses of "Construct". In the psychometric literature, the term *construct* has been used in two ways for two different purposes:

1. to name the psychological characteristics actually estimated by an existing test score or other measurement.
2. to name the psychological characteristics that a test score or other measurement is intended ("designed") to measure.

Thus, the first purpose is usually to find out what a test score actually measures. For example, does this score labeled *mathematical problem solving* actually measure that ability or how should this *mathematical problem solving* score be interpreted? The second purpose is usually to orient the test design process so that the resulting measurement will be interpretable as planned (e.g., develop a measure of *mathematical problem solving* or given this definition of *mathematical problem solving,* assure that the test score resulting from the development process adequately corresponds to it). These two purposes are obviously interconnected. From my perspective, a targeted development process should be iterative (i.e., test items are drafted, tested, and revised iteratively through a sequence of stages. Each of these stages involves, during testing, an assessment of what each item measures and whether it matches the target).

In the original formulation of construct validity (Cronbach & Meehl, 1995), the nomethetic network of interrelations among observables was conceived as dynamic, that is, measurements changed over time so that validity would change as measures were modified and new observables were added. Thus, from my perspective, the *intent* (dynamic) aspect of construct validity as well as the *actual* (static) were built into the concept from the beginning. The point I want to make here is that the word *construct* is used in the measurement literature in two ways, as characterizing what a test measures (e.g., intelligence may be what an IQ test measures, but we need to identify more precisely what that is versus iteratively improving both the construct and its measures, e.g., how well does the SAT9 problem solving score measure problem solving using the New Standards construct definition?) Thus, construct validity has both a static and a dynamic aspect: 1. What does this score measure? vs. 2. Does this score measure what we want it to?

Scores.

Implications for Task Analysis and Scoring. When a performance task uses collections of typical and atypical performances (i.e., student work) to demark kinds or levels of performance in terms of constructs, the result is a mapping of different abilities into differentiable parts of task performance. This allows the multiple learning or assessment goals specified for the task to be more closely aligned with its internal structure. This kind of task analysis makes clear the available information form the task performances about the target abilities. This has important implications for scoring.

Performance Records. The scoring of task performances is always based on scoring records of some kind. However, the criteria for what is included in a scoring record are quite varied. As an example, in a multiple-choice task, only the response category chosen by the respondent is recorded. There are no standard mechanisms for recording the process stages or the preliminary products of multiple-choice tasks. In some experimental work, eye movements have been recorded but this is not feasible under ordinary testing conditions. In computer administered multiple-choice test tasks, it is possible to gather information on search and intermediate processing depending on how the computer program and the task are structured. In research studies, process information can be obtained using think-aloud or stimulated-recall methods to supplement or stand for performance records. These procedures are increasingly used for validity assessment.

Tasks and Task Scores. The purpose of formulating an assessment task to span a construct domain is to have the task evoke responses (i.e., performances) that provide evidence for the utilization of the psychological processes represented in the domain. Establishment of criteria for inferring these processes from assessment performance records is the essence of valid scoring. Confirmation that a task does evoke appropriate responses is the key criterion for task validation. Thus, the critical bases for evidence are the performance records of respondents.

In this conception, task performances and the records that reflect them contain information about constructs that capture their measurement possibilities. This information circumscribes the potential scores that might be extracted from the performance records (e.g., if a task requires conceptual understanding of linear equations for its solution then information about a respondent's understanding should be contained in the performance record if the task has structured the response record to reflect it). Given this, a scoring rubric could be constructed to extract this information. (See Wiley & Haertel, 1996, for a discussion of performance records.) In general, a scoring record for a task may contain information about multiple constructs if the task requires performers to use processes or knowledge that contribute to more than one construct.

What is a Construct Domain? How Should Domains Be Defined, Organized and Structured? How Should Constructs Be Selected and Specified in Domain Terms?

Tasks and Construct Domains.

The specifications of the constructs to be measured by a test would seem to be a necessary prerequisite to its construct validation. Performance assessment has been characterized as being more "authentic" than traditional modes of assessment. As Messick (1994) asserted:

> Authentic assessments aim to capture a richer array of student knowledge and skill than is possible with multiple choice tests; to depict the processes and strategies by which students produce their work; to align the assessment more directly with the ultimate goals of schooling; and to provide realistic contexts for the production of student work by having task and processes, as well as time and resources, parallel those in the real world. (Arter & Spandel, 1992)

Messick (1989, 1994) discusses two major threats to validity for tests generally and performance assessments in particular. These are "construct irrelevant variance" and "construct underrepresentation". Authentic assessments, in Messick's view, are intended not to leave out relevant constructs and construct aspects, minimizing construct under-representation.

All systems for specifying construct domains, implicitly or explicitly, use categories for delineating the constructs in the domain. But there are important differences between category systems for constructs and those for test tasks. One is that the application of a construct category system to a test can result in tasks relating to multiple categories. This seldom happens with task category systems as they are usually designed to produce classifications that are mutually exclusive and exhaustive of the task domain.

In traditional specifications for tests, a category system for test tasks is selected or created that is intended to apply to the domain or universe of tasks that represent all of the possible tasks that could have been used to construct the test. Consequently, the categories are used to classify the tasks actually constituting the test. Specification categories are typically restricted to describe content, not process. Content, in this sense, refers to characteristics of successful products of task performance. *Successful* means that the performance product matches the performance goal as specified in the task and communicated to the respondent (Wiley & Haertel, 1996). Because of this focus on the task itself and its successful performance products, traditional test specifications typically ignore process (i.e., they leave out aspects or parts of the performance leading to the product). To the extent that specific psychological processes underlying performance characteristics constitute part of the desired construct, traditional test specifications and test specification categories may lead to serious construct underrepresentation in the tests for which they are used. This is the case because the content of the test is either (a) *evaluated* by matching each task in the test to the categories and evaluating the resulting distribution of tasks over categories, or (b) *designed* by specifying this distribution. To the extent that the categories are inadequately or incompletely characterized with respect to the desired constructs, a test will appear to be more valid than it is, and will actually underrepresent key constructs or construct aspects.

Rigney, Petit, Mapus, and Atash (1995) have identified a number of performance task characteristics influencing or reflecting process that are not accounted in usual content specification categories. Some of these are grouped into a larger class labeled *challenge*. These provide salient examples of process and performance aspects usually omitted in traditional content categories. In my view, these are task characteristics associated with important process aspects of assessed constructs. Some of these "challenge" characteristics are: *openness, scaffolding, generalization,* and *complexity*.

1. *openness:* the degree of openness in the task, ranging from closed tasks with only one approach and one successful solution to open tasks with many approaches and many successful solutions.

2. *scaffolding*: the degree of structure within a task, (e.g., inclusion of leading questions) as related to cueing the student's selection of approach or strategy for arriving at a successful solution.
3. *generalization*: the degree to which the task demands generalization in order for a student to arrive at a successful solution.
4. *complexity*: the number of different concepts a student must use to arrive at a successful solution.

Without trying to specify here all of the aspects of process and performance necessary to minimize construct underrepresentation through adequate specification of construct categories, clearly the supplementation of traditional content descriptions with additional information of this type on the character of the desired construct would likely improve the fidelity of the assessment.

Fidelity here means validity in the sense of match between constructs assessed and constructs desired. At the level of an assessment (task, form, test, instrument, etc.), this concept denotes the match between the desired mixture of constructs from the domain and the mixture produced by the task score or task score aggregation defining the test score. At the level of the task, fidelity denotes the centrality and scope of the constructs represented in the particular *task* score to the overall mixture desired for the *test* or subtest score. As such, task fidelity might also be called task quality.

Recently, in the United States, the educational reform movement has stimulated growth of performance assessment and along with that has also stimulated the creation of "content standards" to guide curriculum and assessment development. In assessment terms, these standards can be viewed as approximations to content specifications, because they provide categories for the classification of content and performance. Viewed in this way, they do not suffer from some of the defects of traditional specifications. First, they are not simple classifications of tasks or items. This is because they are intended to affect performance as well as traditional content, they tend to incorporate process or performance aspects such as those described previously. Also they tend to be descriptive and are not exemplified by tasks or performances. This latter problem has led the New Standards Partnership (1995) to formulate performance standards with two distinct elements:

Content & performance descriptions—Descriptions of what students should know and the ways they should demonstrate the knowledge and skill they have acquired.

Work samples & commentaries—Samples of student work selected for their capacity to illustrate the meaning of the content and performance descriptions together with commentary that shows how the content and performance descriptions are reflected in the work sample.

The inclusion of student work is central to the development of performance standards. The role of these work samples is partly one of exemplification. The value of content and performance descriptions is limited unless the descriptions are accompanied by samples of actual student work that demonstrate what is meant by the expectations set out in the descriptions. The value of these samples of student work is greatly enhanced if they are accompanied by commentary that sets the context for the work: how the task was presented, the kind of support the student received and so on. It is further enhanced if the commentary includes discussion of the qualities and characteristics of the work, and is annotated with reference to the content and performance descriptions to show how the work illustrates the descriptions.

Once samples of student work and commentaries are included in this way, it becomes apparent that their role extends well beyond exemplification. They form an essential part of the articulation of the standard itself, since it is only through cross-referencing to the samples of student work and their accompanying commentaries that the content and performance descriptions take on shared meaning. In other words, the samples of student work anchor the standards in a way that allows for their consistent interpretation (NSP, 1995).

It should be noted that "samples of student work and accompanying commentaries" means, in this context, (a) full specification of the task the student was to successfully complete, (b) inclusion of the performance record (i.e., student work), (c) evaluation of work against both the task's performance goal and its measurement goal (i.e., the intended construct). See Wiley (1991), Haertel and Wiley (1993), and Wiley and Haertel (1996) for a fuller discussion of these concepts.

Thus, two ways of more completely specifying and anchoring construct categories have been identified: specifications of additional task characteristics reflecting process and performance aspects of intended constructs (Rigney, Petit, Mapus, & Atash, 1995) and inclusion of samples of student work and accompanying commentaries (NSP, 1995).

Building on these concepts, Kopriva's theory of tasks and task performance dimensions (Kopriva, 1997b) represents the beginnings of a theory of construct domains, especially for educational achievement. It elaborates, applies, and differentiates the content/process, performance depth, and accessibility aspects of tasks and constructs. Thus, Kopriva's theory expands and reorients several of Messick's (1989) aspects of construct validity.

Beyond the identification and exemplification of constructs defining a category, the category may need further specification in terms of the relative degrees of centrality of importance of the various constructs in the category. Also category boundaries may need delineation to clearly separate related categories.

New Standards Examples of Construct Definitions.

To guide task and test development, the New Standards Project has formulated construct definitions in mathematics and English/Language Arts (NSP, 1997). At this stage, the construct domains have not been fully explicated. Following are definitions for mathematics:

Conceptual understanding tasks are broadly described as those that usually create the opportunity for students to analyze an idea, to reformulate it, and to express it in their own terms. Tasks designed to assess conceptual understanding are usually nonroutine, short, and cast in a context. Conceptual understanding tasks can be thought of as "idea probes". Usually the accomplishment of a conceptual understanding task draws heavily on reconstruction rather than on recall; solutions are characterized by representation or explanation rather than by the manipulation. Often a short written explanation is sufficient to accomplish the task. These are the kinds of tasks that student can do easily if they understand the mathematics involved.

Mathematical skill tasks are broadly described as those that create the opportunity for students to apply a well practiced and important routine or algorithm. Tasks or parts of tasks designed to assess skills are routine, always short, and often not cast in a context. Accomplishment of this type of task draws heavily on recall and solutions are characterized largely but not entirely by manipulation. Tasks designed to assess mathematical skill generally have a single correct answer. It is likely that students will have learned how to solve mathematical skills tasks in class.

Problem-solving tasks are described as those that create the opportunity for students to select and deploy problem-solving strategies. Tasks designed to assess problem solving are usually nonroutine, long, and cast in a context. One way of thinking about the assessment of problem solving that is useful to us, is to think of it as a measure of what students can do with the mathematics that they have learned one or even two years previously. Our most successful problem solving tasks make high-level use of well assimilated facts, concepts, and skills. Appropriately cast problem solving tasks ensure that students are given the opportunity to formulate an approach to the problem and the opportunity to work purposefully.

How Should Test Be Developed to Measure These Specified Constructs?

Currently, a cohesive technology does not exist for developing construct-valid tests for measuring prespecified constructs. To overcome this, Kopriva, Wiley, and Schmidt (1997) outlined a set of studies aimed at creating such a viable test development technology.

These studies were to involve a consortium of 3 states, a test publisher, and a small group of measurement academics and professionals. The practical purposed of the project was help states and others to effectively design standards-based assessments that faithfully align to content standards, and to the types of learning they are expected to engender.

This involved establishing the validity of test that contained open ended, short answer, multiple choice, and hands-on performance items. The subject areas and grade levels to be studied were reading, mathematics, and science, and one grade each in elementary, middle school, and high school.

The studies: focused on enhancing our understanding of construct validity and providing a technology and tools for articulating how to build and evaluate the construct validity of items and test. These studies included analyses across item types, and testing systems. They proposed defining and evaluating construct validity at the item and test levels. The main components consisted of creating methods for:

- evaluating and promoting content standards to item specifications match
- ensuring item alignment in the item development process
- identification of skills and abilities needed in items that are ancillary to intended constructs
- rubric analysis

- balance over items and construct elements to ensure tests/forms alignment to standards
- evaluation of accessibility in tests/forms.

This set of studies were broken down into two major strands—investigations with the goal of producing effective means of identifying constructs and evaluating completed items/rubrics to ensure alignment; and investigations for producing efficient methods (and associated materials) of building the effective construct alignment into large scale item and test development. The proposed studies were to develop, refine, and use the methods and materials to evaluate construct identification, with components built in to evaluate the effectiveness of the identification, the construct alignment, and the methodology.

How Should Domain-Based Specifications of Constructs Be Utilized in Validation of Scores Developed From Them?

In order to validate a performance task and its accompanying scoring rubrics in terms of intended constructs, several approaches may be taken. One method of construct validation is to (a) systematically modify assessment tasks and task specifications, (b) administer them to small groups of students, and (c) analyze the resulting student work to compare performances across different versions in order to assess the effects of the modifications on performance. These effects would be used to infer how different performance capabilities are evoked by tasks. Because the purpose is to validate performance tasks by inferring which performance capabilities they can be used to assess, these activities help accomplish this goal. The second method is to gather additional data directly from the respondents about their performance. This can be accomplished with "think aloud" protocols, post-performance interviews or, in some cases, through questionnaire responses. See Kopriva, Wiley, and Schmidt (1997) and Kopriva (1997a) for elaboration. (In the context of the New Standards Project, see Young, Resnick, & Wiley, 1997, and Wiley, Kopriva, & Shannon, 1997).

Assessments and Assessment Scores. Assessments are not single tasks, however, they are collections of tasks together with rules for aggregating scores on component task to overall scores on the collection. Thus the construct validation of a test, as opposed to a task, must focus on these aggregation rules.

In practice, typical performance tasks—especially those of longer duration—will be informative about multiple constructs. An aggregation rule is a function that maps a pattern of scores across tasks onto a total score for the task collection. For example, in traditional multiple choice testing, test items are each scored only once as correct (score=1) or incorrect (score=0); the total score for a collection of items is usually simply the sum of the item scores. In performance assessments, rubric scores for tasks are typically graded scales of performance, and summary scores may take the form of task mappings, (California Learning Assessment System [CLAS], 1994; Wiley, 1993). The New Standards tasks may be used to assess more than one construct—on single or multiple rubrics for a given task. A task collection may therefore have more than one aggregation rule. In general, there will be a distinct aggregation rule for each construct measured by the task collection. Because tasks may have more than one scoring rubric, the number of score types potentially entering an aggregation rule is equal to the sum—over tasks—of the number of rubrics used for each task. An aggregation rule groups task performance patterns into score pattern groups with all the patterns in a group considered as equally informative about the construct. The only logical constraint typically imposed on aggregation rules is that if one pattern represents equal or uniformly higher task performance than another, then the corresponding aggregate scores should be greater or equal (e.g., $f(2, 3, 1) \geq f(2, 2, 1)$). In common practice, aggregation rules are linear and additive. Two major patterns of rules have emerged, both linear and additive. One is where each task is scored on a single "holistic" rubric (h_t): Here, each task is given a weight ($w_{tc} \geq 0$) on each construct and the construct score is a weighted sum of task scores [$s_c = \Sigma_t w_{tc} h_t$]. A second is where tasks are given rubrics that address different constructs. So if a task has a rubric for a construct we define a rubric indicator ($u_{tc} = 1$, if rubric for c; = 0, if not). A construct rubric score for a task is v_{tc} and the construct score (r_c) is a weighted sum of rubric scores [$r_c = \Sigma_t w_{tc} u_{tc} v_{tc}$].

Under this schema, w_{tc} or $w_{tc} u_{tc}$ represent the estimated information in the performance record of task t about construct c. Validity of the assessment construct scores is clearly dependent on the validity of the pieces used in the aggregation, i.e., $s_c = \Sigma_t w_{tc} h_t$ and $r_c = \Sigma_t w_{tc} u_{tc} v_{tc}$ so that validity of the aggregate score rests on the validities of w_{tc}, h_t, u_{tc}, and

v_{tc} (i.e., on the validity of the task scores and weights). We note that the validity assessment here must be multivariate (i.e., must depend on the full array of w_{tc}, h_t, u_{tc}, and v_{tc}, because the construct target will usually be a mixture of subconstructs defined across the overall construct domain).

Validation of task scores was briefly discussed above. Task weights are usually based on judgements about the centrality and coverage of the intended construct reflected in the rubric scores; also weights sometimes reflect the amount of time given to performance. Validation of weights should come about via performance records. One possibility when the measured constructs are not highly interdependent is to segment sampled performance records by construct and estimate average amounts of evidence in order to cross validate the weights.

As an overall validation strategy that does not directly depend on the task or weight validities, using cross-assessment relationships among construct focused scores is appropriate as a convergent and discriminant validation process. Consistent with their reliabilities, measures of the same construct should be more highly related across assessments than measures of different constructs.

Constructing Tests: Some Hints to Minimize Construct Underrepresentation

Below I briefly comment on three arenas in test construction that are currently educationally prominent:

1. *example: teacher tests (construction not explicit)*. When teachers construct tests for classroom use, they often draft test items around an instructional unit for which they are evaluating learning. The items span the instructional unit, but the construct being measured is not explicitly articulated. In this case a posterior analysis might frame constructs in terms of the instructional goals of the teaching unit, but this is not usually done prior to test construction.

2. *example: publisher tests (constructs via test specifications)*. When test publishers construct tests for clients or public sale, they usually develop test specifications prior to item development. For achievement tests, the current form of these specifications is often a content by process matrix. These specifications are not equivalent to a full specification of the constructs to be measured by the test, but are usually explicit enough that they could be used to formulate a partial specification of constructs.

3. *example: new standards project/ state assessments: standards→ constructs→ tests.* The educational reform movement of the past 15 years advocates improving classroom instruction by specifying what is important for students to know and to be able to do (i.e., what learning outcomes are expected of students). The vehicle for accomplishing this has become content standards. Content standards are supposed to affect the instructional process by changing the goals and foci to which instruction is directed. A major method for accomplishing this has been through assessment. Assessments should test what is defined to be important in the standards, and, because teachers teach what is being evaluated, this in turn would encourage the focus on certain types of information and performances in the classroom.

VALIDITY OF CONSTRUCTS

What Conceptual Schema Can Be Profitably Used to Frame Questions About Test Use and the Consequences of Such Use?

When we approach the construct validity of a test score, we are taking a distinctive view of that score by the very nature of the notion of *construct*. Implicit in the idea that a score can measure a construct, is a decomposition of the score into *construct* plus *other* (i.e., $s = c + o$). Usually, we conceive of the *other* as the discrepancy between the score and the construct. Sources of discrepancies may be (a) errors of measurement—in the traditional sense, (b) construct underrepresentation (Messick, 1989), (c) ancillary abilities (Wiley, 1991; Haertel & Wiley, 1993) leading to construct-irrelevant variance (Messick, 1989); i.e., invalidity). Note that I am lumping traditional sources of unreliability with sources of lowered validity to constitute *other* or *invalidity*.

This perspective leads to the concept that validity of measurements should be decomposed into two subconcepts. (1) The validity of the construct to be measured, and (2) The validity or invalidity of the score used to measure the construct. The notion here is that the traditional concept of validity applies jointly to the construct being measured and to the score used to measure it. The analogy is that of joint and conditional probability, that is, $P(A, B) = P(B)P(A/B)$. This decomposes the joint probability of A and B into the marginal probability of B and the conditional probability of A given B. Analogously, if we denote the joint validity of a score and the construct it measures by $V(S, C)$, then we can denote the conditional validity of the score for the construct (ii.) by $V(S/C)$

and the validity of the construct itself (i.) by V(C). I do no wish to imply by this that there must be validity indices such that V(S, C) = V(C)V(S/C), and which are scaled like probabilities (i.e., $0 \leq V \leq 1$), although this is a possibility. My intent is only to allow separation of the evaluation of the validity of the score for the construct from the evaluation of the construct itself.

These aspects of validity require more complete definition. The definition of the joint validity of score and construct, that is, V(S,C), is to my mind, the same as the definition implicitly used by Messick (Messick, 1989, 1994) and thus involves all the validity aspects he identifies (e.g., content, consequential). To understand the decomposition better, I define the V(S/C) aspect as the limited definition of construct validity of a score focused on how well the test score measures the construct, (i.e., whether or not the score has construct-irrelevant variance or construct under-representation). To better understand the meaning of by V(C), let's assume that the score validity for the construct is perfect. This eliminates score imperfections as factors lowering validity and reliability and under these hypothetical conditions V(S,C) = V(C). The aspects of validity influencing V(S,C), under these conditions, and therefore V(C), generally, are primarily consequential.

To repeat what I said in the introduction; this chapter has a twofold origin. First, in *Test validity and invalidity reconsidered* (Wiley, 1991), I expressed a preference for separating validity questions about test use and consequences from those concerning the relations between test scores and constructs. My rationale, at the time, was that investigations concerning test use and its consequences involved the psychology of individuals. I now find it less useful to sharply separate these perspectives and as this new perspective has evolved, an integration now seems more productive.

What Role Should Constructs Play in This Schema?

Two Aspects of Consequential Effects: Interpretation of Construct Versus Interpretation of Score.

Validity is at base about interpretations. In the most traditional sense (e.g., Cronbach 1988, 1989); (AERA, APA, NCME, 1985) this interpretation is of scores. I would like here, however, to propose an expansion of targets of interpretation in a validity frame to include constructs as well as scores.

1. *construct→interpretation (of construct) [social] validity of construct.* In one sense a construct is, itself, an interpretation. However, as I discussed previously, construct is generally used in measurement to denote either (1) what a score measures or (2) what a score could measure. In either case, a construct bears a specific relationship to some score and in traditional measurement frameworks relations between these construct-laden scores and other criteria have evidential value for construct validity. Because of this, my perspective in this chapter is that the notion of construct is specific enough to support a conception that the score is an (errorful) mathematical function of a hypothetical construct score (previously). Thus, the interpretation of the construct should (at least in part) derive from the construct itself.

2. *construct→ score[psychometric]: construct validity.* The relationship of the construct to the score is the major part of construct validity.

3. *score→interpretation (of score) [social]*

4. *interpretation (of construct) →interpretation (of score) (social).* Score interpretation is a contextually mediated function of both (1) the score value and (2) the interpretation of the construct.

5. *interpretation(of score)→decision/action (social).* Finally, the consequential decision or action resulting from these interpretations is a direct outcome of the interpretation of the score's value.

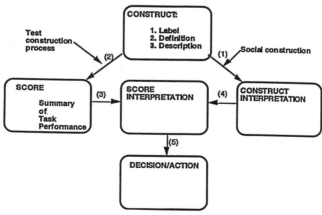

FIG. 12.1

Note that Figure 12.1 in summary exhibits two routes between Construct and Decision/Action. One (2-3-5) is primarily psychometric. The other (1-4-5) is primarily social. Both are necessary, however to understand the validity of any particular consequence of test use.

The diagram describes only the central part of the process determining consequences. Prior to this is the process of construct selection itself. Here we have very little formal knowledge. One very gross global picture might be:

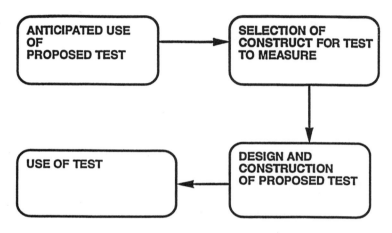

FIG. 12.2

Here we know very little about how anticipated uses determine construct selection or even if they do.

The other part we know little about is how score interpretations affect decisions and actions about individuals. We have very few formal studies about how people interpret and impart meaning to test scores with particular labels. We have even fewer studies of either how construct and score interpretations are acquired or of the social processes linking interpretation to decision and action.

Core validity concepts used in this chapter were drawn from Kopriva, Wiley, and Schmidt (1997), which have been developed in Kopriva (1997a, 1997b, and 1997c). The perspective presented in this chapter continues a program of research earlier begun by Wiley (1991), Haertel and Wiley (1993) and Wiley and Haertel (1995).

REFERENCES

Arter, J. A., & Spandel, V. (1992). Using portfolios of student work in instruction and assessment. *Educational Measurement: Issues and Practice, 11*(1), 36–44.

California Learning Assessment System. (1994). *Technical Report.* Monterey, CA: CTB/McGraw-Hill.

Cronbach, L. J., & Meehl, P. E. (1995). Construct validity in psychological tests. *Psychological Bulletin, 52*, 281–302.

Haertel, E. H., & Wiley, D. E. (1993). Representations of ability structures: Implications for testing. In N. Frederiksen, R. J. Mislevy, and I. I. Bejar, (Eds.), *Test theory for a new generation of tests.* Hillsdale, NJ: Lawrence Erlbaum Associates.

Kopriva, R. (1997a). *Building a construct validity technology for assessments.* Discussion paper.

Kopriva, R. (1997b). *Using three lenses to Reconceptualize test specifications in large-scale assessment: Defining item coverages as a function of content/process, performance depth, and accessibility.* Discussion paper.

Kopriva, R. (1997c). *Getting real about accuracy: Insuring accessibility in testing for everyone.* Discussion paper.

Kopriva, R., & Wiley, D. (1996). *Validating and comparing Assessments: Analyzing Linkages between content /performance standards and assessment systems.* Discussion paper.

Kopriva, R., Wiley, D., & Schmidt. W. (1997). *Building a construct validity Technology for Standards Based Assessment.* A proposal submitted to OERI.

Messick, S. (1989). Validity. In R. L. Linn (Ed.), *Educational measurement (3ʳᵈ Ed).* New York: ACE/Macmillan.

Messick, S. (1994). The interplay of evidence and consequences in the validation of performance assessments. *Educational Researcher,* 23(2), 13–23.

New Standards Project. (1995). *Performance standards* Version 5.1. Pittsburgh, PA: National Center on Education and the Economy.

New Standards Project. (1997). *The New Standards Reference Examination Standards-referenced scoring system.* Pittsburgh, PA: National Center on Education and the Economy.

Rigney, S., Petit, M., Mapus, L., & Atash, N. (1995, June). *Challenge presented by the task. Grade 8.* CCSSO Large Scale Assessment Conference.

Wiley, D. E. (1991). Test validity and invalidity reconsidered. In R. Snow, and D. E. Wiley (Eds.), *Improving inquiry in social science.* Hillsdale, NJ: Lawrence Erlbaum Associates.

Wiley, D. E. (1993, June). Combining Scores into Overall Levels of Performance: Mappings from Products of Chains to Chains. Paper presented at the California Assessment Program. Kenilworth, IL: Beacon Institute.

Wiley, D. E., & Haertel, E. H. (1996). Extended assessment tasks: Purposes, definitions, scoring, and accuracy. In R. Mitchel, (Ed.), *Implementing Performance Assessments: Promises, Problems, Challenges,* Hillsdale, NJ: Lawrence Erlbaum Associates.

Wiley, D., Kopriva, R., & Shannon, A. (1997, February). Standards-based validation of performance assessments. Paper presented at the annual meeting of the American Association for the Advancement of Science, Seattle, Washington.

Young, M. J., Resnick, L., & Wiley, D. E. (1997). *What is a standards-referenced assessment?* Paper presented at the symposium on New Standards Implementation of Standards-Referenced Assessment. Chicago, IL: NCME

IV

VALUES—
THEORY AND ASSESSMENT

13

Constructs and Values in Standards-Based Assessment*

Robert L. Linn
University of Colorado at Boulder

*An earlier version of this chapter was presented at a conference in honor of Samuel Messick, "Under Construction: The Role of Constructs in Psychological and Educational Testing," Princeton, NJ: Educational Testing Service, September 19, 1997. Preparation of this chapter was partially supported under the Educational Research and Development Center Program PR/Award Number R305B600002, as administered by the Office of Educational Research and Improvement, U.S. Department of Education. The findings and opinions expressed in this publication do not reflect the position or policies of the National Institute on student Achievement, the Office of Educational Research and Improvement or the U.S. Department of Education.

Although I was quick to say yes when Ann Jungeblut asked me to participate in this celebration of Sam Messick's contributions to educational and psychological measurement, I must admit it is a bit intimidating to think of talking about issues of validity, constructs, and values in this context. Many people have contributed to the refinement of the way that the field thinks about validity. Two people, Sam Messick and Lee Cronbach, however, stand head and shoulders above the crowd in this regard. In the space available, it would be difficult to do justice to a summary of the ways in which Sam has advanced our thinking about the interplay of constructs and values or the process of validating inferences and actions based on test scores. The intimidation, however, comes from the desire to build and extend his work in these complex areas with him sitting here. Nonetheless, I, of course, told Ann that it was a great idea and wouldn't miss the chance to participate.

Although it may not be evident from my remarks, I have learned a great deal from Sam. I am indebted to him for the support he gave me early in my career when I was at ETS. He always gave me encouragement and the freedom to pursue my research interests. In addition to teaching me a lot about validity, Sam also taught me some more mundane and practical things. For example, he taught me that an ETS Senior Research Psychologist (the title he held when I was new to ETS in 1965) is obviously equivalent to a full professor because we always waited for him to arrive full 15 minutes after the time he set for the start of a meeting. When he became a vice president, I learned that there is no university equivalent of that exalted title, because no one would wait that long in a university setting. I also learned as editor of the Third Edition of *Educational Measurement*, that although a chapter by Sam will certainly not arrive on the editor's desk on schedule, it will be clear when it does arrive that the contribution it makes is more than worth the wait. Although I haven't checked it, I am confident that Sam's chapter is the most cited, and certainly the most influential chapter in the Third Edition of *Educational Measurement*.

Of course, there were good reasons people were willing to wait for Sam to show up for a meeting just as there are for an editor of a book to be willing to wait for a chapter. Most important of these reasons is that the quality of his thinking on issues ranging from the mundane bureaucratic ones to the profound. Sam's contributions to the discussion are consistently worth the wait. It is no wonder that when ETS has had a problem or issue that required the best the organization had to offer, Sam has long been the person that every ETS President (Henry Chauncey, Bill Turnbull, Greg Anrig, and now Nancy Cole) has turned to for help. Thus, there was no answer other than "yes" when Ann Jungeblut asked me to participate in this celebration. I am delighted to be part of it.

The focus of my chapter is on issues of values, constructs, and validity in the context standards-based assessment programs. I take as my starting point, Sam's one sentence definition of validity in his 1989 chapter in the third edition of *Educational Measurement*, which Shepard (1993) describes as the currently "most cited authoritative reference on the topic (p. 423). "Validity is an integrated evaluative judgment of the degree to which empirical evidence and theoretical rationales support the *adequacy* and *appropriateness* of *inferences* and *actions* based on test scores or other modes of assessment" (Messick, 1989, p. 13, emphasis in original). This statement, which is the first sentence of Sam's influential chapter, is so packed with meaning that it took him 91 pages of an oversized book with relatively small type to elaborate the concept.

As I'm sure is familiar to most readers, Sam's comprehensive definition of validity is elaborated in a two-by-two table corresponding to the adequacy/appropriateness and inferences/actions distinctions of the definition. The two rows of the table distinguish two bases of support for validity claims—the evidential basis and the consequential basis that are used to support claims of adequacy and appropriateness. The two columns of the table distinguish between interpretations of assessment results (e.g., the latest NAEP history results show students have a "striking lack of knowledge about their heritage", Innerst, Washington Times, November 2, 1995) and uses of results (e.g., the cash awards given to teachers in Kentucky based on increases in assessment scores by successive cohorts of student).

Although there is some disagreement in the field regarding the desirability of including consequences as a part of validity (see, for example, Green, 1990; Moss, 1994; Wiley, 1991), there is broad consensus both with other parts of Messick's comprehensive formulation and with the importance of investigations of consequences as part of the overall evaluation of particular uses and interpretations of assessment results (Baker, O'Neil, & Linn, 1993; Cronbach, 1980; 1988; Linn, 1994; Linn & Baker, 1998; Linn, Baker, & Dunbar, 1991; Moss, 1992, 1994; Shepard, 1993). Of course, affirmation of primacy of validity based on a comprehensive framework is one thing. Validity practice is quite another. Validity practice is too often more in keeping with outmoded notions of validity that base validity claims on a demonstration that test items correspond to the cells of a matrix of test specifications or the demonstration that scores on a test are correlated with other relevant measures (e.g., teacher ratings, or another test administered at a later time). Although both content-related evidence and criterion-related evidence are relevant to validity judgments, they do not provide a sufficient basis for the kind of "integrated evaluative judgment" that Messick demands.

Standards-based assessments currently being introduced in states around the country are frequently introduced by legislation that includes a requirement that assessments be "valid, reliable, and fair." However, the approach to validation is often limited to comparisons of the assessment content to the content standards that are supposed to determine what gets assessed. In old terminology, the actions suggest that content validity, or what Sam would prefer to call content relevance and content representativeness, are treated as if that was sufficient. The new slogan for that emphasis of content relevance and representativeness is alignment. There is considerable emphasis on developing assessments that are aligned with content standards. Far less attention is paid, however, to accumulating evidence needed to judge the adequacy and appropriateness of interpretations and uses made of assessment results.

There are a number of reasons for the large discrepancy between the theory and practice of validity. When taken seriously, the job of validation can be quite daunting and may seem to be overwhelming due to its comprehensiveness. Because of the scope of validity, it is often useful to identify a series of components or facets of validity.

The CRESST validity criteria (Baker, O'Neil, & Linn, 1993; Linn, Baker, & Dunbar, 1991) were developed in response to questions being raised by new emphases on the forms of assessment that were seen in the early 1990's. In particular, the movement toward an increased reliance on performance-based assessments characterized by judgmentally rated student responses on a relatively small number of open-ended tasks was stimulated by changing priorities. The changing priorities demanded increased attention to the consequences of uses made of assessment results and fundamental questions of fairness. The judgmental aspects of scoring and the limited number of tasks also gave new salience to questions of generalizability and transfer. Questions of content quality, the adequacy of content coverage, the cognitive processes being measured, were also highlighted.

It is not that different forms of assessment require different conceptions of validity. Messick (1994) has cogently argued that "performance assessments must be evaluated by the same validity criteria, both evidential and consequential, as are other assessments. Indeed, such basic assessment issues as validity, reliability, comparability, and fairness need to be uniformly addressed for all assessments because they are not just measurement principles, they are social values that have meaning and force outside of measurement wherever evaluative judgment and decisions are made" (1994, p. 13). New forms of assessment that were emphasized in the early 1990s did require new technical approaches, not only as the result of changes in forms of assessment, but as the result of shifts in emphases and intended uses of assessments that together provided a different context for raising validity questions. The challenge, however, remains to establish priorities for validity studies that will provide adequate evidence for making the overall evaluative judgment that Messick calls for in his definition of validity.

In the time remaining, I focus on current standards-based assessment programs and try to identify some of the issues that would seem to demand high priority in planning validation efforts. I will use as a prime example the Voluntary National Tests (VNT) in 4th grade reading and 8th grade mathematics that the Clinton administration is trying to make a reality. Although the VNT are not based on government adopted national content standards, a reasonable case can be made that they follow a standards-based approach to assessment using as the starting place the frameworks of the National Assessment of Educational Progress (NAEP). That is, the NAEP frameworks are expected to play the role of their close cousin, national content standards, and the NAEP achievement levels play the role of performance standards. Indeed, the NAEP framework was selected as a starting point in an effort to finesse the question of what content standards should be used as the basis for developing the VNT and thereby jump-start the development process so that it could meet the fast-track expectations to have operational test in the field in the spring of 1999.

The kinship between national content standards developed and promulgated by discipline groups epitomized by the NCTM (1989) mathematics standards and the NAEP frameworks is not accidental. Both the process of development and the overlapping membership on the development committees that developed the discipline area content standards and the NAEP frameworks assured some degree of consistency. The same can be said of a comparison of national content standards and the multitude of state content standards, frameworks, and benchmarks that have been developed during the past few years. There is, of course, a big difference between saying there is overlap and the claim that they are interchangeable. As I will argue, differences become most evident when standards are actually used as the basis for the development of assessments. That is so because assessments make differences in interpretations of content standards and in priorities for different aspects of student understandings and performance that shape the measurement constructs.

Standard-Based Reform

Before getting into issues specific to the validity of assessments, it is useful to consider some aspects of the standards-based reform context that is the basis for the types of assessments that are the focus of my chapter. A 1995 report of the National Academy of Education Panel on Standards-Based Education Reform described the vision of the movement as follows.

> The intentions of standards-based reform are best captured in the slogan 'high standards for all students.' Unlike previous reforms focused on the attainment of minimum competencies, setting higher academic expectations is expected to ensure that students have more complete mastery of challenging subject matter and the ability to apply what they know to solve real-world problems. Standards-based reform also reflects a strong commitment to educational equity: The same high expectations are to be established for all students, even groups who have traditionally performed poorly and received watered-down curricula. (McLaughlin & Shepard, 1995, p. xvi)

Values questions are evident in this characterization of standards-based education reform. So too, are issues about the nature of constructs that assessments based on standards consistent with this description are intended to measure. The same curricula and same high standards for all students, although easy to accept at a rhetorical level, obviously may conflict with the desire of parents to have the best for their children. The recently released annual Phi Delta Kappa/Gallup education poll (Rose, Gallup, & Elam, 1997), for example, reported that while roughly three-fourths of the respondents approved establishing national standards for measuring the academic performance of the public schools (77%) an approximately equal proportion favored moving chronic "troublemakers" into alternative programs (77%). Apparently, all students does not include troublemakers in the minds of the survey respondents or they don't agree with the dual goals of the leaders of the standards-based reform movement. Moreover, two out of three favored ability grouping (66%). Although ability grouping is not, in principle, inconsistent with the same "high standards for all students," considerable experience suggests that it is inconsistent in practice (e.g., Gamoran & Berends, 1987; Oakes, 1990).

Value conflicts over the weight to be given to the equity goal as well as over acceptable or desirable approaches to achieving that goal provide potential sources of conflict regarding the standards-based reform effort. These conflicts are less visible, however, than value conflicts over what should be emphasized in the standards and, therefore, taught and assessed. As is evident from the heated debate about the Voluntary National Tests, value conflicts about constructs that are to be assessed have considerable salience. This is so, in part, because it is less socially acceptable to question the goal of equity than to question the vision of a discipline such as history, or even, the less controversial discipline of mathematics.

The standards movement has pushed new concepts of the disciplines that generally downplay the accumulation of facts and procedural skills in favor of conceptual understanding and problem-solving processes. Mathematics was in many respects the lead discipline. It is almost a decade since the National Council of Teachers of Mathematics (NCTM, 1989) published the *Curriculum and Evaluation Standards for School Mathematics*. Although it is hardly the case that the instruction envisioned in the NCTM Standards has been incorporated into the daily practices in most classrooms, there is little doubt that those standards have been influential. They have received a great deal of praise by politicians as well as educators, have served as a model for mathematics standards developed in most states as well as standards in other subject areas at the national and state levels, and are now routinely claimed to be a source of guidance by textbook and test publishers.

The broad support enjoyed for a number of years NCTM Standards was never there for some of the other content areas. The history and English-language arts standards, in particular, were subject to harsh criticism (e.g., Diegmueller, 1994). As the NCTM standards have become more influential and as assessments designed to be aligned with the standards have started to make the constructs and values of the standards more explicit, however, the NCTM standards also have come increasingly under attack. This point is illustrated by the exchange in *the New York Times* in which Lynn Cheney (1997) attacked what she called the "fuzzy math" or "whole math" encouraged by the NCTM standards and Tom Romberg (1997) defended the standards and the mathematics that they envision. That and other recent criticisms have taken place not only in the context of the debate about the Voluntary National Test, but in the context of several state assessment programs and efforts to revise state content frameworks or standards.

Although academics sympathetic to the national content standards of the disciplinary groups are sometimes quick to dismiss attacks such as Chaney's as representing only a small fraction of the extreme right, there is considerable evidence that "the questions opposition groups raised reflect broader public concerns. For example, recent surveys about teaching of mathematics and writing point to fundamental difference between the curricular values of education reformers and large segments of the public" (McDonnell, 1996, p. 31). Large segments of the public favor such basics as factual knowledge, phonics, and facility with arithmetic calculations without the aide of a calculator. Furthermore, a large fraction of the public is not adverse to such familiar approaches as memorization and drill-and-practice as ways of accumulating those skills. Leading education reformers, on the other hand, place much greater emphasis on conceptual understanding and are likely to favor constructivist notions of effective learning.

It is not surprising that standards, especially ones that actually have an influence on things that matter such as assessments, textbooks, and instructional programs, are controversial. To be of educational value, standards must specify what knowledge and skills are of greatest value within a content area. It is the specificity of what is of most worth that makes standards valuable guides of curriculum and instruction, but specificity also makes them potentially contentious. As Cremin (1989, p. 9) has aptly noted, "standards involve much more than determinations of what knowledge is of most worth; they also involve social and cultural differences, and they frequently serve as symbols and surrogates for those differences."

The emphasis in standards-based assessment is on (1) clear specifications through "content standards" of what students should know and be able to do in specific content or subject matter areas at identified points of their education (e.g., 4th grade reading, or 8th grade mathematics) and (2) clear specifications through "performance standards" of the level of performance that students are expected to achieve in relationship to the content standards. In other words, content standards specify what is to be learned and measured whereas performance standards answer the question: "how good is good enough?"

Performance Standards

Sadler (1987) distinguished among four methods of specifying and promulgating performance standards. These are (1) numerical cut-offs, (2) tacit knowledge, (3) exemplars, and (4) verbal descriptions. Numerical cut-offs are the most familiar and widely used. They have the advantage of specificity and apparent precision, but they do not aide understanding of what is required by the standard. By itself, knowledge that a score of 80 on a test is required to meet the "proficient" standards does not tell either the teacher or the learner what needs to be done to achieve a proficient performance.

Sadler's second method, tacit knowledge, is best illustrated by connoisseurship. Experts who have the tacit knowledge of the standard may achieve relatively high degrees of agreement, but that is of little aide to the novice if the standards continue to depend on tacit knowledge possessed only by experts. Tacit knowledge can be used successfully to grade student work by consensus among experts, possibly using formal moderation procedures. More is needed than consistent grading, however, if students and other novices are to understand what is required to meet the standard and hence be able to judge performances against the standard.

The third method, the use of exemplars of performance that does or does not meet standards, is usually instituted in an explicit effort to communicate what the standards entail to a broader audience. "The exemplars are not the standards themselves, but are indicative of them; they specify standards implicitly" (Sadler, 1987, p. 200). Because there are innumerable potential examples and a host of contextual and other factors that may influence performance, many exemplars are needed and a heavy interpretation burden is placed on anyone attempting to infer performance standards from a collection of exemplars.

Verbal descriptions attempt to provide explicit definitions of performance standards. Some verbal descriptions make heavy use of adverbs and adjectives to define levels of performance (e.g., *clearly*, *concisely*, *logical*). Other verbal descriptions rely on verbs (e.g., *demonstrate*, *provide*, *make*). For example, the Proficient level for fourth grade students in reading is defined as follows for NAEP.

> Fourth-grade students performing at the Proficient level should be able to demonstrate an overall understanding of the text, providing inferential as well as literal information. When reading text appropriate to fourth grade,

they should be able to extend the ideas in the text by making inferences, drawing conclusions, and making connections to their own experiences. The connection between the text and what the student infers should be clear. (Campbell, Donahue, Reese, & Phillips, 1996, p. 42)

Unlike the precision of numerical cut-offs, verbal descriptions are "fuzzy standards." Yet, it is verbal descriptions and associated exemplars that most influence interpretations of assessment results. Hence, those descriptions and exemplars deserve much more attention in validation efforts than they usually receive.

Three of the four methods described by Sadler are used in an effort to implement and communicate the NAEP performance standards. Verbal descriptions, such as the one just illustrated, are accompanied by numerical cut-offs that operationalize the performance standards on the NAEP score scale, and by exemplar items and student responses. Apparent discrepancies between these different approaches to specifying performance standards sometimes arise and lead to challenges to the validity of the standards.

Verbal descriptions and the use of exemplars as a way of defining performance standards have important implications for the construct interpretations of assessments designed to determine whether students meet those standards. The fact that verbal descriptions are fuzzy standards implies that there is a fuzziness in the constructs measured by the assessment used to determine the performance level achieved by a student.

Variation in Content Standards

The prospect of the Voluntary National Test has caused concerns in some states about the degree to which the tests will match their own content standards. Educational leaders in some states that have invested heavily in the development of standards and put great stock in aligning their assessments to those standards worry that the Voluntary National Test will usurp their state assessments and content standards and become the de facto driver of curriculum and teaching.

Discipline-based efforts to improve curriculum and instruction through the development and promulgation of content-standards are reinforced by standard-setting efforts in almost every state. The National Academy of Education Panel on Standards-Based Education Reform, for example, reported that by 1995 all but one of the 50 states had "developed or were in the process of developing curriculum frameworks; some of these have been impressive enough to influence national standard-setting efforts" (McLaughlin & Shepard, 1995, p. 3).

Among other things included in NCTM standards 10 and 11 dealing with statistics and probability, the Standards say that students in Grades 5-8 should be provided with instructional experiences so that students can

- "construct, read, and interpret tables, charts, and graphs;" (from NCTM Standard 10, Grades 5 through 8)
- "model situations by devising and carrying out experiments or simulations to determine probabilities;" (from NCTM Standard 11, Grades 5 through 8).

As can be seen in Table 13.1, there is considerable overlap between what is expected according to state standards and the NCTM standards with regard to these specific topics. There is also considerable consistency with regard to these topics between the state standards and those of the New Standards Project, the NAEP framework, and, most importantly, the draft specifications for the Voluntary National Test in eighth grade mathematics. As can also be seen in Table 13.1, the July 25 Draft of Item and Test Specifications for the National Voluntary 8th Grade Mathematics Test includes the following in strand D: Data Analysis, Statistics, and Probability.

2. Use a variety of graphs and plots to organize and display data, and make inferences from organized data. The items themselves should push students to compare different representations, select appropriate representations, determine reasonable scales for graphs or plots, and justify their selections, and to solve problems using the representation they select. Analysis or generalizations could be called for across multiple representations. Items could also involve multiple data sets or multiple representations of a single data set. [Example 9, METRO RAIL, Ch. 5]

Table 13.1
Comparison of Selected National and State Standards in
Statistics and Probability for Eighth Grade Students*

Source	Area of Standard	
	Statistics	Probability
NCTM Standards	construct, read, and interpret tables, charts, and graphs	model situations by devising and carrying out experiments or simulations to determine probabilities
Colorado	reading and constructing displays of data using appropriate techniques (for example, line graphs, circle graphs, scatter plots, box plots, stem-and-leaf plots) and appropriate technology	determining probabilities through experiments or simulations
New York	systemically collect, organize, describe, and interpret data, including grouped data as well as individual data	model situations by devising and carrying out experiments and simulations to determine probabilities
North Carolina	apply knowledge of statistics in problem solving situations, selecting an appropriate format for presenting data	find the probability of simple and compound events using experiments, computer simulations, random number generation, and theoretical methods
Texas	uses statistical procedures to describe data [and is expected to] ... construct circle graphs, bar graphs, and histograms, with and without technology	applies concepts of theoretical and experimental probability to make predictions [and is expected to] ... use theoretical probabilities and experimental results to make predictions and decisions; and select and use different models to simulate an event
Virginia	use information displayed in line, bar, circle, and picture graphs and histograms to make comparisons, predictions, and inferences	analyze problem situations, such as games of chance, board games, or grading scales, and make predictions, using knowledge of probability

New Standards Project	collects and organizes data and displays data with appropriate tables, charts, and graphs	recognizes equally likely outcomes, constructs sample spaces, and determines probabilities of events
NAEP Framework	2. Organize and display data and make inferences -- Use tables, histograms (bar graphs), pictograms, and line graphs -- circle graphs and scattergrams -- stem-and-leaf plots and box-and-whisker plots -- Make decisions about outliers	8. Determine the probability of a simple event -- Estimate probabilities by use of simulations -- Use sample spaces and the definition of probability to describe events -- Describe and make predictions about expected outcomes
NVT Test Specifications	2. Use a variety of graphs and plots to organize and display data, and make inferences from organized data. The items themselves should push students to compare different representations, select appropriate representations, determine reasonable scales for graphs or plots, and justify their selections, and to solve problems using the representation they select. Analysis or generalizations could be called for across multiple representations. Items could also involve multiple data sets or multiple representations of a single data set.	7. Determine probabilities, describe events, and make predictions using simulations, sample spaces, and the definition of probability. Determine fairness of games. Use probability as it relates to independent and dependent events. In the assessment of probability, situations should be simple enough for students to demonstrate what probability means as well as apply addition and multiplication rules for probability.

* State, NCTM, NAEP, and NVT statements are taken from the following web sites: http://www.mprinc.com/nationaltests /math.html and http://putwest.boces.org/StSu/Math.html. The NSP statements are from the New Standards Project *Performance Standards.*

7. Determine probabilities, describe events, and make predictions using simulations, sample spaces, and the definition of probability. Determine fairness of games. Use probability as it relates to independent and dependent events. In the assessment of probability, situations should be simple enough for students to demonstrate what probability means as well as apply addition and multiplication rules for probability. [Example 6: ZARK'S PATH, Ch. 5]
(See web site: http://www.mprinc.com/nationaltests/math.html).

Of course, analyses of other topics or strands in eighth grade mathematics or of the standards and specifications for fourth grade reading might show far less consistency than the ones I picked for illustrative purposes from the areas of probability and statistics. The key point, however, is that detailed analyses are needed for a state that takes seriously its own content standards to be convinced that the Voluntary National Test has specifications that are consistent or aligned with their content standards.

Assessments

The question of what should be assessed is and should be of central importance. Traditionally, publishers of widely-used test batteries have developed content specifications for their tests using a process that relied heavily on the review of current textbooks and other instructional materials. Those reviews are supplemented in a variety of ways by recommendations of subject-matter experts, feedback from users, and experience with previous editions of the test battery. For obvious reasons, market forces play a prominent role. Even if a publisher, for example, would like to do away with a separate arithmetic computation score and make calculators an assumed tool for its mathematics test, it is unlikely to do so as long as the marketplace wants scores to show how well students do arithmetic computations by hand. Real and perceived market forces can and often push in the direction of the status quo. The conventional is safer than the new and overly innovative, especially when the new comes with a substantially higher price tag.

The standards movement has done a great deal to rock the boat. Assessments make explicit particular interpretations of the standards. They provide operational examples of what is expected by the statement that students "should understand . . . ," or "should be able to . . .." The scoring criteria and cut scores required for a student to be at the "basic" level in history, the "advanced" level in mathematics, or the "proficient" level in reading also make explicit how good is good enough and what is required to be considered excellent. In other words, it is through assessments that both content standards and performance standards become concrete.

Because of the diversity of opinion on what is most important for students to learn and what is legitimate for schools to teach, it is essential that the process of development engage the broad public so that the diverse range of views can be heard. Basic skills such as spelling, phonics, multiplication tables, historical dates and locations that are valued by sizable segments of the public must be considered. They can be ignored in standards because educational reformers believe in "constructivist" learning theories only at the peril of the whole enterprise. Building a broad consensus requires, not just public hearings and a period of time for public review and input, but a process that ensures that concerns are heard and a balance is struck in the standards and assessments that attends to major concerns of the public.

Neither the voluntary national tests nor important state assessments can escape this debate. Indeed, it is already underway. As Ravitch (1997a) noted, "the Internet is humming with charges that the national tests will be stacked to favor 'whole language' theories of reading and against phonics and to promote 'fuzzy math' (where the process of problem-solving, not the right answer, matters most) and against computation" (p. A15). Although she stated that she did not know if these charges were valid, she used the concern to argue forcefully for Congressional authorization for the voluntary national tests and the assignment of responsibility for determining what should be assessed by the tests to a nonpartisan board. She argued for the action taken by Congress to establish an expanded National Assessment Governing Board (NAGB) for this purpose. The key point is that the tests need to be protected from partisan views and political swings.

Standardization

Standardization has long been thought of as a foundation for building tests that were valid, reliable, and fair. The first edition of Anastasi's (1954) widely used textbook, *Psychological Testing*, described a psychological test as "a standardized measure of a sample of behavior" (p. 22). She elaborated the concept of a standardized measure as follows. "Standardization implies uniformity of procedure in administering and scoring the test. If the scores obtained by different individuals are to be comparable, testing conditions must obviously be the same for all. Such a requirement is only a special application of the need for controlled conditions in all scientific observations" (p. 23). Other well-known authorities presented similar arguments. Cronbach (1960), for example, emphasized the standardization of procedure and defined a standardized test as "one in which the procedure, apparatus, and scoring have been fixed so that precisely the same test can be given at different times and places" (p. 22).

Popular use of standardized tests often has other meanings. It may, for example, be the term used to refer to a published, multiple-choice test, but such characteristics are not fundamental to the concept. An essay test can have a relatively high degree of standardization of procedures (e.g, instructions, timing, and scoring), whereas a multiple-choice test can be administered in unstandardized ways (e.g., with different instructions, under different conditions, and with different time constraints).

It is hardly surprising that uniformity of procedure would be emphasized when the goal is fair and valid comparisons among individual test takers. It would obviously be quite unfair in the administration of an essay test scored for content, spelling, and grammar to allow some job applicants to type their responses at a word-processor with access to a spell-checker, a thesaurus, and a grammar checker whereas other applicants were required to write their essays by hand without access to such resources. Traditionally, it would also be considered unfair to allow one test taker 90 minutes to complete a test whereas other test takers with whom they are competing were held to a strict time limit of 60 minutes. Such traditional notions of standardization are being challenged with increasing frequency, however.

The goal of including students in assessments who would have been excluded in the past because of a disability or because of lack of facility in English has raised questions about the essential and nonessential aspects of standardization. This is fundamentally a values-laden construct validity problem. The most commonly requested and used variance from stipulated administration conditions in state and national assessments is extra time. Other adaptations and accommodations that are used with increasing frequency include oral presentations of assessments to students, individualized administration, and translations of assessments into languages other than English. The plan for the 8th grade voluntary national test in mathematics, for example, includes a provision for the creation of a Spanish language version of the test. A number of states are following a similar path.

The expanded emphasis on adaptations and accommodations that allow greater numbers of students to participate in assessments raise fundamental issues about standardization not just for the students for whom the variations in procedures are intended, but for all students. Uniformity of procedure should be recognized as a means to the ends of validity, reliability, and fairness rather than an end in itself. Simplistic examples, such as being allowed to use eye glasses when taking a test, make it clear that complete uniformity was never the intent. Indeed, most people would agree that it would be unfair to deny a person who wears glasses the use of this accommodation when taking a test. Similarly, there is little debate about the fairness of the use of large print or Braille versions of a test. Implicit in the allowance of such accommodations is the belief that they are not relevant to the construct being measured. Or conversely, the unaided visual acuity that may contribute to variability in test performance is an ancillary ability (Haertel & Linn, 1996) that contributes construct-irrelevant variance to test scores (Cook & Campbell, 1979; Messick, 1989).

In a similar vein, the decision to make a Spanish version of the 8th grade voluntary national test in mathematics is predicated on the notion that the specific language used for presentation of problems and for constructing responses by test takers involves language skills that are ancillary to the mathematical knowledge and skills that the test is intended to measure. Presumably the limitation to either English or Spanish rather any language preferred by a student is based on practical considerations of numbers and cost rather than principle. Note that the same decision was not made for the 4th grade voluntary national test in reading where the Department of Education plan prior to the transfer of responsibility for the test content to NAGB called for the test to be printed only in English. Given that position, it is obvious that the measurement intent is not simply the ability to read, but the ability to read in English.

It is worth noting that both the plan to develop a Spanish language version of the 8th grade mathematics test and the plan not to do that for the 4th grade reading test were challenged. Advocates for linguistic minority children argued that the reading test needs to be given in Spanish to allow children who have received instruction in Spanish to participate in the reading test. On the other hand, the plan to give the 8th grade mathematics test in Spanish was called a "terrible idea" by those who argued that "[s]tudents in American schools must learn to function in the larger society, which requires knowledge of English language" (Ravitch, 1997b, p.64).

Although the allocation of the likely effects on performance to construct-relevant and construct-irrelevant sources of variance is straight-forward and noncontroversial for some variations in administration procedure (e.g., the use of eye glasses), in most cases there is uncertainty. First, there is controversy about the choice of construct should it be reading in English, doing mathematics in English, or should it be reading or doing mathematics in the language of a student's choice? Second, there is uncertainty about the degree to which skills intended to be ancillary (e.g., reading on a mathematics test) influence performance for different students.

The evidence to support or refute a specific allocation of variance as construct relevant or irrelevant is generally weak or nonexistent. Does the extra time allowed a student diagnosed as having a particular learning disability make the test performance a better reflection that student's skills and knowledge the test is intended to measure than it would be under standard time limits? Would a similar increase in time make the test a more valid measure of those intended skills and knowledge for other students who were not diagnosed as having a learning disability? Both questions are relevant to judgments validity and fairness of the accommodation. If the answer to both questions is yes, then it may be considered unfair to allow extra time only for students diagnosed to have a particular learning disability although it would enhance the validity of the measure for those students.

Two key ideas that direct the search for evidence relevant to an evaluation of the validity of the interpretations and uses of an assessment are the concepts of construct underrepresentation and construct-irrelevant variance (Cook & Campbell 1979). As Messick's (1989) elaboration of these ideas makes clear, the nature of the evidence relevant to these two ideas may be multifaceted and quite complex. The basic ideas, however, are relatively straight forward and intuitively reasonable. Content under-representation occurs to the degree that the assessment excludes or gives inadequate attention to aspects of the intended domain of measurement (e.g., ignores hard-to-measure skills and understandings specified in the content standards). Construct-irrelevant variance refers to the degree to which scores are dependent on ancillary skills that are irrelevant to the intent of the measure (Haertel & Linn, 1996).

Although one might like a measure to be pure in the sense that it depends only on the single ability the test is intended to measure, in practice, performance always depends to some extent on ancillary abilities. That is, there are some construct-irrelevant sources of variability in the performance of test takers. Considerable effort is put into minimizing the effects of ancillary abilities. For example, the reading level on a mathematics test may be reduced well below the typical level of students at the target grade of a test in an effort to minimize the effect of reading ability because it is considered ancillary to the intent of measurement. Such efforts can effectively eliminate this ancillary ability as a source of noncomparability for most students, and may reduce its effect for other students, but there are limits. Obviously, this approach does not help for students who read and speak a different language. A mathematics task presented in English is obviously unfair to students who speak only another language and receive their mathematics instruction in that other language. In this case the unfairness is the result of scores that are systematically biased downward for members of one group but not of another.

In general, ". . . any single task that relies on ancillary abilities that one group of students possesses and another group does not will be biased in favor of the first group" (Haertel & Linn, 1996, p. 67). Although easily stated, this general conclusion is difficult to evaluate and even more difficult to eliminate in practical assessment situations.

The language example, though real and important for substantial numbers of students in the U.S., is in some ways too easy. Differential familiarity with specific aspects of tasks on an assessment is more subtle and more pervasive.

Test Fairness

Standardization used to be almost synonymous with test fairness when the latter "was viewed mainly as the administration of objective tests under standard and secure conditions to protect individuals from prejudiced or capricious high-stakes decisions" (Willingham & Cole, 1997, p. 6). As Willingham and Cole (1997) have recently noted, however, the concept of test fairness has evolved. They argued that the concept of test fairness was made more complicated by the addition of requirements that the test be "unbiased" and that the uses of test results be "equitable and just." They went on to make the case that "fairness is an important aspect of validity . . ." and that "[a]nything that reduces fairness also reduces validity" (p. 6). They concluded that "test fairness is best conceived as comparability in assessment; more specifically comparable validity for all individuals and groups" (pp. 7–6).

Equating test fairness with comparable validity for all individuals and groups places some constraints on the concept that may not be compatible with certain views of equity or justice. The formulation by Willingham and Cole, however, provides a useful lens for analyzing quite a range of fairness issues. Test fairness as comparable validity implies a great deal for the ways in which evidence can be brought to bear on fairness questions and challenges some older ways of thinking about fairness.

Although popular discussions often speak of validity as if it were an all or nothing characteristic of a test, there is broad professional consensus that validity is neither a property of the instrument nor an all or nothing characteristic. Inferences and actions based on test scores are validated— not the test itself—and validity is always a matter of degree. The same could be said of fairness. Thinking of the concept as a matter of degree rather than an all-or-none characteristic, however, may be even farther removed from common usage in the case of fairness that in the case of validity. It may also be more foreign to think of fairness as residing not in the test but in the inferences or decisions based on test scores.

Evidence about construct-irrelevant variance is especially important to an evaluation of the fairness of an assessment because groups may differ in a wide variety of attitudes, experiences, and capabilities that are not explicitly a part of the intended focus of measurement. The assessment would have reduced validity and be less fair to the degree that those ancillary skills and characteristics affect performance on the assessment. It should be noted that skills that are considered ancillary or sources of construct-irrelevant variance for one interpretation or use of assessment results may be relevant for part of the intent of measurement for another interpretation.

The final issue I want to mention before closing is an important one, but also a very complex and messy issue. That is the notion of opportunity to learn. Although it may be fair to include material students have not had an opportunity to learn for some uses of the assessment results (e.g., monitoring system progress or system-level accountability), the same assessment may be considered quite unfair for other purposes (e.g., making a consequential decisions about individual students) without evidence that students had had an adequate opportunity to learn.

Unfortunately, with the Voluntary National Test the variations in consequences associated with uses of the test from one state to the next or one district to the next are unknown. The Administration has been in such a strong promotional mode so far that little serious attention has been given to the question of appropriate and inappropriate uses.

The committee that developed the draft specifications for the eighth grade mathematics test made some fairly strong assumptions about the learning opportunities that students would have had before they take the test. According to the Mathematics Test Specification Committee, for example,

> Students should have had extensive experience in gathering data, organizing data into tables and graphs, and interpreting data from a variety of situations. Since the early elementary grades, they have interpreted, used, and made basic bar graphs, pictographs, and line graphs, although often these experiences may have been teacher led in terms of making decisions about form, scale, axes, units, and so on. Students should have been previously assessed on basic reading and constructing of such graphs to organize data. Consequently, it is assumed that they are ready to be assessed at a more in-depth level than making a bar graph on provided axes or reading information from a line graph.
> (http://www.mprinc.com/nationaltests/math.html).

The committee also assumed that students should have had opportunities to use calculators on a routine basis. They viewed calculators as a standard tool that should be available to students and hence pushed for allowing students to use calculators of their choice when taking all parts of the Voluntary National Mathematics Test. Of course, not all students will have had an adequate opportunity to learn how or when to use calculators. Nor will all students even have access to calculators when taking the test. Although the specifications call for test items that can be done either with or without the calculator, I believe that the committee's permissive stance on the use of calculators raises fundamental issues of validity and fairness that could cause serious problems in any high-stakes uses of the test that might be mandated by a state or district. Serious validation will require close attention to the social consequences of such uses.

CONCLUSION

Serious evaluation of the "adequacy and appropriateness of inferences and actions" based on results of the Voluntary National Tests will require the concerted efforts of many researchers and users of the tests. Of course, that could be said of any test. Because these tests will have the benefit of substantial financial support for development from public funds, will bear the government imprimatur, and are a prominent part of the Clinton Administration's education agenda, the validity requirements should be more stringent than they are for a typical test sold for use at grades 4 or 8.

The political prominence of the tests will only heighten the value conflicts and exacerbate the difficulties of conducting rigorous validation studies. For these reasons, I think it is critical that the measurement profession and organizations such as ETS get actively involved in fostering rigorous validation work starting with the 1998 field tests and continuing into the operational use of the tests in 1999 and beyond. Measurement professionals cannot answer the question "Should the test be used for this purpose?" that underlies Messick's call for an overall evaluation of "adequacy and appropriateness." But it is incumbent upon the measurement profession to accumulate evidence regarding the consequences of particular uses of tests, especially when those uses involve major decisions such as the certification of an individual (Linn, 1982, p. 25). As Cronbach aptly put it: "Our task is not to judge for nonprofessionals but to clarify, so that in their judgments they can use their power perceptively" (Cronbach, 1980, p. 100).

REFERENCES

Anastasi, A. (1954). *Psychological testing.* New York: Macmillan.

Baker, E. L., O'Neil, H. F., Jr., & Linn, R. L. (1993). Policy and validity prospects for performance-based assessment. *American Psychologist, 48,* 1210–1218.

Campbell, J. R., Donahue, P. L., Reese, C. M., & Phillips, G. W. (1996). *NAEP 1994 Reading Report Card for the Nation and the States: Findings from the National Assessment of Educational Progress and Trial State Assessment.* Washington, DC: National Center for Education Statistics.

Cheney, L. (1997, August 11). Once again, basic skills fall prey to a fad. *New York Times,* Monday, August 11, p. A13.

Cook, T. D., & Campbell, D. T. (1979). Quasi-Experimental Design and Analysis Issues for Field Settings. Chicago: Rand McNally.

Cremin, L. A. (1989). *Popular education and its discontents.* New York: Harper & Row.

Cronbach, L. J. (1960). *Essentials of psychological testing* (2nd ed.). New York: Harper and Row.

Cronbach, L. J. (1988). Five perspectives on validation argument. In H. Wainer, & H. Braun (Eds.), *Test validity* (pp. 3–17). Hillsdale, NJ: Lawrence Erlbaum.

Cronbach, L. J. (1980). Validity on parole: How can we go straight? *New Directions for Testing and Measurement, 5,* 99–108.

Diegmueller, K. (1994). Panel unveils standards for history: Release comes amid outcries of imbalance. *Education Week, 14*(9), pp. 1, 10.

Gamoran, A., & Berends, M. (1987). The effects of stratification in secondary schools: Synthesis of survey and ethnographic research. *Review of Educational Research, 57,* 415–435.

Green, B. F. (1990). A comprehensive assessment of measurement. *Contemporary Psychology, 35*(9), 850–851.

Haertel, E. H., & Linn, R. L. (1996). Comparability. In G. W. Phillips (Ed.), *Technical issues in large-scale performance assessment* (pp. 59–78). Washington, DC: National Center for Education Statistics Report NCES 96-802. U. S. Government Printing Office.

Innerst, (1995, Nov. 2). *Washington Times.*

Linn, R. L. (1982). Two weak spots in the practice of criterion-referenced measurement. *Educational Measurement: Issues and Practice, 1,* 12–13, 25.

Linn, R. L. (1994). Performance assessment: Policy promises and technical measurement standards. *Educational Researcher, 23,* no. 9, 4–14.

Linn, R. L., & Baker, E. L. (1998). Can performance-based student assessments be psychometrically sound? In J. B. Baron & D. P. Wolf (Eds.), *Performance-based student assessment: toward access, capacity and coherence. Ninety-third Yearbook of the National Society for the Study of Education.*

Linn, R. L., Baker, E. L., & Dunbar, S. B. (1991). Complex, performance-based assessment: Expectations and validation criteria. *Educational Researcher, 20* (8), 15–21.

McDonnell, L. (1996). *The Politics of State Testing: Implementing New Student Assessments.* (Technical Report). Los Angeles: UCLA Center for the Evaluation, Standards, and Student Testing (p. 31).

McLaughlin, M. W., & Shepard, L. A. (1995). *Improving education through standards-based reform.* A report by the National Academy of Education Panel on Standards-Based Education Reform. Stanford, CA: The National Academy of Education.

Messick, S. (1989). Validity. In R. L. Linn (Ed.), *Educational Measurement,* 3rd ed. (pp. 13–103). New York: Macmillan.

Messick, S. (1994). The interplay of evidence and consequences in the validation of performance assessments. *Educational Researcher, 23,* 13–23.

Moss, P. A. (1992). Shifting conceptions of validity in educational measurement: Implications for performance assessment. *Review of Educational Research, 62,* 229–258.

Moss, P. A. (1994). Can there be validity without reliability? *Educational Researcher, 23*(2), 5–12.

National Council of Teachers of Mathematics. (1989). *Curriculum and evaluation standards for school mathematics.* Reston, VA: Author.

Oakes, J. (1990). *Multiplying inequalities: The effects of race, social class, and tracking on opportunities to learn math and science.* Stanta Monica: Rand Corporation.

Ravitch, D. (1997b, May). Yes to national tests. *Forbes*, p. 64.

Ravitch, D. (1997a, August). National Tests: A Good Idea Going Wrong. *The Washington Post*, p. A15.

Romberg, T. (1997, August 11). Mediocre is not good enough. *New York Times*, p. A13.

Rose, L. C., Gallup, A. M., & Elam, S. M. (1997). The 29th annual Phi Delta Kappa/Gallup poll of the public's atttudes toward the public schools, *Phi Delta Kappan, 79*(1), 41–56.

Sadler, D. R. (1987). Specifying and promulgating achievement standards. *Oxford Review of Education, 13*, 191–209.

Shepard, L. A. (1993). Evaluating test validity. *Review of Research in Education, 19*, 405–450.

Wiley, D. E. (1991). Test validity and invalidity reconsidered. In R. E. Snow & D. E. Wiley (Eds.), *Improving inquiry in social science: A volume in honor of Lee J. Cronbach* (pp. 75–107). Hillsdale, NJ: Lawrence Erlbaum Associates.

Willingham, W. W., & Cole, N. S. (1997). *Gender and fair assessment.* Mahwah, NJ: Lawrence Erlbaum Associates.

14

Assessing Six Assumptions in Assessment

Michael Scriven
Claremont Graduate University

In order to make progress in developing a scientific discipline it is often necessary to turn to an examination of the foundations of that discipline, although the hard-core empiricists in the discipline often oppose this move. Familiar examples of such a move are provided by the Copenhagen School when it faced the mind-bending threat of the Uncertainty Principle and Bohr felt he had to turn back to the Athenian philosophers for guidance; and by Einstein who was forced, by what he called Mach's philosophical questions about the ether to explore a physics based on denying its existence. We see it again in Sam Messick's career, which took him beyond the maverick and gadfly role to that of a serious critic of the foundations of the applied science of assessment. This is nowhere more evident that in the 1982 paper in *Educational Measurement*, where he criticized the assumptions of the National Academy report on testing. He saw and followed the need to connect the foundations of testing to the foundations of ethics, to the concepts of justice and fairness.

In so doing, he led us to a new perspective and indeed new dimensions of assessment, dimensions that he illuminated further in the *Handbook* essay. Like any significant innovator, this has of course led to some spectacular misunderstandings by others, such as the ascription to him of the concept of *consequential validity*, a term he never uses referring to a concept he does not endorse. He does endorse examination of the consequences of testing—social consequences being of particular importance. These are to be considered, he says, in order to determine whether our tests—including their selection, use, interpretation, administration, and scoring—have managed to build in one bias or another, this to be judged by the usual, preexisting, standards of validity. The consequences, however socially undesirable, are not to be considered as grounds in themselves for conclusions about validity.

In passing one should also note that we owe thanks to his employer for having the good sense to see him as someone clearing ground that had to be cleared if progress was to be made, rather than—as others have sometimes suggested—criticizing testing at a time when it needed little more of that. ETS thus aligned itself with those other enlightened employers such as IBM and Bell Labs in their golden days, who supported serious research by their staff even if it opened up prospects of having to rethink the assumptions on which much of their business practice depended. In the case of ETS, as with the others, this policy commanded a respect in the educational research community that could not be bought at any price.

Having paid some well-earned compliments, I can no do, albeit mainly in sketch form here, is to follow Sam Messick's example and push still harder at the value assumptions underlying paradigmatic standardized testing. I will pick up six examples of places where I think we need to reconsider our present assumptions. I should start by emphasizing that in this kind of enterprise, the issue is not whether I get all these points right. That would be more than one can reasonably expect in such an enterprise, which challenges conventional expertise on so many issues. It would at most be reasonable to hope that some few of these suggestions lead to serious reconsideration of current theory and practice. But don't let that concession to reality be seen as grounds for casually dismissing any of these points as catcalls from the bleachers. I do not put them forward with any sense that the arguments for any of them are slight or merely probative. I will argue very hard for each point: these are serious charges and the stakes are huge, because these arguments attack the foundations of great structures of theory and practice in assessment.

TEST VALIDITY

Let's begin with this core notion, because other assumptions depend on it. In the 1982 paper, Sam Messick pointed out the extent to which the NAS report is committed to what he called the 'institutional perspective': a focus on the selection and employment functions of testing. Against this he suggests that we should pay more attention to the use of testing for diagnostic and instructional purposes—and he mentions some other possible frameworks in which it might be placed, with a particular eye on preserving equity, parity, and fairness. These are admirable moves toward being more aware of the framework we are assuming. But I want to suggest or at least support a more radical perspective. As so often happens, this is also a much more conservative position.

To begin with, what I suggest will seem like a rather pedantic effort to restrict common usage in talking about test validity. As we'll see, however, it turns out to be a good deal more than that: it's an essential corrective to a confused conceptualization. It's related to some proposals that have gone before, but I have difficulty in interpreting these, so I will just use my own words. Perhaps the most interesting consequence of what I am going to suggest is that construct validity is not the key underlying notion at all. However, although I reject this view about the primacy of construct validity, which Sam Messick favors, I do so for a number of reasons that he supports and diverge from him less on several of his related conclusions, for example, in the recognition of the importance of the utility, validity, and distinction.

In fact, a slightly oversimplified way to characterize what I am about to propose is one more effort to distinguish validity from utility.

The validity of a test is a matter of what it is a test of—a matter, we might say, of its logical meaning. A well-designed typing test, when scored in the usual way, is in fact a test of typing speed and accuracy, a.k.a. a valid test of those things. This is a logical truth about it; it is not based on correlation studies but on analysis of the content of the test, the understanding of the test by the testees, and the actions of those taking the test. This is related to Messick's "content relevance," perhaps also to Gulliksen's "intrinsic validity," and also, although not simply, to face validity. But I'm not sure exactly what those relations are, and in what follows we soon diverge from the way those notions are developed.

The utility of a test is a matter of the practical importance of the inferences that can be drawn, from results on the test to states of affairs about which we want to know—a matter of what the test can be used for. A good score on a typing test may thus be said, on the basis of the usual evidence, to support—to a limited degree—a useful inference to future performance in a word processing pool. But the typing test is not a valid test of that performance; it's simply an indicator, an empirical indicator, of it.

Thus, the GRE is a valid test of certain skills, both quantitative and qualitative; but its utility derives not from that fact, where its logical validity resides, but from the fact that valid inferences can be drawn from scores on it to future performance in graduate school. It is not correct to refer to the GRE as a valid test of future graduate school performance, essentially because no test can be a valid test of something that has not yet happened. When we talk of its use as a predictor, the more exact formulation would be to say that the GRE is a valid indicator of future graduate school performance (i.e., we can make valid, although of course only probabilistic) inferences from the test to future performance. It is not a valid test of those matters, although it's easy to see how we are tempted to talk that way.

In medical diagnostics, we have a number of tests for cancer. In the sense that we are using here, the biopsy is a logically valid test, because it involves direct visual identification of cancer cells directly removed from the patient's body. The others—for example, the mammogram—are just useful tests of various states of affairs that provide us with information from which we can make inferences of modest to good validity about the presence of cancer. (In the Cronbach and Meehl terminology, this is of course concurrent validity rather than the predictive validity of the GRE; for Messick, it's 'diagnostic utility' an excellent way to describe it.) One might think that at least a positive mammogram is also logically valid because it is commonly thought to be an example of 'seeing' the cancer; but the false positive rate is high just because benign tumors present almost identically. And of course the false negative rate is very high: neither is possible with logical validity. (The same problem of (possible) 'pseudo-seeing' applies to tests of teacher competence that are based on what experienced teachers say they see in the candidate's performance.)

Note that logical similarity between test content and criterion is not the only relation that supports test validity; a mercury thermometer is a valid instrument for measuring temperature even though the volume of mercury is not a sample of the thermodynamic concept of temperature. It is valid because it is calibrated so as to exactly exhibit an aspect of variations in temperature—and nothing else. When cows lie down in the fields, although that is said to be an indicator of coming rain, it is surely not an aspect of it. In general, there are no valid tests of future affairs, only indicators. Current states of affairs, however, are directly and validly accessible by tests like the thermometer.

Validity in mathematics is like validity in tests: it has to be supported by logically valid proofs. The judgment of good mathematicians as to the truth of unproved hypotheses like Fermat's Last Theorem is highly correlated with their actual truth; but that does not make it proper to call their judgment a type of proof. So one should not call the reliability of inferences from results on test X to condition Y a kind of test validity; it's just a diagnostic inference, a shadow of coming events, not part of them.

Although Messick wants to move to what he calls unified validity, he takes this to include both of what are, I suggest, properly called validity and utility:

> The essence of unified validity is that the appropriateness, meaningfulness, and usefulness of score-based inferences are inseparable and that the unifying force behind this integration is the trustworthiness of empirically grounded score interpretation, that is, construct validity. (1989, p. 5)

By contrast, although I also want to move to a unitary notion, it's a unitary notion of validity only. I want to do this by separating off the validity from the utility. This means abandoning all serious efforts to identify separate notions of validity—construct validity, predictive validity, etc.—and recommending that we regard them as matters of utility not validity, and that we restrict the use of the concept of validity to the original and proper notion. We got seduced by talk of 'the nomological network' into regarding all legitimate inferences from test results as part of the validity of the test, instead of being a separate issue of inference validity. (I was also seduced, which got my name in the attribution footnote to the original Cronbach and Meehl paper, so this can be seen as a slightly belated postscript to that essay.)

A test is a valid test of X if and only if it directly tests for X, that is, it calls for performance correctly described as X or an essential part of X, when administered and scored in the prescribed way to the prescribed population, etc. Predictive or concurrent inferences are useful applications of a test, but not separate types of validity. Content and face validity are considerations in identifying valid tests, but not separate types of validity in themselves. Construct validity is an illicit combination of test validity and indicator validity (i.e., the validity of inferences from the test to other conclusions).

So, a test of X that is useful in predicting Y should not be advertised as a test of Y or even as a test for Y; it can be advertised as a test that is a good indicator of Y, or as a test (that can be used) for predicting Y. Further examples: (a) A projective test is a test of one's response to inkblots, etc., not of psychodynamic state; (b) The Meyers-Briggs can correctly be called an inventory; (c) The MMPI tests people's belief in various claims (thanks to the lie scale), and indicates something important about their classification in a rather antiquated but not useless taxonomy; (d) The SAT may or may not be an aptitude test but it's no longer seen as staking much on that aspect of its title, and it is a valid test of certain scholastic knowledge and skills, with some predictive utility as an indicator of later scholastic performance; and (e) The Stanford-Binet can be called a valid test of intelligence because, first, the sub-tests require intelligence; and second, (if this is still true) because it correlates as well or better, across large numbers of cases, with the mean judgments of balanced panels of experienced teachers who know the individuals tested, and clinicians, who know the usual sources of error, as does the judgment of any one rater.

This carelessness with the term *validity* should be seen as one more example of the linguistic imperialism, proclaimed by the positivists, that has made statistics a nightmare for beginning students. The other leading examples are: (a) the careless redefinition of reliability as different from validity; (b) the redefinition of significance as not involving effect size and the other contextual variables that define importance; and (c) the redefinition of bias as involving error rather than a disposition to error. I am here making one more call back to common sense, a call to make us focus on the fact that there really are valid tests of abilities, such as the ability to multiply two three-digit numbers, to construct a foundation wall, or to type legal documents at 45 wpm (discounted for errors); and that validity in this core sense is quite different from utility, which requires an extensive and different kind of empirical verification of the kind that ETS religiously undertakes before making the usual claims about its tests.

Now, why should we bother to police this kind of linguistic persnicketyness? My hope is that doing so will help stop the cheapening of the notion of validity. Doing so will tie in with analogous efforts in other areas such as the recently renewed efforts to be more careful about the notion of significance in psychological research. It will do this by helping us to see the absolutely crucial nature of the distinction between criteria— which are logically connected to the parent notion—and indicators—which are empirically connected. In program evaluation today, for example, there is a tremendous push by governments and agencies across the world for what is called *performance evaluation*. This consists largely in identifying some indicators of good performance and using them to evaluate programs and projects. Of course, these indicators are quickly abused, worked around, and outdated; they were only indicators of program merit, not criteria of program merit. The substitution of indicators for criteria has to be seen for what it is, something useful within limits, but only of ephemeral use. Being careful with the concepts is the first step—and an important one—toward this recognition. Talking as if high-stakes testing invalidates tests is another symptom of confusion here; what it does is to encourage the violation of the standard conditions for one use of the test.

In the evaluation of teachers, the discovery of correlations between certain features of teaching styles and successful causation of learning in students led to the use of those styles, which are only indicators of good teaching, as tests of good teachers. This became known as the 'research-based model of teacher evaluation' and has been widely built into the standard evaluation procedures, often with state endorsement. This is a completely inappropriate procedure because we have—or can readily get—evidence about criterial performance. This reminds us that any use of indicators (i.e., variables that justify an inference in some cases) can only be justified when we cannot get or cannot afford to get criterial evidence (i.e., variables that define the quality we are seeking to identify); and this is indeed the case with the predictive use of academic tests.

In the testing world, we tend to forget that teacher-made tests are by far the largest proportion of tests in use. And validity as I have described it, not validity in the sense of what distant matters can be inferred from the results, is exactly the standard to which they should be held. In the world of commercial testing, we are today far more sensitive to looking at the consequences of testing than we were, and at looking at contextual modifiers: both of these remind us that the long-chain inferences from test scores to future performance are fragile. We should demarcate the use of tests as providing data for such inferences from the validity of the tests themselves, a much more robust property of tests. One should not be suggesting, as is too common today, that the validity of a test is that fragile; we were wrong to tie validity to these weaker inferences, just as we were wrong to tie program merit at all strongly to performance indicators, or teaching merit to teaching styles. The validity of tests should be seen as something tied logically, not correlatively, to the test.

It is not a trivial matter to determine the validity of tests (i.e., the proper description of them, even in this narrower sense). The GRE Mathematical Reasoning Test, for example, developed by an ETS team including Carol Dwyer, can't be validated by just checking whether its items are all good mathematical items. The desired label here—calling it "a test of mathematical reasoning"—is not easy to attain: one must show that all significant types of mathematical reasoning are covered, and that there is not too much emphasis on one rather than another. But that's a feasible project, much less expensive than validation in the sloppy sense (i.e., validation of inferences to future performance). So, test validity is indeed a matter of whether the test tests what it says it tests, as the textbooks all say, but only if what it says it tests is what it *directly* tests.

TEST SCORING

Naturally, the validity of a test depends not only on its content, as we stated previously, but also on the way it is scored (and administered, etc., but we will here concentrate on the scoring). Considerations of fairness, a commendably favorite topic of Sam Messick's and an important element in validity considerations, suggest that a requirement that I called the *Point Constancy Requirement* (PCR) should often be given center stage in the discussion of the test scoring component in validity. The PCR simply says that a point, however it is earned on the test, should represent an equal increment of merit on whatever it is the test is said to be a test of. We'll never attain this ideal in practice, but we can certainly get reasonably close to it: the paradigm is a test of basic arithmetic skill. It should be treated as an ideal in the design of all scoring keys (a.k.a. rubrics). Moreover, it is an ideal that should be approximated, not treated as extremely remote. (For convenience, we can focus on quantitative scoring, although the same principle extends to qualitative assessment, e.g., most grading.) Note that the PCR does not involve claims about item (-success) difficulty, only item-success merit. The two are connected, of course, but it's easier to argue that all basic two-by-two multiplication items are of equal merit, in the domain of arithmetic competence, than that they are of equal difficulty; and one can do it from one's armchair, which helps the development budget significantly.

The PCR is a principle that governs test validity, but its ethical aspect surfaces when we look at the continuing failure of students in less-well-funded schools to receive any training in test-taking skills. This means, for example, on the usual multiple-choice tests, that they are not taught to: (a) put in answers by guessing, when they don't know or have time to work out the correct answer; and (b) answer the easy questions first. Immediately, we have adverse impact: and, for SM and MS as well as all the enthusiasts for consequential validity, we have test invalidity. Not because of the adverse impact, however, although that must be studied, as SM stressed, because it often serves to warn us of invalidity, but because the test is in fact a test of two quite different skills, although its results are being treated as if the test only tested one of these skills. Students from the wealthier districts or parents are getting extra scores on that skill by virtue of having (purchased) the other skill; a clear violation of the PCR. The worst violation of the PCR, however, involves a more general problem, mentioned as item (a) above. Blind guessing on the usual multiple choice test has an expectancy of 25% and a merit of zero, a flagrant violation of the PCR. Now, the adverse impact of this can be reduced by applying a "correction for guessing" (a misnomer since the usual version is a correction for not guessing). But the validity of the test cannot be saved by this process, because the blind guesser still gets 25% of the total score for knowing nothing at all. Hence, in case you were getting a little sleepy by now, it is provable that all standard multiple-choice tests are invalid. I'll later indicate how to correct this without plunging off the straight and narrow path of sound testing into the swamps of pseudo-authentic testing.

The second argument for this conclusion concerns item (b) above; the awarding of a single point for all correct answers, when in fact a correct answer may be much more meritorious on one rather than another question. I'll now extend our list to include a third breach of the PCR. This is (c) the failure to distinguish between the score for incorrect answers (i.e., zero), when in fact, on some items (not all) some incorrect answers are very close to being as correct as the official correct answer, whereas other distractors would only be chosen by someone with essentially no knowledge of the topic. (Note that there are test items, e.g., in competency testing for surgical or airline pilot skills, in which one wants to say that any answer besides the correct one is equally and absolutely valueless; but these are the exception rather than the rule.)

In terms of our list of assumptions for assessment, under the heading of test scoring we are now addressing three common assumptions of standardized testing (two of them are not entirely independent): the assumption that blind guessing can legitimately yield 25% (in the usual case; 20% in some other cases); the assumption that all correct responses should be equally weighted in the scoring key; and the assumption that all incorrect responses should be equally weighted. These will bring us up to a total of four assumptions that we will have discussed.

I will propose relatively easy fixes for each of these problems; the main functions of the proposals are to show that fixes are not impossible, and to stimulate discussion, rather than suggest these are the only or best ways to fix the problems. But first I need to head off the usual dismissal of any attempts to fix them. It is commonly said—forgive them, Lord, for they know not what they do—that such changes have been shown repeatedly to have little effect on the rank ordering of testees. Justice is not done by dismissing low body counts as negligible. If one of your children did not make it to college because of a sloppy scoring key, even if it is only occasionally sloppy, you would not regard this as an acceptable argument, and I strongly recommend making that the test for acceptability. Of course, this recommendation assumes that the costs for remediation are not beyond our means.

These errors are not just methodological ones, but, because of the predictably adverse effects on some people, ethical ones. But there is also the practical issue. To this enlightened company of colleagues, I am sure I need not stress that the days of thinking that tests are to be rated purely or even mainly as instruments for discriminating (rank-ordering) are over. We are interested in criterion-referenced testing as well as norm-referenced, not always but often. We need the total score on a test to be an indication of competency, not just of relative competency. This has some significant consequences (e.g., that we need to avoid the old practice of incestuous validation in which we threw out items that did not correlate well with other items, without thorough exploration of the possibility that they were probes into untouched regions of the domain). (In the critical thinking area, for example, they often were just that.) In the present case, we want a score that represents the actual value of the testee's knowledge or skills as well as is practicable. So we must set up the scoring key to measure that knowledge as accurately as we can, as always with due respect to cost feasibility. Ranking will always follow from grading, but should not be the primary function of most tests, and discrimination power should not be the key index of merit in items. The crucial question about a criterion-referenced test, analogous to the question of how many testees are wrongly ranked, becomes, "How accurate and how efficient is our estimate of total knowledge?" Some rough calculations suggest a surprising figure. In round numbers, our present scoring system often throws away 50% of the information that is on the answer sheet turned in by the testee. We can recover most of that extra information by adding estimates of variable item merit, variable error merit, and by scoring the test so as to eliminate any expectancy for guessing.

The fixes for this wastage that I am going to suggest involve three fairly simple procedures, but no pretense is made that they do not involve any extra costs. There is no completely free lunch in this business, and recovering twice as much information will often take about 50% more effort in a typical case, not a bad ratio. However, the suggestions here are not all-or-none; one can recover very large amounts, perhaps half of what is possible, for less than a proportional amount of investment, perhaps a 15% surcharge. These estimates are very rough, however, and we need more evaluative studies of these alternatives.

The three recommendations are these. (a) We should weight items at least roughly for the amount of valuable information (or the degree of competence on the skill) that is required in order to give the correct answer (perform the required task). This is loosely related to what we might call the standard difficulty of the item (i.e., its difficulty for the median student; and also loosely related to the time that it takes the median student to answer correctly, but must not be equated with either or a combination of these). (b) We should weight errors by the amount of useful information they contain, a natural generalization of the idea that we score choices as correct because they contain the most valuable information of the options available. (This is what we already do with constructed responses.) (c) We should adjust the weighting of answers so that the expectancy from blind guessing is zero.

Item Weighting. We have to proceed very circumspectly with this, because the use of a long weighting scale (e.g., 1 to 10, leads to an unacceptable lack of interjudge reliability). We will use a very modest scale of 1, 1.5, and 2; and the ROI (return on investment) estimates above are based on this. Nevertheless, it should be born in mind that the 1 to 10 scale may be closer to an accurate representation in many cases. In reviewing the published LSAT items for the company a few years ago, I found that items took me between 10 seconds and 8 minutes to deal with, despite my ex-law school faculty skills in legal reasoning. (That experience precipitated me into some serious exploration of differential weighting.) The beginning posture here is for an instructor to estimate the relative merit; the estimate is easily improved by quick-and-dirty item analysis; and further significantly improved by carefully using (i) peer and (ii) candidate input. For published tests, one would of course supplement this with expert-level item design and item weighting. But let's not get lost in the details: the basic fact is that virtually every multiple-choice test is invalid because it incorrectly scores every question as of equal weight. Teachers may have some trouble using a scale of 10; they have very little trouble with the scale of 1:1.5:2; and they have none at all in rejecting with good reasons the legitimacy of the assumption of equal weight.

Only a profound confusion about the nature of validity could obscure this kind of invalidity. It was presumably supported by a double argument:

the negative argument was that getting interjudge agreement on weights was difficult, hence no differential weights could be justified. The positive argument was presumably that because certain predictions from the level-weighted tests were modestly successful, then they were valid (or valid enough). On our account, the situation is much simpler: the test is valid only if its scores match its title. It may be useful for certain purposes without meeting that requirement; but that match is what is required for validity. It is likely to be more useful, for criterion referenced evaluation, if we make the scoring more defensible.

Near-Miss Scoring. In general terms, there are two ways to produce improved tests that take some of these suggestions into account: test conversion and test creation. The first means improving the scoring of existing tests; the second means improving the instrument itself in the course of creating it. Item weighting is easily used in conversion; near-miss weighting can be used either way. In the conversion scenario, using the existing distractors, inspection will usually reveal that some of them are only subtly different from the correct answer, whereas others would only be chosen by someone who was extremely confused about the subject or knew little or nothing about it and was essentially guessing. The suggestion here is that in many cases it is more appropriate to reward the testee for grasping the difference between nearly the best option and the worst options by awarding half a point for the near-miss. From the diagnostic point of view there is obviously considerable value in knowing this, in order to adjust future teaching: more on this in a moment. In the construction scenario, we can engineer the items so that they illustrate this distinction more clearly since it is an important distinction.

An independent reason for making these efforts is that they all contribute to improved *face-validity* which leads to much improved user relations, as we have discovered in evaluating tests in the personnel evaluation field. The changes described do something to avoid the many complaints about what is often described as the "rigid" and "unforgiving" nature of standard multiple-choice tests.

At this point, we need to say something more about the diagnostic use of these reweighted items. By running a computer analysis that identifies the number of near-misses in the score total versus the number of "far-misses" versus the number of correct options chosen; and between the number of points scored on single-weighted items by contrast with those weighted 50% and 100% more, we can often identify a pattern that is helpful for instructional purposes. For example, we might be able to suggest that an inordinate number of responses are in the near-miss category and that the testee needs to focus more on getting exactly the right form of expression or the right qualifications into their understanding of a matter. Or we might be able to classify someone as doing very well on basic items (merit level = weight = 1) by contrast with those worth double the points. We should also be able to identify the fingerprint of the (largely) random guesser even if s/he is doing rather better than the expectancy for that approach.

When in the construction mode, it will also be desirable to try to restrict the actual range of item difficulty to the range we are recognizing with our 200% spread (i.e., to avoid items that are much more than twice as hard or meaty than any other item). This will improve the absolute accuracy of our scoring as an estimate of merit (and the accuracy of our estimate of information gained over the standard approach), although the superiority of near-miss scoring over the standard method of level scoring will not be impaired, or improved, in the slightest. Ethically, as well as epistemologically, the advantage of doing this is to reduce the payoff from the testwise strategy of doing easy items first. (Of course, there will still be an advantage in doing items first that are easy for you.)

Far-Miss Scoring. Now we come to the feature of our scoring reform plan that eliminates pay-for-guessing. Let's begin with a plan we won't stay with but which indicates the approach. Suppose we are converting or creating an item with four options, one correct, one near-miss, one plain wrong answer without redeeming features (but not ridiculous), and one far-miss (i.e., hopelessly wrong/absurd answer). If this is a typical item, and if we score one for the correct answer (subject to the multiplier from the weighting of the item), half for the near-miss, zero for the plainly wrong answer, and minus 1.5 for the absurd answer ("absurd" only if you understand the field), the expectancy from blind guessing goes to zero, and with it the benefits of testwise training in this respect. Or you could deal with an item that had two far-miss answers by scoring the responses 1, .5, -.75, -.75, with the same net effect. And so on for near-misses. The possibility of a net negative score on some items creates the possibility that the testee loses points that were legitimately gained on other items. At first sight this seems "unfair"; however, it is only the total score that is used for test-dependent actions, or that is relevant to test validity, and the total score more accurately reflects merit if this constraint is imposed on it. (For diagnostic purposes, the teacher can look at each item of interest and see quickly what kind of errors were made.)

It is significant that this approach eliminates the need to apply, or argue about applying, a "correction for guessing". If someone does not guess, they get zero points; if they do guess, their expectancy is zero points, so there is no need to correct for what they do or do not do. If a student gets an overall negative score on a test, this will almost certainly represent a situation in which they were doing a lot of blind guessing, and it's an appropriate indication of that fact. It does not means that they knew "less than nothing" in the sense of getting nothing right; only that their bad guesses outweighed their good knowledge.

Note also that the introduction of negative scoring of far-misses flags something of some diagnostic interest, because we can quickly pick up the number of times that choosing far-misses cut into legitimate scoring on other items. This is the "penalty for blind guessing" that we are imposing as a counter-measure to the misleading payoff and invalidity of the standard scoring rubric. In the real world, blind guessing usually involves either a considerable risk or a definite avoidable penalty, for example in matters of health and investment. That means you typically hazard something you already have when you make blind guesses; and in our rubric, what you already have are the hard-earned gains from demonstrated knowledge or skill gained on other items.

Negative scoring is an option that is wholly independent of near-miss scoring and item weighting. If it upsets an instructor or test designer, it can be left out of their rubrics without losing the advantages of the other modifications. But it is an important part of the alternative paradigm we are presenting here, which we might call the 'modified multiple-choice' test paradigm, or MMC. This model has half a dozen signficant advantages over the present standard procedure (MC), by comparison with other alternatives that have been proposed.

1. It does not involve abandoning objectively scorable tests, and hence it keeps us out of the serious financial trouble that adoption of most so-called authentic alternatives would involve.
2. It reduces some of the antagonism inspired by standard MC tests.
3. It minimizes the advantage of testwise testees (thereby reducing adverse impact).
4. It provides no reward for blind guessing, thereby avoiding one source of gross invalidity, and avoiding positive reinforcement of the undesirable practice of faking knowledge when it's not present. (Of course, the kind of

guessing that is based on a good knowledge of the subject but uncertainty about how to answer a particular question still makes sense, given the research on it, and will pay off; we can think of this as "informed guessing".)

5. It avoids one of the pressures towards grade inflation. It's common to give C- or at worst D grades for 35% scores, which represent a true knowledge level of 10%, hardly appropriate for a pass. Worse, a score of even 45% on a teacher-made test will often reflect 10% or more from overcueing or other errors of design as much as it does knowledge, so even that score level may represent 10% or less of true knowledge. Using the scoring system suggested here would make it harder to justify any given level of grade because they would not all be pushed upward by a false lower bound.

   Now, if one did not use negative scoring of the kind suggested here, one could alternatively just subtract 25% from each testee's score as a "correction for guessing" that would make (blind) guessing an incorrect strategy. The results would no doubt be politically exciting. Fortunately, this approach is invalid for other reasons. However, the kind of grade inflation due to bad MC test scoring may be one main reason that people report that U.S. education is in trouble nationally, although they also say that the schools their children attend are good: their children are getting good grades (only because inflated as above) but they are alarmed by the reports they read about the state and nation, which are based on more analytical studies.

6. It facilitates better feedback to testers, teachers, and testees for a given duration of the test. It shares this advantage with computer-interactive testing, but for completely different reasons. It squeezes considerably more information about the testee from the footprint of the same test answer sheets, using the same test items. We have made a good deal of the efficiency payoff from computer interactive testing, but it appears we can provide an independent gain of at least the same magnitude by redoing our analytic procedures.

ITEM DESIGN

The next assumption on our list is one that has received remarkably little critical scrutiny. It is the common textbook claim that multiple-choice items are the most general type of "objective" test (i.e., "objectively scorable" item). Here of course, "objectively scorable" simply means scorable by the examiner—once designed, delivered, and completed by the testee—without use of skilled judgment or knowledge, i.e., machine scorable or template scorable. The term "objective" is misleading since the scoring key used may be laced with racism, sexism, or religious prejudice. All that's objective is the scoring process; we here use the term *machine scorable* instead. It's an important enough claim without exaggerating it; after all, most large-scale testing would be virtually impossible to finance if we used essay items throughout.

Returning to the claim being considered, it is true that the multiple-choice item is more general than a number of other machine-scorable item types such as the true-false item or the matching item. But it's a long way from being the most general machine scorable item type. In this section, we briefly review another and considerably more general type of item that offers some powerful advantages over the multiple-choice item (which is a special case of it), not in all cases but in many. It may or may not be combined with the three modifications to the standard scoring rubric that are built into what we have called the modified MC item (MMC), discussed in the previous section. This type of item is called the multiple-rating (MR) item, and is considered at greater length in Fisher and Scriven (1997).

A multiple-rating item is typically presented in a format that is rather similar in format to a multiple-choice item. It begins with a text stem followed by a set of short, numbered, text passages. But what the testee is called on to do with it is completely different. First, the short passages following the stem (they are called stubs) are not options from which the best is to be picked; each is to be dealt with separately. Hence, none serve the throw-away role of distractor, and we get more mileage out of each; a stem with four stubs is formally equivalent to four MC items, which saves time and trees. Second, what is to be done with them—the stubs—is not to choose one from the set, but to rate each one using a rating scale provided (hence the term multiple-rating item, MRI). The rating scale might be the usual grading scale A-F with suitably defined anchors; or it might be a merit ranking scale; or it might be an ad hoc scale such as a set of cost-effectiveness or storm weather categories. Any item may have any grade; so, for example, there may be no As or all As. For teacher-made tests, the student can write the appropriate letter into a single box that is provided; for machine scoring, a list of the rating options (e.g., the letters A to F) would be printed next to each stub and the testee would circle one of these.

One advantage of this type of item is that it cuts straight to testing higher order thinking skills, notably evaluation and critical thinking skills, but also—with a suitable choice of items—synthesis skills. This represents one advantage over the more typical kind of MR item, although MR items are in principle capable of similar testing. Another advantage of the MR item is that it undercuts many of the other tricks of the trade taught in test-taking seminars, such as looking for subtle grammatical cues as to the right choice, or eliminating options without having even recognition skills with respect to the right answer ("I don't know what this option means, but the rest are sure wrong.") A third is that the evaluation task is much more realistic than the choice task; in the real world, we are rarely offered a small set of options of which one is guaranteed to be correct: in this sense, MR items are more authentic than MC items. A fourth is that many of the usual errors of amateur item-writers are avoided; for example, one does not have to worry about grammatical cueing.

Types of Multiple-Rating Items. An important kind of example of the multiple-rating item, although no more typical than many others, would look like this. The stem would be a half-page passage of complex prose from, let us say, a technical report. The four stubs (although it might also be two or six) would be attempted summaries of it, about a quarter as long, aimed for use in a condensed field manual or textbook. The grading scale would have five anchors like: (a)essentially complete and easily readable; (b)complete but not highly readable; (c)readable but missing some significant content and so on. Another example would present an argument for banishing inflammatory speech on campus as the stem; the stubs would represent critiques of the argument. They might of course all be equally good or bad, or any intermediate mix. There is no way of pulling off the testwise trick of eliminating alternatives in order to increase one's chance of getting the right answer, despite having no understanding of the remaining options. A third example, of a kind that one might say is made for this format, would be likely to find its home in a school of education; it would provide a stem that is an assignment for an eleventh-grade class in American History, the stubs being transcriptions of five student answers obtained from the university's lab school the previous semester, and the grades being defined as whatever is appropriate for such a class. Given that few schools of education give any training in grading, this would be a highly authentic—but still machine-scorable—kind of test.

The example just given, which is readily generalizable to other instructional contexts—certainly in junior high and up—illustrates three points of some importance. First, it illustrates a useful and labor-saving source for items (i.e., the set of stubs with a stem), namely, earlier answers to a related essay version of the same question. One can mark or note a few of these when grading them the previous term, as illustrating important or common confusions or distinctions. Second, using materials from student test responses as objects for evaluation makes the task set by the MR item into one that the student understands as useful for them because it requires them to emulate and learn something about the teacher's grading behavior. Third, having the student role-play the instructor in grading mode, is one step in the process of internalizing quality standards, a key pedagogical payoff. This an advantage that also helps bridge the testing and teaching gap, so destructive in many classrooms, and the reverse of what it should be; thus it bears on Sam Messick's recommendation that we look for instructional uses of testing.

Rubrics for MR Items. The basic scoring key for each stub (sub-item) would be to award one point for the correct grade and zero for the rest, if using the traditional approach. Using the recommended near-miss system, it would award half a point for a grade only one grade away from the correct grade, zero for the rest. If that were the only innovation in the rubric, however, intelligent blind guessing would still bring in a substantial reward—it could in fact bring in 40% by using the optimal strategy which is to always guess C. But using the recommended guess-control system of scoring (i.e., negative scores for far misses), we would set a score of minus two points for being two or more off the correct grade (e.g., for selecting C when the correct grade is A or F). If you construct the items so that about an equal number of them have each of the five possible answers (A through F) as the correct answer, that "negative one" rubric will guarantee at best a zero expectancy for blind guessing. If using item-weighting, you would also want to arrange that in the long run this arrangement holds across each group of items of comparable difficulty/merit level.

For a teacher-made test, it's hardly worth taking that much trouble about balancing the correct answers, unless constructing a cumulative item pool, in which case the trouble is relatively small for any one run of the test. If a teacher just ignores balancing, the results are likely to be only minor deviations from the ideal: The expectancy from guessing will vary slightly, ranging from slightly negative to slightly positive, which should ensure that the guessing strategy will not be worth following, thus protecting the PCR.

For those with an interest in diagnostic use of testing, and in deeper pedagogical insights from it, there is a powerful variation on the multiple-rating item called the 'two-stage MR' item. In this type of item, we seek the reasons that testees have for their ratings, if any. For a given stem (i.e., down the right-hand margin next to the list of its stubs (a.k.a. sub-items), we provide a list of ten or a dozen possible reasons for the answers given). This list may or may not include correct reasons for each correct answer; it usually does provide some that are correct for one or more answers, and incorrect or absurd for others, and a number that are incorrect for all answers. The testee then proceeds to rate each stub as usual, by selecting one of the grades (etc.) listed next to the stub, then writes in, next to the grade, the letters that label his or her reasons (or, for machine scoring, circles the appropriate letters from a list provided for each stub). For a teacher dealing with small classes, it is useful to leave a line between stubs on which the student can write in a reason if it is not seen as one of those on the list. This approach quickly pinpoints guessing, and also helps to identify lines of incorrect reasoning that may explain any surprising failures to get the right answer. I think it's fair to say that there is a common assumption in assessment circles that one cannot eliminate the possibility of guessing when using "objective" tests; and I think it's clear that the two-stage MR item eliminates it about as well as the usually constructed-response, e.g., essay test, and better than most of them.

I hope enough has been said here to indicate that the MC test is a long way from being the most general machine-scorable test, and that there are interesting and useful possibilities in these further reaches of the testing universe, without the need for and cost of computer interactive testing or panel grading. In head-to-head comparisons with simulation testing, the most authentic of all authentic tests, multiple-choice tests of the highest technical quality have done remarkably well; my thought here is that improving the scoring system for them, and supplementing them (not replacing them) with some, perhaps almost as many, multiple-rating items, can lead us to a new and significantly higher level of practical testing methodology without the need for computer equipment and its attendant costs and without the need for moving into the quicksands—and the even higher costs—of most of the other, allegedly authentic testing approaches.

TEST APPLICATIONS

It seems clear enough from the research that the best one-shot test of composition skill is a cloze test. The result strikes nonprofessionals as bizarre, but professionals know that when you have low test-retest reliability, a relatively stable even if content-invalid indicator can average closer to the mean of the criterion measures than any measures of one true criterion sample. Nevertheless, although it's apparently better, as a predictor of what we want to predict, we should not use it, and in fact we no longer do use it as the principal predictor of the criterion ability. Why? The usual assumption is that the correct answer is simply that it's politically unacceptable (because most people don't have the background to understand the true situation), even though scientifically superior. That assumption is incorrect.

The cloze test should not be used, because the score on it is only an indicator, not a criterion, and you are only justified in using an indicator on a high-stakes test if it is not feasible to get at a criterion. Since you can get at a criterion—namely, a sample essay—even though marking it is much more expensive, the discussion is at an end. In the bad old days, of course, we did use the cloze test, because of the saving of time and money, and the fact that it's a more accurate indicator, on balance. But how would you like to be turned down for Princeton because of your weakness in English Composition, when the tests on which the decision was based did not include writing an essay? You may in fact be one of the people, and the statistics makes clear they certainly exist, who write very good essays, essays that are obviously very good, although you find cloze tests very hard and do badly on them. The unfairness to you is so gross that we will no longer accept a decision based only on cloze testing, despite the fact that a larger number of people will be inaccurately diagnosed by the usual rather inaccurate procedure of judging essays. This is not a political but an ethical constraint.

We use the SAT and the GRE for admission decisions, even though their utility for that purpose, like that of the cloze test, is only statistically supported—not true in every case. But there are two differences. First, their content is a simulation, in fact a true work sample of the kind of task that the testee will have to do in college or grad school: hence there is no lack of direct (i.e., concurrent) validity for them, by contrast with the cloze test. Second, there is no feasible alternative, given the limits on what can be charged for such testing services. Testing the wide range of skills that the SAT/GRE cover by more "authentic" methods would delay results unacceptably (because of the slow scoring procedures) as well as producing an overall massively reduced "predictive validity."

The same point applies to the use of computerized grading of essay samples, an approach which has made significant gains in accuracy in recent years. Even if it wins on the statistical game, it loses on the validation side. This issue is confused by the fact that we treat two types of statistical inference as if they are epistemologically equivalent; the inference from current observations to the current state of X and the inference from that to the future state we are trying to predict. But I think I've gone on long enough to make the point, which is simply that there are depths below what we have previously regarded as the floor of the ocean, depths well worth exploring.

REFERENCES

Fisher, A., & Scriven, M. (1997). *Critical thinkng; defining and assessing it.* Inverness, CA: EdgePress. and Centre for Research on Critical Thinking, University of East Anglia.

Messick, S. (1989). Validity. In R. L. Linn (Ed.), *Educational Measurement,* (3rd ed. pp. 13-103). New York: Macmillan.

15

Constructs in Student Ratings of Instructors

Anthony G. Greenwald
University of Washington

My career has been strongly influenced by various mentors, but strangely with much delay from the time at which their influence was first encountered. Perhaps the delay was my way of indicating intellectual independence, not to adopt the approaches of my mentors while I was still in their presence. When I worked with Elliot Aronson at Harvard, I stayed away from his favored cognitive dissonance theory, but started writing articles on the topic 15 years later. Gordon Allport advised my work on a dissertation problem that I devised to be quite remote from his topic interests and preferred research methods. Fifteen years later, however, I was working on one of his favorite topics, the self, and after nearly another 15 years I was working on prejudice, another of Allport's major topics. It is therefore no surprise to me to recognize that, many years after being exposed to Sam Messick during a few formative postdoctoral years at Educational Testing Service, I developed a research program that combines three of his career-long passions, psychological testing, construct validity, and educational psychology. How these influences worked themselves out in my research of the past several years, in a fashion that I hope will please Sam, is what this chapter is about.

The psychological test in which I became interested is a set of procedures known as *student ratings of instruction*. Anyone who teaches at a university in the United States has been exposed to these, as have those who teach in many other countries. In 1989 and 1990 I received widely divergent ratings for teaching the same course in 2 successive years, using the same syllabus, text, course requirements, meeting format, etc. Although the discrepancy could conceivably have been nothing other than sampling error, it was impressive in degree—my average ratings were separated by 8 deciles (about 2.5 standard deviations) on the university norms that accompanied the ratings reports I received. Searching for an explanation, I naturally suspected that the ratings were influenced by something other than the qualities of the instructor, which should have been almost as similar as possible over the two offerings of this particular course. Perhaps it was significant that I first approached this topic as an outsider who had no previous research involvement in the topic. My first research on the topic therefore had some of the character of the naive child seeing the Emperor's New Clothes.

HISTORICAL TRENDS IN RESEARCH ON STUDENT RATINGS

Electronic search made it possible to arrive quickly at a summary of the history of research on validity of student ratings. The search revealed that ratings validity had been the focus of much research, peaking 15 to 20 years ago. Figure 15.1 characterizes a sample of that research in the period from 1971 to 1995. It can be seen in Figure 15.1 that, over the entire 25-year period, more publications favored validity than invalidity. It can also be seen that the research changed sharply in character around 1980.

Prior to 1980, research was frequently critical of the validity of student ratings. The major validity-related criticism of the pre-1980 period was a concern that instructors who graded leniently received inappropriately high ratings. As can be seen in Figure 15.1, 1980 marked the beginning of a decline in research activity on student ratings. This was a decline specifically of studies that remained neutral (dropping from 31 to 16 between 1976–1980 and 1981–1985) and those that were critical (dropping even more drastically, from 15 to 3). At the same time, the number of studies supporting validity remained the same, and these increased in proportion from a minority of 35% (25/71) between 1976 and 1980 to a majority of 57% (25/44) between 1981 and 1985. By the 1990s, research on validity of ratings had diminished to such a low level that it is easy to infer that earlier contributions had resolved the major issues. Articles published from about 1980 on do indeed give the impression that some major questions about ratings validity were considered to have been answered. Researchers were willing to proclaim the validity of student ratings in remarkably general

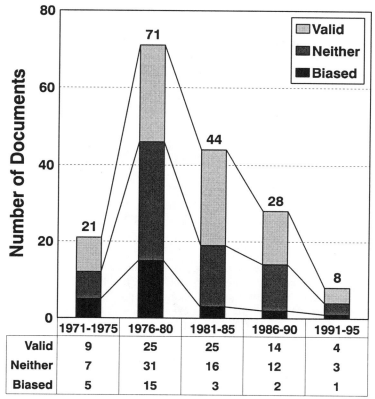

FIG. 15.1. Shifting appraisals of validity of student ratings. This figure summarizes the author's categorization of study conclusions on the basis of abstracts retrieved from electronic searches of PsycINFO and ERIC, using for both data bases the search query, *(student rating$1 or teaching evaluation$1) and (bias or valid$3 or invalid$3).* The *$n* suffix included in the search any words found by appending up to *n* letters after the stem. Categorization as "biased" indicates study conclusions that student ratings of instruction are contaminated by one or more extraneous influences. The ERIC search was limited to unpublished reports, in order not to have the two searches produce duplicates.

fashion. The opinions of several prominent reviewers, concerning grading leniency as a possible source of invalidity of ratings, are well summarized in this quotation from McKeachie (1979):

> In general, . . . most of the factors [that] might be expected to invalidate
> ratings have relatively small effects . . . . Some studies have found a
> tendency for teachers giving higher grades to get higher ratings. However,
> one might argue that in courses in which students learn more the grades
> should be higher and the ratings should be higher so that a correlation
> between average grades and ratings is not necessarily a sign of invalidity . . .
> My own conclusion is that one need not worry much about grading
> standards within the range of normal variability. (McKeachie, 1979, pp.
> 390, 391)

1970s: Research Questioning Validity of Student Ratings

Although research published in the 1970s covered a variety of concerns
about validity, the major concern of that period was the possible effect of
grades on ratings. The concern with grade-induced bias is apparent in the
following quotes.

> The present evidence, then, supports a notion that a teacher can get a
> "good" rating simply by assigning "good" grades. The effect of obtained
> grades may bias the students' evaluation of the instructor and therefore
> challenges the validity of the ratings used on many college and university
> campuses. (Snyder & Clair, 1976, p. 81)

> The implications of the findings reported are considerable, and it is
> suggested that the validity of student evaluations of instruction must be
> questioned seriously. It is clear that . . . an instructor [who] inflates grades
> . . . will be much more likely to receive positive evaluations. (Worthington
> & Wong, 1979, p. 775)

These were conclusions from experiments in which grades had been
manipulated upward or downward, and the manipulated grades were
observed to result in raised or lowered student ratings, correspondingly.
Several such experiments, mostly in the 1970s, were conducted in actual
undergraduate courses (Chacko, 1983; Holmes, 1972; Powell, 1977; Vasta &
Sarmiento, 1979; Worthington & Wong, 1979). On reading these field
experiments side by side in the 1990s, it is easy to conclude that, in
combination, they make a powerful case that ratings can be biased sharply
by arbitrary grading practices. Those experiments are difficult to repeat in
the 1990s, because their grade manipulations imposed stresses and used
deceptions that university human subjects review committees do not now
look kindly on. However, the best argument for not replicating these

experiments 20 years later is that it hardly seems necessary to do so—the results of the older studies were clear enough so that there seems little doubt about what new replications would find.[1]

This is a strange situation. On the one hand, experimental results reported during the 1970s appeared to demonstrate that grading practices influence student ratings. Contemporary folklore among academicians also endorses the conclusion that one can raise ratings by inflating grades. On the other hand, concern about the possibility that grading practices can distort student ratings largely disappeared from the scholarly literature on student ratings after about 1980. How did research manage to quiet concerns that ratings could be biased by manipulating grades?

1980s: Demonstrations of Convergent Validity of Student Ratings

Since 1980, research on student ratings has mostly been in the form of correlational construct validity designs. Three kinds of studies provided evidence that has supported the construct validity of student ratings.

Multisection Validity Studies. In the best of the largest group of construct validity studies, multiple sections of the same course are taught by different instructors, with student ability approximately matched across sections and with all sections having identical or at least similarly difficult examinations. Using examination performance as the criterion measure of achievement, these studies have determined whether differences in achievement for students taught by different instructors are reflected in the student ratings of the instructors. The collection of multisection validity studies has been reviewed in several meta-analyses. Although the meta-analytic reviews do not agree on all points concerning the validity of student ratings, nevertheless it is clear that multisection validity studies yield evidence for modest validity of ratings. Correlations between ratings and exam-measured achievement average about 0.40 (see the overview of meta-analyses by Abrami, Cohen, & d'Apollonia, 1988, esp. pp. 160–162).

Multisection validity studies favor construct validity of ratings by supporting an interpretation of observed grades-ratings correlations in

---

[1]Contemporary reviews of student ratings literature either omit treatment of these natural classroom experiments on effects of manipulated grades on ratings, or mention them only in the context of suggesting that they are collectively flawed (e.g., Marsh & Dunkin, 1992, p. 202).

terms of common effects of a third variable, teaching effectiveness. If grades correlate with ratings simply because good teachers produce both high grades and high ratings, then all is well with the validity of student ratings.[2]

Path-Analytic Studies. The second type of correlational construct validity study also explores the idea that effects of third variables on both grades and ratings explains their correlation, but considers third variables other than teaching effectiveness. For example, Howard and Maxwell (1980) applied path analysis techniques to show that grades and ratings were both related to measures of students' level of motivation for courses, from which they concluded that

> the relationship between grades and student satisfaction might be viewed as a welcome result of important causal relationships among other variables rather than simply as evidence of contamination due to grading leniency. (p. 810)

In another example of this type of study, Marsh (1980) observed that

> A path analysis demonstrated that students' Prior Subject Interest had the strongest impact on student ratings [and] accounted for about one-third of the relationship between Expected Grades and student ratings . . . . Expected Grade was seen as a likely bias—albeit a small one—to the ratings, and even this interpretation was open to alternative interpretations. (pp. 219, 236)

Multitrait-multimethod studies. The third type of construct validity study seeks to demonstrate that student ratings possess both convergent and discriminant validity—that is, to demonstrate that they correlate (a) relatively well with measures based on other methods for assessing the construct of quality of instruction, and (b) relatively less well with measures assumed to assess other constructs (e.g., Freedman, Stumpf, & Aguanno, 1979; Howard, Conway, & Maxwell, 1985; Marsh, 1982). Such multitrait-

---

[2]Interpretation of this approximate .40 correlation as reflecting processes other than, or in addition to, validity of student ratings has also been suggested. For example, Marsh and Dunkin (1992, pp. 173ff.) note that this correlation could be contributed to either by motivational variations among students in different sections or by greater student satsifaction with higher grades.

multimethod studies typically have reported evidence for both convergent and discriminant validity of student ratings, although they usually have done so without considering expected grades as a source of contamination.

Overview: The Question of Discriminant Validity Remains

As previously suggested, there is an Emperors' Clothes quality to the research literature on validity of student ratings. The researchers of the 1970s, who demonstrated experimentally that grade manipulations affected ratings, declared in effect that the student ratings emperor had a wardrobe problem. Researchers of the mid 1970s to mid 1980s, who reported construct validity studies, concluded that the emperor was in fact clothed. If one reads carefully the latter construct validity studies, it becomes apparent that they did not declare the emperor to be *fully* clothed. The question of what was left exposed translates, in construct validity terms, to the question of discriminant validity of student ratings. Construct validity studies have established that student ratings do, to a moderate extent, measure what they're supposed to measure. But one wants to know also how well student ratings measures avoid bias resulting from sensitivity to things that they're not supposed to measure—which is to say that one wants to know about their discriminant validity.

When there is good discriminant validity, having only modest convergent validity means that one has an unbiased, even if noisy, measure. For example, think of weighing people on a scale that will produce a value somewhere within 10 pounds of their correct weight. If a series of these weights has an independent normal distribution that is centered on the correct weight, then one can get a very good measure simply by being patient enough to take multiple readings and average them. If student ratings have moderate convergent validity accompanied by good discriminant validity, one might be reluctant to treat individual-course ratings as highly accurate, especially ratings obtained from small classes, but one should not otherwise be concerned.

The situation is importantly different when moderate convergent validity is accompanied by some failure of discriminant validity. Consider, for example, what happens when economists report seasonally adjusted monthly indexes of unemployment. The raw figure of percent of people out of work fluctuates seasonally due to school schedules and the influences of weather on employment in building construction schedules and farm harvests, etc. These systematic fluctuations are irrelevant to the overall state of the economy, and make the raw unemployment rate misleading (i.e., discriminantly invalid) as an indicator of economic health. Fortunately, this discriminant validity problem of the raw unemployment rate does not render those data useless. If one applies appropriate adjustments for known seasonal effects, then the adjusted unemployment rate can provide a valid measure of the overall economy.

Student ratings measures are now used in most undergraduate institutions without any adjustments. In other words, student ratings are treated as if they have excellent discriminant validity. It is assumed that student ratings do not suffer from any substantial contaminating influences (as asserted, e.g., in the previously quoted remark by McKeachie, 1979). On the one hand, this seems implausible, because convergent validity with nonratings measures of quality of instruction has never been shown to be more than moderate, and also because replicated experiments, conducted in actual classroom settings, have repeatedly demonstrated that grading policy variations substantially affect student ratings. On the other hand, however, for the past 20 years well respected researchers have repeatedly asserted that student ratings are construct-valid measures of instructional quality. This is a paradox.

THEORIES AND FINDINGS

An acceptable response to the paradoxical status of the literature on student ratings is to attempt to subdue the paradox with theoretical analysis and new data. Toward that goal, a series of data collections was conducted at University of Washington starting in 1992. These studies sought to choose among the alternative theoretical interpretations that were central to pre-1980 concerns about ratings validity (see review by Stumpf & Freedman, 1979).

Figure 15.2 shows the grades-ratings correlation in the form of a structural model that relates two measures of expected grades to two measures of course and instructor evaluation. Figure 15.2's data were obtained in a series of three studies at University of Washington during the 1993–1994 academic year. These studies used a new rating form (Form X, see Gillmore & Greenwald, 1994) that added several measures to forms previously in use at University of Washington. Data were obtained from 200 or more courses in each of several academic terms. Although these were university-wide samples of courses that were diverse in subject matter,

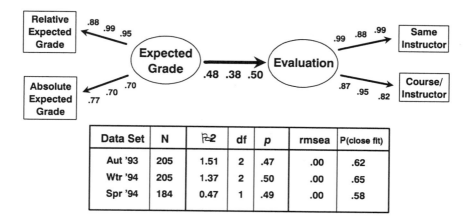

FIG. 15.2. Structural model including two measures of expected grade and two measures of evaluative ratings of course and instructor. The three coefficients on each path are standardized values (i.e., on the same −1 to +1 scale as correlation coefficients) shown in left-to-right order for the three data sets. Statistics report major tests of fit for this structural model. Nonsignificant ($p > .05$) chi-square values indicate satisfactory fit. Chi-square values have an extra degree of freedom (df) when the computational routine added a constraint to avoid a negative variance estimate. 'rmsea' is the root-mean-square error of approximation index of fit that has been described by Browne and Cudeck (1993) and by MacCallum, Browne, and Sugawara (1996). These authors characterize rmsea < .05 as indicating "close" fit, .05 − .08 as "close to fair" fit, .08 − .10 as "mediocre" fit, and rmsea > .10 as "poor" fit. 'P(close fit)' values greater than .05 indicate satisfactory fit.

class size, and academic level, the courses were also self-selected by virtue of instructors having volunteered to use the new rating form. Results from undergraduate courses for which at least 10 students provided ratings responses are summarized in the figure. The positive grades-ratings correlation is measured by the standardized path coefficient (averaging +.45 for the three samples) that links the two latent variables of Expected Grade and Evaluation.

Five Theories of the Grades-Ratings Correlation

The existence of this grades-ratings correlation of course prompts a suspicion that ratings can be increased by the strategy of increasing grades. That conclusion assumes a causal influence of grades on ratings. However, observed correlations such as in Figure 15.2 by no means demand the conclusion of a causal influence of grades on evaluative ratings. Each of the first three of the following five theories explains the grades-ratings correlation in noncausal fashion by hypothesizing that a third variable influences both grades and ratings. The remaining two theories do assume a causal influence of grades on ratings.

1. *Teaching Effectiveness Influences Both Grades and Ratings.* This is the one theory that is fully based on the presumed construct validity of student ratings (see McKeachie, 1979, pp. 390–391). The central principle of the teaching effectiveness theory is that strong instructors teach courses in which students both (a) learn much (therefore they earn and deserve high grades), and (b) give appropriately high ratings to the course and instructor. Instructional quality is thus a third variable that explains the grades-ratings correlation in a way that raises no concern about grades having improper influences on ratings.

2. *Students' General Academic Motivation Influences Both Grades and Ratings.* Compared to unmotivated students, students with strong academic motivation should both (a) do better in their course work and (b) more fully appreciate the efforts of the instructor, possibly even inspiring the instructor to superior performance. Courses that attract highly motivated students should give higher grades (because the students work harder) and should get higher ratings (because the motivated students appreciate both course and instructor). Student motivation has been suggested as the operative third variable in several research investigations of student ratings (e.g., Howard & Maxwell, 1980; Marsh, 1984).

3. *Students' Course-Specific Motivation Influences Both Grades and Ratings.* This theory differs from the preceding one by supposing that a student's motivation can vary from course to course rather than being a fixed characteristic of the student. Because the two motivation theories credit the relation between grades and ratings to a characteristic of students, they appear not to support a teaching effectiveness interpretation of ratings. However, if student motivation is itself credited to the instructor—for example, the instructor either attracts highly motivated students or motivates them once they are in the course—these theories retain the interpretation that ratings measure teaching effectiveness.

4. *Students Infer Course Quality and Own Ability From Received Grades.* Social psychological *attribution* theories describe how people make inferences about both their own traits and the properties of situations in which they act by observing the outcomes of their actions. Research in the attribution theory tradition shows that favorable outcomes for one's own behavior typically lead to inferences that one has desirable traits, whereas unfavorable

outcomes may lead one to perceive situational obstacles to success. A simple summary of these attributional principles is that people tend to accept credit for desired outcomes while denying responsibility for undesired outcomes (Greenwald, 1980). Applying this principle to student ratings leads to an expectation that high grades will be self-attributed to intelligence and/or diligence, and low grades to poor instruction. Social psychological attribution theory matured after the peak of research activity on student ratings, perhaps explaining why this interpretation has been little mentioned in research on student ratings. Some recent discussion of attribution interpretations appear in papers by Gigliotti and Buchtel (1990) and Theall, Franklin, and Ludlow (1990); see also the recent overview by Feldman (1997).

5. *Students Give High Ratings in Appreciation For Lenient Grading.* The idea that praise induces liking for the praiser (especially if the praise is greater than expected) is familiar in social psychology (Aronson & Linder, 1965). The translation of this familiar principle into the ratings context is that the instructor in effect praises the student via a high grade, and the student's return liking is expressed by providing high ratings. This *leniency* or *grade satisfaction* theory has been a focus of much controversy in past research on validity of student ratings. The leniency interpretation was advocated by researchers who were critical of ratings validity in the 1970s, including those who published demonstrations in natural class settings that grade manipulations affected student ratings (Chacko, 1983; Holmes, 1972; Powell, 1977; Vasta & Sarmiento, 1979; Worthington & Wong, 1979). However, support for the leniency theory dropped sharply in the wake of correlational construct validity research conducted in the late 1970s and early 1980s. Mentions of leniency or grade-satisfaction theories in post-1980 publications appear mostly in the context of asserting that leniency may account for only minor and ignorable influences on student ratings (in addition to McKeachie's [1979] already-quoted comment, see Marsh, 1984, pp. 741, 749; Howard et al., 1985, p. 187; Cashin, 1995, p. 6).

Four Theory-Diagnostic Patterns in Correlational Student Ratings Data

Table 15.1 presents four data patterns that, as a collection, can discriminate among the five theoretical interpretations of the grades-ratings correlation. For completeness, the grades-ratings correlation also appears as a fifth (but first-listed) pattern in Table 15.1.

With the exception of one that was tested only during a single academic term (the third one listed below), the four diagnostic data pattern of Table

15.1 have been corroborated as findings in separate data collections over three or more academic terms in university-wide samples of courses at University of Washington. As each finding is described, its use to evaluate the five theories is explained.

1. *Positive Grades-Ratings Relationships Within Classes.* In addition to between-classes grades-ratings correlations as described in Figure 15.2, grades-ratings correlations are also routinely obtained *within* classes (Stumpf & Freedman, 1979). In the University of Washington data, the within-classes relationship has been observed very reliably. Because, in the teaching effectiveness theory, the variable that influences both grades and ratings is a constant (the instructor) within any classroom, that theory does not explain the within-classes positive correlation of grades and ratings. By contrast, the two third-variable theories that relate student motivation differences to ratings differences are able to explain the within-classes grades-ratings correlation. That is, within each class, the more highly motivated students may both get higher grades and give higher ratings. Also, of course, the attribution and leniency theories very directly explain why students who get higher grades in a course should evaluate that course more positively than others.

2. *Stronger Grades-Ratings Relationships With Relative (Than Absolute) Measures of Expected Grade.* Figure 15.2's structural model included two measures of expected grades, *absolute* and *relative* expected grades. The absolute measure used class medians on the 0.0 (E or fail) to 4.0 (A) grading system in use at University of Washington. The relative measure used class medians on a measure that asked each student to report the relation of the grade expected in the rated course to the student's average grades in other courses. The stronger weight of the relative measure on Figure 15.2's Expected Grade latent variable reflects the finding that the grades-ratings relationship was stronger for the relative-grade measure than for the absolute-grade measure. In regression analyses that predicted ratings simultaneously from both of the expected grade measures, the relative grade measure yielded a substantial gain in percent of ratings variance explained, over and above that explained by the absolute expected grade measure. By contrast, the absolute grade measure accounted for very little beyond what was explained by the relative grade measure. The superiority of the relative grade measure was evident in both between-course and within-course analyses. The use of a relative grade measure was a novel feature of the University of Washington research. Consequently, this finding—that the grades-ratings correlation is stronger for the relative-grade measure—was previously unreported in the student ratings research literature.

TABLE 15.1

Success of Five Theories in Explaining Five Patterns in Student-Rating Data

Type of explan-ation	Hypothesis	Established pattern	Four diagnostic patterns			
		Positive between-classes grades-ratings correlation	Positive within-classes grades-ratings correlation	Greater correlation for relative than absolute grade	Grade correlation radiates to peripheral items (halo)[a]	Negative between-classes grades-workload correlation
Third variable affects both grades and ratings	Third variable is instructor's teaching effectiveness	✓	X	X	X	X
	Third variable is student's general academic motivation	✓	✓	X	X	X
	Third variable is student's course-specific motivation	✓	✓	✓	X	X
Grades influence ratings	Attribution: Grades provide information about course quality and student ability	✓	✓	✓	✓	X
	Leniency: Students reward/punish instructors who give high/low grades	✓	✓	✓	✓	✓

Notes: ✓ = hypothesis predicts result; X = hypothesis predicts either a null or opposite-direction result.
[a]This halo effect is a positive grade-ratings correlation (across students, within courses) for items that, rationally, should be evaluated in the same way by all students in the same class (i.e., independently of their grades).

The teaching effectiveness interpretation does not explain any within-classes grades-ratings correlation, let alone the greater strength of this correlation for the relative-grade than the absolute-grade measure. The general academic motivation theory, which ties ratings to the student's assumed stable level of motivation, also has trouble explaining superiority of the relative grade measure, unless it is (very implausibly) assumed that highly motivated students always report that they expect to obtain grades that are above their average grade. By contrast, the course-specific motivation theory and the attribution and leniency theories readily explain why ratings associated with a specific course are higher when the grade in that course is relatively high for the student.

3. *Grade-Related Halo Effect in Judging Course Characteristics.* In Winter Quarter of 1994, approximately 100 instructors at University of Washington agreed to add a small set of items to their regular rating forms. The added items included three judgments that, a priori, were unlikely to be more than weakly related to quality of instruction. These three items sought students' judgments of (a) legibility of instructor's writing, (b) audibility of instructor's voice, and (c) quality of classroom facilities to aid instruction (such as an overhead projector). There was no evidence of a grades-ratings relationship in the between-course analyses of these responses, consistent with the assumption that these items are peripheral to judgments of instructional quality. However, within-courses analyses showed clear positive relationships (Greenwald & Gillmore, 1997a, pp. 1212–1213). Although these within-courses relationships were not large, they were nevertheless very stable statistically. Because all students in the same classroom saw the same instructor's handwriting, heard the same instructor's voice, and had the same classroom teaching aids, the observation of these within-sections correlations is remarkable. The content of items on which these grade-halo effects occurred—especially their noncentrality to most conceptions of instructional quality—suggests the potency of grade influences on student ratings.[3]

---

[3]Previous findings that front-of-class seating is associated with higher grades (e.g., Knowles, 1982) provide the basis for a possible student-motivation interpretation of the within-courses relationships of expected grades to ratings of instructor voice and legibility, although not the relationship to ratings of classroom facilities. The author thanks Lloyd K. Stires (personal communication, October 26, 1995) for noting the relevance of the classroom seating variable to these data.

All three of the third-variable theories have difficulty with these grade-related halo effects. For the teaching effectiveness theory, if there are any grade effects on the legibility, audibility, and class facilities items, those effects should appear in between-classes analyses (but they do not) and they should not appear in within-classes analyses (but they do). The two student-motivation third-variable theories are strained in attempts to account for the pattern of grade-related effects on these three items. To spell this out: One might suppose that highly motivated students are more likely to read the instructor's handwriting easily, to hear the instructor clearly, and perhaps even to notice the classroom facilities. Given either student-motivation interpretation, however, these effects should have appeared in between-courses analyses, as well as within courses. The two social psychological theories that credit grade influences on ratings to irrational motivated judgment processes are quite consistent with radiation of the grade-halo effect to peripheral judgments.

4. *Negative Grades-Workload Relationship Between Classes.* It seems reasonable that students should work harder in courses in which they receive high grades than in ones in which they receive low grades. The reasonableness of this expectation rests on two assumptions: (a) that grades awarded in a course provide an indicator of student achievement or learning in the course, and (b) that students work harder in courses in which they learn much than in courses in which they learn little. From these two assumptions it follows that students should tend to work harder in courses that give high grades than in courses that give low grades. However, this expected positive relationship between grades and course workload has been repeatedly disconfirmed in data obtained at University of Washington. To the contrary, the data consistently display a substantial negative relationship between expected course grades and workload. That is, students report doing more work in courses with low expected grades than in courses with high expected grades. This relationship, based on data obtained at University of Washington in the three consecutive terms of the 1993–94 academic year, is shown in the structural model of Figure 15.3 (a model that also includes evaluative ratings). Tests of the relationship between expected grades and course workloads have rarely been reported by previous researchers. However, other studies have indeed observed the same surprising negative relationship between expected grades and workload in between-course analyses (e.g., Marsh, 1980, pp. 234–235).

The three third-variable theories all imply nonnegative relationships between expected grades and workload. This is most readily seen for the two motivational theories. If students earn high grades by virtue of high motivation (i.e., by working hard) then a positive relationship between

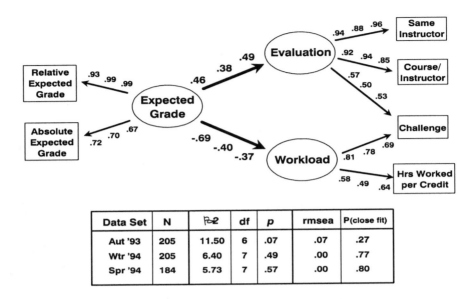

Data Set	N	χ2	df	p	rmsea	P(close fit)
Aut '93	205	11.50	6	.07	.07	.27
Wtr '94	205	6.40	7	.49	.00	.77
Spr '94	184	5.73	7	.57	.00	.80

FIG. 15.3. Structural equation model replicated on three data sets from the 1993–1994 academic year. The "Challenge" and "Hours Worked per Credit" measures are based, respectively, on Items 20 and 26 of the University of Washington's Form X (see Gillmore & Greenwald, 1994). The negative between-course relationship between Expected Grade and Workload is measured by the standardized coefficients (average = –.45) for the path linking their latent variables. See additional explanatory information in Figure 15.2's caption.

expected grades and workload is clearly expected. For the teaching effectiveness theory, it might be assumed that effective teachers manage to get their students to do more work and, thus, if high grades are explained by effective teaching, a positive relation between expected grades and workload is expected. If, on the other hand, it is assumed that effective teachers are just more efficient in imparting knowledge to students, then expected grades should be unrelated (but not negatively related) to workload. The attribution theory is equivocal in regard to the grade-workload relationship because it is possible either for students to attribute a *high* grade to hard work or for them to attribute hard work to a *low* expected grade. Only the leniency theory readily explains the observed negative relationship. The explanation is that strict-grading instructors induce students to work hard in order to avoid very low grades.[4]

Summary Evaluation of the Five Theories. Each theory predicts a different subset of the four diagnostic data patterns of Table 15.1, ranging from the teaching effectiveness theory predicting none of them to the leniency theory predicting all (see Table 15.1). Each of the three third-variable theories fails to explain at least two of the four findings. The two direct-cause (grades influence ratings) theories fare best as a class and, of these two, the leniency theory is favored by virtue of being the only theory to explain the negative relation between grades and workload.

CONCLUSIONS

The findings described previously, considered in the context of much previous research on student ratings, justify the following conclusions:

1. *Inflated Grades Produce Inflated Ratings.* The conclusion that grades influence ratings appears to be decisively established on the combined basis of (a) experimental studies that show impact of grades on ratings, (b) replicable correlational data patterns that are explained only by theories that suppose a causal influence of grades on ratings, and (c) the existence of well-established theories (attribution and reciprocal attraction) that provide plausible social psychological interpretations of this causal influence. The evidence certainly does not warrant the conclusion that giving high grades is, *by itself*, sufficient to assure high ratings. Nevertheless, it does support the conclusion that, if an instructor varies nothing between two course offerings other than grading policy, higher ratings should be obtained in the more leniently graded section.

2. *With Statistical Adjustment, Student Ratings May Be Very Useful.* Their failing of discriminant validity (i.e., their contamination by grading leniency) notwithstanding, student ratings have repeatedly been shown to have modest convergent validity. In other words, at the same time that student ratings provide a distorted measure of instructional quality, they also have a moderate level of valid correlation with instructional quality. The valid

---

[4]The analyses of competing interpretations of the relationship between expected grades and workload have been described in more detail by Greenwald and Gillmore (1997b, pp. 743–744).

component of ratings may be enhanced to the extent that it is possible to statistically adjust for the sources of discriminant invalidity.

3. *Workload Measures Are Useful.* The consistent finding of a negative relationship between course grades and workload (illustrated in Figure 15.3) is disturbing. Although this relationship may exist at many colleges and universities, it has never become a focus of research attention, perhaps because workload measures are not routinely included in student ratings. The inclusion of workload estimates in course evaluation forms can assure that this important aspect of differences among courses does not continue to escape attention.

The Baby and the Bathwater

This examination of psychological processes underlying student ratings might be interpreted as sufficient basis for abandoning the whole enterprise of obtaining student ratings. However, there are three good reasons to conclude just the reverse—that even more attention should be paid to ratings.

First, in many cases there is no practical alternative method for evaluating instruction. Although expert appraisals and standardized achievement tests might, in principle, provide more valid assessments, unfortunately both of those alternative methods are considerably more costly than student ratings. Their present very limited use probably stands as an appropriate indicator of their relative impracticality.

Second, the evidence for convergent validity of student ratings should not be dismissed. Although student ratings are overlaid with some misleading artifacts, they nevertheless also contain useful information. Theory-based statistical adjustments can make that information more usable than it presently is.

Third, even a worst-case scenario suggests that student ratings can provide useful information. In this worst-case scenario, one might conclude that adjusted student ratings provide information only about how well students like a course, and nothing at all about how much students are learning from the course. Still, this assessment of liking or attitude should be very useful, in the same way that an assessment of bedside manner is useful in evaluating a physician. The assessment of bedside manner doesn't describe the physician's success in preventing or curing illness, but it does give information that may predict a patient's willingness to adhere to prescribed treatments and to return for future treatment. Similarly, knowledge of how much a teacher is liked should provide information that can predict a student's willingness to do assigned work and to register for further course work from that teacher.

In summary, there very likely *is* an instructional quality baby in with the bathwater of grades-ratings correlations and other possible contaminants of ratings. It seems much, much wiser to give that baby a bath, to clean it up and make it presentable, than to abandon the baby in the process of discarding the bathwater.

ABSTRACT

Higher education relies heavily on student ratings to evaluate faculty teaching, largely because the alternatives (expert peer appraisals or objective performance criteria) are costly or unavailable. Because student ratings are crucial not only to improving instruction, but also in making or breaking faculty careers, it is important to assure that they provide valid indications of instructional quality. Problematically, findings summarized in this chapter show that student ratings suffer from artifacts that lead to underestimation of teaching ability for instructors who grade strictly and overestimates for those who grade leniently. Some likely system impacts of this distortion of ratings are to guide (a) instructors toward lenient grading, and (b) students toward nonchallenging courses. The bright side of this picture is that the usefulness of student ratings can be improved statistically.

ACKNOWLEDGMENTS

Portions of this chapter were first presented as an address for the Donald T. Campbell Award from the Society of Personality and Social Psychology, presented at the 1995 meetings of the American Psychological Association in New York. The research on which this chapter is based was greatly facilitated by the Office of Educational Assessment at University of Washington, and was conducted in collaboration with Gerald M. Gillmore, who is co-author of some of the more detailed reports based on this collaborative research (Greenwald, 1997; Greenwald & Gillmore, 1997a, 1997b). Some material from those other reports has been reproduced in this chapter with permission of American Psychological Association. Additional support was provided by Grant SBR-9422242 from National Science Foundation, and by Grants MH 41328 and MH 01533 from

National Institute of Mental Health. For comments on various previous drafts of related material, the author thanks Robert D. Abbott, Philip C. Abrami, Kenneth A. Feldman, Gerald M. Gillmore, Joe Horn, George S. Howard, Herbert W. Marsh, Scott E. Maxwell, Jeremy D. Mayer, Robert S. Owen, Lloyd K. Stires, and John E. Stone. Correspondence may be addressed to the author at Department of Psychology—Box 351525, University of Washington, Seattle, WA 98195-1525, and by electronic mail to agg@u.washington.edu.

REFERENCES

Abrami, P. C., Cohen, P. A., & d'Apollonia, S. (1988). Implementation problems in meta-analysis. *Review of Educational Research, 58*, 151–179.

Aronson, E., & Linder, D. E. (1965). Gain and loss of esteem as determinants of interpersonal attractiveness. *Journal of Experimental Social Psychology, 1*, 156–171.

Browne, M. W., & Cudeck, R. (1993). Alternative ways of assessing model fit. In K. A. Bollen & J. S. Long (Eds.), *Testing structural equation models* (pp. 136–162). Newbury Park, CA: Sage.

Cashin, W. E. (1995). Student ratings of teaching: The research revisited. IDEA Paper No. 32. Manhattan, KS: Kansas State University, Center for Faculty Evaluation and Development.

Chacko, T. I. (1983). Student ratings of instruction: A function of grading standards. *Educational Research Quarterly, 8*(2), 19–25.

Feldman, K. A. (1997). Identifying exemplary teachers and teaching: Evidence form student ratings. In R. P. Perry & J. C. Smart (Eds.), *Effective teaching in higher education: Research and practice* (pp. 368–395). New York: Agathon Press.

Freedman, R. D., Stumpf, S. A., & Aguanno, J. C. (1979). Validity of the Course-Faculty Instrument (CFI): Intrinsic and extrinsic variables. *Educational & Psychological Measurement, 39*, 153–158.

Gigliotti, R. J., & Buchtel, F. S. (1990). Attributional bias and course evaluations. *Journal of Educational Psychology, 82*, 341–351.

Gillmore, G. M., & Greenwald, A. G. (1994, April). *The effects of course demands and grading leniency on student ratings of instruction.* Paper presented at meetings of American Educational Research Association, Orlando, FL.

Greenwald, A. G. (1980). The totalitarian ego: Fabrication and revision of personal history. *American Psychologist, 35*, 603–618.

Greenwald, A. G. (1997). Validity concerns and usefulness of student ratings. *American Psychologist, 52*, 1182–1186.

Greenwald, A. G., & Gillmore, G. M. (1997a). Grading leniency is a removable contaminant of student ratings. *American Psychologist, 52*, 1209–1217.

Greenwald, A. G., & Gillmore, J. M. (1997b). No pain, no gain? The importance of measuring course workload in student ratings of instruction. *Journal of Educational Psychology, 89*, 743–751.

Holmes, D. S. (1972). Effects of grades and disconfirmed grade expectancies on students' evaluations of their instructor. *Journal of Educational Psychology, 63*, 130–133.

Howard, G. S., Conway, C. G, & Maxwell, S. E. (1985). Construct validity of measures of college teaching effectiveness. *Journal of Educational Psychology, 77*, 187–196.

Howard, G. S., & Maxwell, S. E. (1980). Correlation between student satisfaction and grades: A case of mistaken causation? *Journal of Educational Psychology, 72*, 810–820.

Knowles, E. S. (1982). A comment on the study of classroom ecology: A lament for the good old days. *Personality and Social Psychology Bulletin, 8*, 357–361.

MacCallum, R. C., Browne, M. W., & Sugawara, H. M. (1996). Power analysis and determination of sample size for covariance structure modeling. *Psychological Methods, 1*, 130–149.

Marsh, H. W. (1980). The influence of student, course, and instructor characteristics on evaluations of university teaching. *American Educational Research Journal, 17*, 219–237.

Marsh, H. W. (1982). Validity of students' evaluations of college teaching: A multitrait-multimethod analysis. *Journal of Educational Psychology, 74*, 264–279.

Marsh, H. W. (1984). Students' evaluations of university teaching: Dimensionality, reliability, validity, potential biases, and utility. *Journal of Educational Psychology, 76*, 707–754.

Marsh, H. W., & Dunkin, M. J. (1992). Students' evaluations of university teaching: A multidimensional perspective. *Higher Education:Handbook of Theory and Research, 8*, 143–233.

McKeachie, W. J. (1979). Student ratings of faculty: A reprise. *Academe, 65*, 384–397.

Powell, R. W. (1977). Grades, learning, and student evaluation of instruction. *Research in Higher Education, 7*, 193–205.

Snyder, C. R., & Clair, M. (1976). Effects of expected and obtained grades on teacher evaluation and attribution of performance. *Journal of Educational Psychology, 68*, 75–82.

Stumpf, S. A., & Freedman, R. D. (1979). Expected grade covariation with student ratings of instruction: Individual versus class effects. *Journal of Educational Psychology, 71*, 293–302.

Theall, M., Franklin, J., & Ludlow, L. (1990). Attributions and retributions: Student ratings and the perceived causes of performance. *Instructional Evaluation, 11*, 12–17.

Vasta, R., & Sarmiento, R. F. (1979). Liberal grading improves evaluations but not performance. *Journal of Educational Psychology, 71*, 207–211.

Worthington, A. G., & Wong, P. T. P. (1979). Effects of earned and assigned grades on student evaluations of an instructor. *Journal of Educational Psychology, 71*, 764–775.

16
Construct Validity and the Language of Inquiry

Philip W. Jackson
University of Chicago

The questions I examine in this chapter have to do with construct validity as a tool of thought. They deal with how well the concept serves us intellectually, what it does or might do to the way we frame our research questions and undertake our investigations. I confess at the start that I do not have great confidence in the answers I shall give to those questions, being neither a test-designer nor a psychometrician. Indeed, I hardly have the right to address the subject, I suppose, at least not in the company of such experts as those contributing to this volume. Yet, like most people who are broadly interested in the social sciences, I have given the matter some thought over the years and have casually discussed it with others on several occasions. Although the judgments I have come to may appear naive or even misguided by those in the know, I am confident that they are not mine alone. Those who may wish to correct them will be aided, I trust, by the following effort to state them as clearly as I can.

For reasons soon to be explained, I take a very circuitous approach to my subject. I devote almost the entire first half of my chapter to the telling of two personal anecdotes that bear illustratively but only tangentially at best on the commentary contained in the second half. The fact that Sam Messick figures directly into one of my stories and was indirectly involved with the other helps to explain why I have chosen to tell them on this special occasion. Following that roundabout path brings me ultimately to the central topic of this volume and to viewpoint alluded to above.

* * * * *

Sam and I became friends during our fellowship year at the Center for Advanced Study in the Behavioral Sciences. Our stay at the Center began in the fall of 1962, just about the time of the Cuban Missile crisis, when John Foster Dulles and Nikita Khrushchev stared each other down, eyeball to eyeball, while the world trembled in fear of the consequence. For a reason soon to be made known, I had occasion to fly from California to the east coast during those tense days, a trip made with some trepidation I must say, and one whose attendant feelings I still vividly recall.

The international crisis aside, it was a great year to be at the Center. In fact, Sam and I to this day boast of it having been one of the greatest years in the Center's history, an audacious claim, to say the least. Whether or not our claim is justified, the year as a whole certainly felt like a once-in-a-lifetime event to the two of us. We were both young enough at the time to be properly impressed by the luminosity of that year's crop of senior fellows, which included Meyer Schapiro, Michael Polanyi, Erik Erickson, Carl Rogers, Renato Paggoli, Fred Mosteller, Lancelot Law Whyte, Fred Harbison, and others. There was also an impressive collection of younger talent on hand, including, among others, Wayne Holtzman, Michael Scriven, Alberta Segal, George Schaller, Irving Devore, and Phyllis Jay. Even the casual visitors who wandered in and out of the Center that year were often noteworthy enough to make us all sit up and take notice. Arnold Toynbee graced us with a one-day seminar, as did Alan Watts, whose writings on Zen were then very popular. More impressive company would be difficult to imagine, I hardly need say.

As new acquaintances Sam and I hit it off from the start. We found that we had a lot in common, both professionally and non-professionally. On the professional side, we were both interested in problems of psychological assessment, particularly the assessment of creativity. I had just co-authored a book with J. W. Getzels entitled *Creativity and Intelligence: Explorations with Gifted Students* (Getzels & Jackson, 1962). Among Sam's many interests at that time were correlates of intellectual performance associated with personality variables, especially those having to do with what was called *cognitive style*.

The closeness of those interests led us to spend a lot of time discussing how creativity was currently being assessed and thinking about how those assessments might be improved. We talked about extending them to include aspects of creative performance that went far beyond the then-popular notions of divergent thinking and verbal fluency. From those discussions came a jointly authored paper entitled "The person, the product, and the response: Conceptual problems in the assessment of creativity," which later was published in the *Journal of Personality* (Jackson & Messick, 1965).

What Sam and I sought to do in that paper was to postulate a set of criteria by which a creative product of almost any kind might be judged. We next asked by what standards those judgments might be made and, furthermore, what kinds of responses those properties of the object might elicit from the person making the judgment. We sought also to name the personal qualities and the predisposing cognitive styles of the individuals associated with each standard and each kind of response. Our effort was ambitious, to say the least. In retrospect I would also call it naive. Neither of us knew much about any of the arts, at least not enough to speak authoritatively about them. Though we drew our examples from diverse sources, including poetry, music, and painting, they by and large lacked richness and subtlety. So did the argument we were trying to make.

It is easy to translate what we were trying to do in our paper into the language of construct validity. Essentially, we were working on the problem of construct under-representation as it applies to creativity. By drawing on our own knowledge of poems, music, novels, and so forth, we sought to identify aspects of creativity that were not then being tested. We also tried to give some order to the qualities we identified. We did so by positing a developmental progression through which such yet-to-be-tested components of the construct might logically pass. That part of our work involved us in what might properly be called the *structural* aspect of the construct of creativity. Another way of describing what we were about will be introduced later.

Meanwhile, in the midst of our work on the paper my own enthusiasm for continuing to do research on creativity suffered a serious setback. It did so as a result of the trip to the east coast that I have already mentioned. The reason for my trip and what I found when I got there are both a bit complicated, so I must explain each in some detail.

In the research described in our book Getzels and I had focused on two groups of students identified from among all of the students, from the sixth grade forward, then attending the University of Chicago's Laboratory School. One group had performed very well on several tests of creativity, so-called, but not nearly so outstandingly on a standard test of intelligence; the other group had a pattern of scores exactly the reverse. We sought to compare those two groups on a wide variety of dependent variables having chiefly to do with their performances in school—variables like teacher and peer ratings, attitudes toward school and family, career aspirations, and so forth. The five tests comprising our "creativity" battery had either been modeled after or were exact copies of tests employed in a wide variety of other investigations of creativity undertaken by investigators such as J.P. Guilford, Raymond B. Cattell, E. Paul Torrence, and Frank Barron. Here is how we described that set of five tests.

> In general, our tests of creativity involved the ability to deal inventively with verbal and numerical symbol systems and with object-space relations. What most of these tests had in common was that the score depended not on a single predetermined correct response . . . but on the number, novelty, and variety of adaptive response to a given stimulus task. (Getzels & Jackson, 1962, 17)

We reproduced four of the five tests in an Appendix of our book, together with simplified scoring instructions.

Our book aroused the interest of a number of psychologists and school people around the country, some of whom were eager to put our tests to work in school settings. Although we emphasized in our book that the use of the tests for such practical purposes was very premature and was not something that we would endorse or recommend, we did not take the additional safeguard of publishing only sample items from each test, for we wanted to make our full set of instruments readily available for inspection and use by other researchers.

As it turned out, an early report of their premature use in a non-research setting came to me shortly after my arrival at the Center. I received a call from the superintendent of schools in a suburb of Boston (let's call it Easton). He enthusiastically described an "educational experiment," as he called it, currently underway in the Easton schools. Near the close of the prior school year his Director of Psychological Services had supervised the administration of our battery of creativity tests to all of the fifth-grade students in Easton. The tests had been scored according to the instructions supplied in our book. Twenty or so of the students who had scored highest on that battery of tests and whose parents had consented to their participation in the study were being bussed to a single classroom in Easton where they were being taught by what the superintendent described as "one of Easton's most creative teachers." He ended his account with an invitation for me to fly to Easton, all expenses paid, to witness at first hand this unusual experiment.

As might be guessed, the superintendent's account triggered mixed feelings on my part. On the one hand, I was annoyed that he had done exactly what we had warned against in our book. On the other hand, I couldn't help but be intrigued by the prospect of seeing what such a group of youngsters looked like and learning something about how they actually behaved in school.

The students Getzels and I had studied—the ones we called our *high creatives*—were mixed in with all the others in our sample and were known to us by test scores alone, which is what made the prospect of seeing a group of such youngsters in the flesh so very attractive. Although I disapproved of how the tests had been used, I had no hand in the process, which helped to assuage my uneasiness. I also reasoned that the students themselves were probably not suffering from having been so identified and might even be benefitting from their new educational arrangement. In the end, my curiosity turned out to be stronger than my sense of disapproval. So I suppressed my misgivings and accepted the superintendent's invitation. I looked forward to what my journey to Easton held in store.

My visit there covered three school days plus a day of traveling at each end. I spent most of the time there sitting in the back of the experimental classroom, watching the town's 25 "most creative" sixth graders and their "most creative" teacher go about their business. What I saw turned out to be interesting, all right, but not at all in the way I had anticipated.

During my first morning's visit I was chiefly struck by how familiar everything looked. The physical classroom, the students, the teacher, they all looked pretty much like their counterparts back in the Laboratory School in Chicago, which, in turn, had looked to me pretty much like the classrooms I had inhabited as child. I had no particular expectations about what I would witness in Easton but somehow I expected it to be different from what it was. The room was bright and cheerful with plenty of colorful charts and samples of student artwork on display. The students seemed eager to participate in whatever activity the teacher introduced. They raised their hands when questioned. They huddled together in small groups to work on projects of one kind or another. They read silently during free reading time. They wrote reports. They moved about the room and chatted comfortably with each other and with their teacher during study periods. And so on. The curriculum too contained nothing out of the ordinary that I could see; just the standard school subjects of math, social studies, language arts, science, and so forth. Long before my first full day of observation had ended I found myself stifling yawns and beginning to wonder whether or not the trip would turn out to have been worthwhile.

Some questions pertaining to construct validity did enter my thinking almost at once on my first day. I worried first of all about how well the testing had been handled. Had the tests been properly administered? Were they accurately scored? (I was not then familiar with the phrase *construct irrelevant variance*, but such is the term I would now apply to the subject of that set of worries.) I also wondered how other differences in the way the students had been selected might have affected the outcome of the selection process. The students Getzels and I had called our *high creatives* had not been equally outstanding on tests of intelligence. They were, one might say, distinctively higher performers on the battery of creativity tests. The school people at Easton had paid no attention to intelligence test scores at all in making their selection. Therefore, there was the obvious possibility that some or even many of the Easton students had scored equally well on both kinds of tests. What difference, if any, might that make? This too was a question having to do with construct validity although, again, I did not think of it in that way at the time. If some of the *high creatives* at Easton were also *high IQs*, that could well be yet another contaminating factor—more *construct irrelevant variance*.

Before the first day's classes were over, however, my thoughts had begun to move in a different direction entirely. I had begun to suspect that questions having to do with how the tests were administered and scored and how the students were selected—questions of a kind that seemed to me almost obligatory to ask from a research design standpoint—were somewhat beside the point in the light of what I was witnessing. The more I concentrated on what was going on and the more I thought about its significance, the more my thoughts began to veer in a new direction, radically different from the one first traveled.

What difference would it make, I mused, how faultlessly administered the tests might be if the construct of creativity had no purchase in such an environment? Let's suppose these youngsters turned out to be psychometrically identical to the ones we called *high creatives* in our Chicago study? So what? The gross features of what was going on in the classroom seemed to have so little to do with creativity or at least with what was being sampled in our tests of the construct that it seemed almost foolish to expect there to be a relationship between the two. The Easton students were not being called on by their teacher to give divergent responses to ambiguous stimuli. They were not being asked to think of new uses for common objects. They were not required to invent clever new morals to attach as endings to familiar fables. None of those tasks came anywhere near what was being demanded of them by their so-called "creative" teacher.

Instead, they were being asked to discuss material they had read in order to demonstrate their understanding of it. They were being presented with facts and then questioned about them. They were being invited to share opinions and past experiences with their teacher and with each other. In all of this, however, the emphasis was on standard replies and correct answers. The teacher often complimented individual students for asking "good" questions but the ones they asked seldom moved the discussion in an unexpected direction or showed any other signs of being highly original. What would it mean to be creative under such circumstances? How might creativity be evinced? What good would it do? This is not to say that what I saw contradicted my expectations. As I have already pointed out, I had no clear expectations to begin with, which is one reason why I wanted to make the trip.

I was, none the less, almost immediately struck by what seemed to be a glaring discrepancy between whatever our so-called tests of creativity were measuring (or what we thought they were measuring) and what was being asked of the students as they sought to fulfill their teacher's expectations and otherwise adjust to the demands of classroom life.

As my thoughts moved along these lines new questions began to replace the ones I had initially asked. The students were so well-behaved and compliant. Where did those shared understandings about what should go on in classroom come from? How were they passed along? What functions did they serve? The shift from one set of questions to another certainly did not occur as smoothly as I am reporting it here, but by the time I left Easton I had the feeling that a very important change had begun to take place in my customary ways of thinking over the course of those three days. I was not sure what the significance of that change might be but I vowed to explore such matters further when I returned to California.

It is possible to translate the change I have just described into the language of construct validity. One might say, for example, that I was on the verge of abandoning my interest in one construct—creativity—in order to pursue a developing interest in another construct—something vaguely denoted by the label *classroom behavior*. What had initially been a kind of criterion variable—the classroom behavior of creative students—had become an object of interest in its own right and, thus, a construct that would ultimately stand in need of validation. Cronbach offers a piece of advice to researchers that comes close to fitting my changed set of circumstances. He says,

> In criterion-related validation we generally should inspect the criterion for contaminants [i.e. the source of construct irrelevant variance] and missing ingredients [i.e., construct under representation]. That is, CV [construct validation] of the criterion is wanted. (Cronbach, 1989, p. 151)

I was by no means looking for contaminants and missing ingredients in what I was witnessing from the back of that classroom in Easton. Therefore it would not be accurate to describe what I was doing as being consciously engaged in the process of construct validation. But that was the direction in which I appeared to be heading from a construct validity point of view. I will return to the advantages and disadvantages of that way of describing my situation in due course.

Soon after I returned to the Center I began to make regular visits to two elementary schools in Palo Alto, where I repeated what I had done in Easton, only this time without any thoughts about the psychological characteristics of the students I was watching. I was not at all sure what I was looking for and it turns out that I never did come to a clear sense of mission rivaling that of my prior test-giving and data-gathering past. (More on that too in due course.) But my new tourist-like gawking seemed like the right thing to be doing and elementary classrooms seemed like the right place to do it.

I am fast approaching the end of my two anecdotal accounts but I cannot resist adding a brief extension to the story I have just told. It ties to one of the things I later want to say about construct validity. In retrospect, I find it amusing, although I did not find it so at the time.

N.L. Gage had just moved from the University of Illinois to Stanford that year. As we were both newcomers to the west coast and had known each other casually before then, we decided to get together on a fairly regular basis to compare notes on our new surroundings and to share some of our common interests. At one of our lunchtime meetings shortly after my return from Easton I announced to Nate my plan to visit some local classrooms just to look around and see what was going on. He stared at me as if I had lost my mind. "Do you know what you're doing, Phil?," he asked incredulously, "You're studying the oil lamp in the age of the electric light!" What he meant, of course, was that any teaching I might observe was soon to be outdated and replaced by an entirely new mode of instruction that would be based on "scientific" research. He and his students at Stanford were then busily engaged in exactly the kind of research that they confidently believed would one day form the basis of a new science of teaching. Numerous others were similarly engaged at universities around the country and throughout the world.

Although Nate did not come right out and say so at the time, I have no doubt that he also believed that what I was proposing to do was unworthy of being called "research," much less "science." He might then have conceded (as he later did in some of his writings) that the kind of unstructured observations that I was about to undertake could possibly lead to science. They might, in other words, become the source of hypotheses that could later be tested but this meant that they were no more than exploratory in nature, something to engage in very briefly before getting down to brass tacks, which is to say: the serious business of doing research. The latter, as both Gage and I at the time would have readily explained if asked, entailed undertaking a carefully designed study, gathering quantifiable data, analyzing it statistically, presenting its findings in tabular or graphic form, and so on.

I confess that at the time Gage's reaction aroused worries that even then had not been very far beneath the surface of my thoughts. I had worked hard at learning how to design and conduct empirical studies. I was moderately pleased with what I had already managed to accomplish along those lines. I was also as confident as was Gage that Science with a capital S offered the only true route to knowledge. I further took pride in being a psychologist, particularly one who did research. The prospect of giving up that identification was not at all attractive, in fact it made me very uneasy, yet that was the direction in which my proposed plan pointed, as Gage's reaction to it clearly implied. I will have something further to say about the source of my uneasiness in due course.

I now want to turn from my two anecdotal accounts to a set of remarks about construct validity as a tool of thought. All that has been said to this point will continue to reverberate as background, I trust, as I move on to what follows.

My concerns are twofold. They have to do in part with what might be called the ontological status of constructs, with what the word *construct* stands for and with how we habitually speak of whatever the term represents. They also have to do with the validation process qua process and with whether and why we should insist on it being perceived as scientific.

The Ontological Status of Constructs.

Do psychological constructs like intelligence or anxiety or creativity refer to entities that truly exist or are they fictional devices, more theoretical than real? The answer to that question, according to philosopher Stephen Norris, depends on one's philosophical pedigree (Norris, 1983). Those who call themselves logical positivists, for example, (a dying breed, it would seem) answer in one way, whereas those who think of themselves as realists (a term of self-reference also not in wide use, it again would seem) answer in another. The former treat constructs as fictions and thereby tend to dismiss them; the latter see them as real and thereby attach great importance to them. Which one is correct? The issue, according to Norris's account, remains open to debate, although not as tendentiously perhaps as was once the case. Moreover, opposing views of the matter are by no means limited to philosophers who attach themselves to one or another school of thought. They also include, among others: psychologists, educational researchers, and test-makers.

It is among the latter, Norris tells us, that we find some of the most egregious forms of ignorance and confusion with respect to this important set of questions. The chief difficulty, we are told, lies in the inconsistency with which test-makers in particular view and discuss the ontological status of psychological constructs. Sometimes they treat them one way (as real) and sometimes another (as fictional). Some, it would seem, want to have it both ways at once. Still others appear not to care very much one way or the other and, therefore, allow themselves to switch from one point of view to the other almost capriciously.

Norris worries that these various forms of inconsistency may lead to unjustified conclusions with respect to the causes of people's test performances. They also may contribute to other forms of mis-communication between and among test-makers and test-users, particularly as the inconsistencies often go unrecognized. In the light of those risks, Norris urges test-makers, collectively and individually, to seek a "consistent foundation" for their theorizing and for their test-making efforts (Norris, 1983, 74).

Messick addresses Norris's worries both directly and indirectly in his overview of validity that appeared in the Third Edition of *Educational Measurement* (Messick, 1989b). In doing so he introduces a number of refinements that complicate and to some extent annul certain features of Norris's depiction of the situation.

He does so chiefly by insisting that the concept of test validation be broadened to include not only "score meaning but also . . . value implications and action outcomes" (p. 13). Thus the interpretation of test performance is made to flow outward as well as inward, to include considerations of social consequences and value implications as well as the more traditional questions having to do with what the test measures. Messick depicted this broadening of the domain of validation as one of adding "interpretive strands to the general construct validity fabric" (p. 20).

Messick further complicated the picture by acknowledging the existence of "constructs that have no supposed reality outside the theoretical system of the investigator" (p. 27). He gives as examples "higher order constructs such as 'ego' or 'self,'" which are employed "as heuristic devices for organizing observed relationships, with no necessary presumption of real entities underlying them" (p. 29). He also mentions "such constructs as 'working class' and 'middle class' or 'childhood' and 'adolescence'" about which the attribution of reality is, as he says, "debatable" (p. 29).

To say that not all constructs refer to a supposed reality leaves us, of course, with the clear implication that some do have such a reference, which would allow plenty of legroom for Norris's worry about test-makers' inconsistency. For it could be that test-makers sometimes attribute reality to constructs that have none, or vice versa. Doing so would not make them inconsistent, exactly, but it would surely make them wrong. The added complexity of Messick's account allows for that possibility.

Another possibility that might yield inconsistency, yet still fit comfortably within Messick's account, might be that test-makers are simply unsure about what to say about certain constructs. They do not know whether to speak of them as real or unreal because the fact of the matter has not yet been established. Messick's saying that the reality of constructs like "working class" or "childhood" remains "debatable" would seem to leave room for factual determination.

Yet a third possibility occurs to me and it is one on which I wish to concentrate. It is that such inconsistencies as occur, if that is what to call them, could well arise neither because of any intellectual laxity nor because of any ignorance on the part of individual test-makers but simply because that is the way language works.

As an illustration of our habitual mixed-up-ness when it comes to speaking about what are usually thought of as psychological traits or dispositions, consider how we have addressed human virtues through the ages, beginning perhaps with Aristotle. Is courage something individuals have (a trait)? Or does it simply stand for how certain individuals typically behave (i.e., courageously)? The same question may be, and has been asked about honesty, generosity, magnanimity, and the rest. Aristotle, for one, used the language of virtue in different ways for different purposes. He called actions virtuous but he called people virtuous as well. He believed that virtue was a habit and that people become virtuous by behaving virtuously. That remains pretty much what most of us believe today. As a result, we sometimes speak of virtue as something people have (i.e., as a noun) and at other times as the way they behave under certain circumstances (i.e., as an adjective or adverb).

Another thing we often do in common speech is to treat certain kinds of relationships as though they were objects. In a word, we "objectify" them. Thus the relationships between the individual and his environment conveyed by words like thinking, believing, loving, and so on are spoken of as though the relationship was itself an object that was somehow interiorized within the thinking, believing, loving, organism. In this way, a declarative statement describing a relationship between two objects, such as "Plato loves Socrates," soon gets transformed into "Plato's love of Socrates," a verb replaced by a noun. Now, is Plato's love real or unreal? The question sounds a bit odd, when phrased in that way. Yet the fact that we use a common noun to refer to the relationship, while at the same time speaking of it as though it were a possession, something Plato now "has," does move it along the road toward reification.

Confronted with these many flip-flops in our ordinary ways of speaking, some whom Norris calls realists may object that those speech habits only describe the way we speak today and not the way we should speak. After all, they might rhetorically ask, "Is it not precisely the task of construct validation to clear up such confusions and to answer such questions once and for all?" Why not allow such investigations to determine what is real and unreal?

Messick obliquely addresses the attraction of such a proposed policy in the distinction he draws between *observed consistency* (of a pattern of test performance, let us say) and a *reified construct* (Messick, 1989b, p. 29). Presumably, the greater the observed consistency, the more confident we become in believing that what is named by the construct refers to something real (i.e., the more willing we are to reify it). But, as he elsewhere points out, such observed consistencies are almost always open to more than one interpretation. Moreover, alternative interpretations need not invariably devolve into a life-or-death struggle to determine which one reigns supreme. When it comes to establishing fruitful ways of thinking about particular constructs, even when one of them posits something real and the other does not, the law of the excluded middle, it would seem, need not always apply.

Lest the previous talk about the laissez-faire character of ordinary speech come across as sounding too permissive to apply within the framework of an empirical investigation, let me return briefly to Norris' warning about the risks involved in test-makers being inconsistent in how they speak about the ontological status of psychological constructs. His worry, we will recall, was that test-takers might ultimately suffer the negative effects of such inconsistencies.

As much as I disagree with the extremely high value Norris attached to the virtue of consistency in such matters, I acknowledge that he had a point about the risks involved. How we choose to speak of this construct or that often does have consequences that need to be taken into account on penalty of doing harm, albeit unwittingly. I would agree with that. It also matters to whom we speak in particular ways. Moreover, the risks involved in different ways of speaking are commonly multiplied by the authority of the speaker. Those who present themselves as experts and who speak in the name of science or research do so from positions of authority that elevate the significance of their words far above that of the ordinary speaker. That being so, they, above all, need be sensitive to what they say and how they say it, as well as to whom they are saying it. This warning is in accord with the spirit of Norris's admonition, though it applies far more broadly than he intended it, or so it seems to me.

While thinking about the potential consequences of different kinds of talk, I recalled Dewey's observation about our ways of speaking of intelligence. In *Democracy and Education* he says:

> How one person's abilities compare in quantity with those of another is none of the teacher's business. It is irrelevant to his work. What is required is

that every individual should have opportunities to employ his own powers in activities that have meaning. (Dewey, 1916, p. 172)

Dewey went on to urge teachers (and others) to think of intelligence as being more like an adjective or adverb than a noun. By so doing, he believed, teachers in particular would be more inclined than they otherwise might be to ask how persons may be encouraged to behave more intelligently in particular circumstances and with reference to particular kinds of materials and subject matter.

In making those suggestions, Dewey was not advocating that teachers be kept in the dark, so to speak, about well-established facts having to do with the relative stability of performances on intelligence tests or anything else of that nature. He was, however, questioning the wisdom of certain practices, such as supplying teachers with each student's score on such a test. He also by indirection was calling into question the kind of talk about intelligence that ascribes to it greater causal potency than the facts allow. We do not have to agree with Dewey's estimate of the risks involved in such practices and such talk to understand what he thought those risks to be. He feared that misinformation and even accurate information, improperly communicated, might inadvertently contribute to a decline in teachers' efforts to do the best they can for each of their students.

The possibility of untoward consequences being associated with certain ways of talking about psychological constructs calls to mind Messick's many discussions of what he calls the *consequential basis* of validity, which refers to the *social consequences* of test use and interpretation (Messick, 1989a, 1989b, 1995). Would Dewey's worries about how teachers might make use of the construct of intelligence fit comfortably within Messick's category of *social consequences?* I see no reason why not. Indeed, they seem to me to provide an almost classic instance of the kind of concerns with which today's enlightened test-makers are increasingly occupied.

Following Dewey's logic, might it be that, in general, adjectival and adverbial ways of referencing psychological constructs are better suited to the kinds of discussions that go on within educational contexts than are the more noun-referenced discussions that typify so many psychology textbooks? I would not support such a conclusion without it having been given a lot of thought and investigation but I do find it to be an intriguing idea, all the same.

This brings me to the word *construct*, which conveniently can serve as either a noun or a verb, depending on its use. "*Construct* connotes construction and artifice," Jane Loevinger declared, back in the days when the term's meaning was being freshly explored by psychologists (Loevinger, 1957, p. 642).

Loevinger's observation is true enough: the term surely *connotes* an act of some kind, an act of construction. But it *denotes* something else. It denotes *a* construction, something put in place and made to endure, something christened, so to speak, with a name.

What shall we say of this process of constructing and naming as a way of characterizing what goes on in inquiry? Is that a sensible way to proceed? It surely seems to be much of the time. We often need to be clear about what we are looking for. Naming helps. But not always. Indeed, there may be times when a lack of clarity may be actually beneficial to the conduct of the inquiry. Under certain circumstances names get in the way. Even the term *construct* may then be more of a hindrance than a help.

Returning to my experience in Easton, I recall my initial sense of puzzlement as I sat in the back of that classroom. I earlier said that as I sat there my interest began to shift from one construct (creativity) to another (classroom behavior). That is certainly one way of describing what went on. But the word *construct* never crossed my mind at the time, nor did *classroom behavior*. Was I remiss in not thinking in those terms? Would I have been better off to have done so? My own answer to both questions is no. There are times, in short, when it seems best to forget about constructs and allow oneself to "hang loose," so to speak, insofar as a precise depiction of what one is investigating is concerned. I feel sure that most experienced investigators would heartily agree with that statement, so perhaps I need not have said it. Yet the ubiquity of advice to the contrary, whether explicitly made or tacitly implied, perhaps justifies making the obvious explicit.

There doubtless are many other circumstances, beyond the one I have described, in which the introduction of *construct* language may be inappropriate, if not actually dysfunctional, when addressing certain audiences or even when thinking to oneself about the conduct of an investigation. In this regard, I recall a casual conversation I had with a member of the ETS staff during one of the coffee breaks at the conference honoring Messick. The staffer was describing a project that had as its goal the development of a licensure exam for one of the health professions. He explained that in working on the project he and his colleagues regularly use *construct* language when talking among themselves but they quickly drop such talk when they go out in the field to discuss their plans with members of the health profession. He did not bother to explain why he felt the change of language necessary and he hardly needed to have done so. the switch made perfectly good sense to me, as it obviously did to him and his colleagues. His report underscores the broader point about there being risks involved in choosing one form of speech rather than another. In certain situations, as in the one I have just described, those risks may be relatively insignificant. In other situations, however, they may become substantial.

I turn finally to the question of whether the process of construct validation as described by Messick and others is or is not scientific. My intention is not to answer that question. Instead, I want to cast doubt on its importance. One of my reasons for doing so is that I find that the criteria of what is to count as being "scientific" are usually too vague and ill-defined to be of much value to investigators. Another is that the words science and *scientific* too often convey little more than eulogistic meaning, as Dewey might say. They are employed, in other words, chiefly as badges of distinction, conveying honor to those awarded them, naturally enough, but little in the way of information to those doing the applauding. This is by no means to advocate that we give up making distinctions between good and poor methods of test validation. On the contrary, it is to insist that such distinctions be made as explicitly and as clearly as possible. It is, however, to deny that the process of making those distinctions is helped very much by talk of science and by invidious comparisons between those who follow something called *the scientific method* and those who do not.

The Scientific Nature of the Validation Process

One way of reading the history of the concept of construct validity is to see it as part of a larger and continuing political struggle to establish and maintain psychology's status as a science. The paper trail of that history is commonly traced to the now classic article by Lee J. Cronbach and Paul Meehl published in 1955 and entitled *Construct Validity in Psychological Tests* (Cronbach & Meehl, 1955). Looking back on the circumstances that gave rise to the writing of that paper, Cronbach in 1989 readily acknowledged their political nature. "The currents of professional politics brought CV [construct validity] into psychology," he reports (Cronbach, 1989, p. 147).

What spurred the American Psychological Association (APA) to form a special Committee on Testing (of which Cronbach and Meehl were members) was the fear among academic psychologists, particularly among those involved in test-making, that their clinical colleagues, with whom they had newly joined ranks to form the APA, had been and would continue to be frightfully lax in the claims made for tests they employed and thus would bring dishonor and ridicule on the entire enterprise of psychology, not to mention the untold harm that might befall test-takers. The goal of the special committee was to devise a set of professional standards and guidelines that would reduce the likelihood of such an outcome.

As part of their effort to make test use and interpretation scientifically respectable, Cronbach and Meehl included within their paper (in a section subtitled "The Logic of Test Use") a lot of talk about "the interlocking system of laws which constitute a theory as a *nomological network*" (Cronbach & Meehl, 1955, p. 290). In brief, such a net was said to consist of laws in which observables were tied to theoretical constructs, either statistically or deterministically. After explaining how such a nomological network might be constructed, a process that entails the application of scientific methodology, Cronbach and Meehl conclude, "The preceding guide rules [sic] should reassure the 'toughminded' who fear that allowing construct validation opens the door to nonconfirmable test claims" (Cronbach & Meehl, 1955, p. 291).

Things did not turn out quite as Cronbach and Meehl had hoped. Not only were not all of the tough-minded reassured by the article's appeal to the criterion of scientific methodology, but, ironically, at least one such tough-minded critic, Harold Bechtoldt of the University of Iowa, was quick to accuse the article's authors of themselves being nonscientific. Bechtoldt wrote:

> The renaming of the process of building a theory of behavior by the new term 'construct validity' contributes nothing to the understanding of the process nor to the usefulness of the concepts. The introduction into discussions of psychological theorizing of the aspects of construct validity [discussed in this article] . . . creates, at best, unnecessary confusion and, at worst, a nonempirical, nonscientific approach to the study of behavior. (Bechtoldt, 1959, p. 628)

The vituperative tone of Bechtoldt's accusation is indicative of the passions that could be easily aroused in those days by any perceived threat to the scientific status of psychology.

Looking back on his jointly written paper some 30 years later, Cronbach sounded apologetic and almost embarrassed by its scientistic flavor. He said,

> Paragraphs on the network and on links between theoretical notions and observables *added dignity* to the CM [Cronbach & Meehl] paper. They *bolstered a virtuous claim* that CV [construct validity] was in line with philosophy of science, and not a nostrum brewed up hastily to relieve psychology's pains. (p. 159, emphasis added).

He then goes on:

> Still it was *pretentious* to dress up our *immature science* in positivist language; and it was *self-defeating* to say that a construct not part of a nomological network is *not scientifically admissible*. (p. 159, emphasis added)

Cronbach's candor is unsparing and exemplary. "Adding dignity," "bolstering a virtuous claim," being "pretentious," and "self-defeating" on behalf of an "immature science"—those are harsh things to say about one's prior behavior, even from the distance of several decades. Yet, although applauding his forthrightness, we must not ignore the question of why he and Meehl might have behaved that way in the first place.

A piece of the answer surely must lie in the aspiration to be tough-minded and to be seen as being so, which, at least back then, translated into the goal of being scientific and of "doing" science. Moreover, that Past, to some degree, remains our Present. No psychologist, then or now, can remain completely indifferent to such aspirations. To do so would cast doubt on his or her entitlement to membership within the community of psychologists.

It was certainly the fear of that happening that made me wary back in 1962 when I turned from giving paper-and-pencil tests to more informal and naturalistic methods of data-gathering. Was I not giving up science in the process? That was the question I asked myself at the time. I feared I was, although I knew that not every psychologist crunched numbers and worked with hard data. In my heart of hearts, however, I harbored little respect for those psychologists who had nothing but words at their command. That lack of respect was widely shared by the majority of the faculty and students with whom I studied, I must say, and remained evident among my collegial associates at Chicago and elsewhere.

In his 1989 overview of the history of construct validity, Cronbach clearly rues the pretensions associated with his earlier effort to pacify the tough-minded and to keep psychology scientifically respectable. Yet if one reads his 1989 paper carefully one can still discern, I believe, traces of the attitudes and biases that partially motivated the earlier work. In 1989 he still spoke almost wistfully of "the community of pure scientists" and of "the very long-run enterprise of pure science" which lives "for the day when truth becomes crystal clear" (p. 163). He also twice uses the term *jawboning* to refer to the test interpretations of those who have no hard data to back their claims. "The good news," Cronbach told us in 1989, "is that today's [test] manuals rarely flood users with jawboning speculative defenses." The innuendo communicated by the slang word *jawboning* goes beyond the empiricist's insistence that talk alone will never suffice. It places talk itself under a cloud of suspicion.

Messick's more recent expositions of what today's fully elaborated process of construct validity entails make clear that simple-minded notions of what it means to be rigorous as an investigator will no longer pass muster. Although he continues to appeal to the standard of science—making specific reference in the titles of his articles to "the science of assessment" and to "scientific inquiry into score meaning" (1989b, 1995)—his emphasis on "interpretation" and "valuation" serves as a tacit acknowledgment that an attitude of let-the-facts-speak-for-themselves will no longer do. Sensitive judgment, whose presentation requires a lot of jawboning, is called for every step of the way.

In 1989 Cronbach also reported that "almost every psychologist writing about construct validity applies to it the word *confusing*" (Cronbach, 1989, p. 147). He called that "a sad fact." Assuming the fact to be true, I am not at all sure how sad it is. It may well be that widespread acknowledgement of being confused about construct validity constitutes a step forward. It certainly sounds better to me than the smug confidence of the mid-fifties. The goal of dispelling some of that confusion is obviously behind Messick's exemplary exegesis of the concept of validity in the Third Edition of *Educational Measurement*. There and elsewhere he repeatedly acknowledges the "conceptual messiness" that such an effort requires.

On the last page of Part II of *Philosophical Investigations*, Ludwig Wittgenstein wrote, "In psychology there are experimental methods and *conceptual confusion*" (Wittgenstein, 1968, p. 232). He continued,

> The existence of the experimental method makes us think we have the means of solving the problems which trouble us; though problem and method pass one another by. (p. 232)

Wittgenstein was referring to the Gestalt psychology of Wolfgang Kohler at the time but his complaint remains as relevant today in certain ways as when it first was made. We still somehow believe that method alone (read: "scientific method," whatever that might mean) will suffice to deliver us once and for all from the torment of trying to determine, for example, whether a "construct" like "intelligence" or "creativity" or "working class" ought to be treated as real or unreal, as discovery or artifice. What we require, of course, as Wittgenstein understood, is to be relieved of the question. A portion of that relief may attend our fretting less than we have in the past over whether what we are doing is scientific and, in place of that, becoming more concerned than ever with doing our damnedest to make sense of whatever it is we are trying to understand. Where special techniques, like convergent and discriminant analysis or talk of nomological networks, can be of help, let us use them, by all means. Where they cannot be of use or promise to provide only the patina of science, let us lay them aside free of regret as we turn our attention to answering the questions that concern us: science be hanged. That, as I read it, is Messick's main message as well, his subsidiary comments about science and the scientific method notwithstanding.

The language of inquiry into human affairs is perforce a versatile tongue. It has to be to fit the complexities of the phenomena it investigates. It must make use of ordinary speech and its pronouncements must ultimately be intelligible to ordinary speakers, because it is in the public interest, for the most part, that such inquiry gets undertaken. That interest makes the study of humans a moral enterprise from start to finish. Recent trends in our understanding of construct validation as a tool of inquiry reveal a growing awareness of the moral consequences of how that tool is employed and its usage elaborated. That awareness brings with it the gradual, though inevitable repeal of some of our older and narrower ways of thinking. For that we can all be thankful to Sam Messick and to those like him, who stand at the forefront of broadening our understanding of this important set of ideas and practices

REFERENCES

Bechtoldt, H. P. (1959). Construct validity: A critique. *American Psychologist, 14*(10), 619–629.

Cronbach, L. J. (1989). Construction validity after thirty years. In R. L. Linn (Ed.), *Intelligence: Measurement, Theory, and Public Policy* (pp. 147–171). Urbana: University of Illinois Press.

Cronbach, L. J., & Meehl, P. E. (1955). Construct validity in psychological tests. *Psychological Bulletin, 52*(4), 281–302.

Dewey, J. (1916). *Democracy and Education.* New York: The Free Press.

Getzels, J. W., & Jackson, P. W. (1962). *Creativity and intelligence: Explorations with gifted students.* New York: John Wiley & Sons.

Jackson, P. W., & Messick, S. (1965, September). The person, the product, and the response: Conceptual problems in the assessment of creativity. *Journal of Personality, 33,* 309–329.

Loevinger, J. (1957). Objective tests as instruments of psychological theory. *Psychological Reports, 3*(Monograph Supplement 9), 635–694.

Messick, S. (1989a). Meaning and values in test validation: The science and ethics of assessment. *Educational Researcher, 18*(2), 5–11.

Messick, S. (1989b). Validity. In R. L. Linn (Ed.), *Educational Measurement: Third Edition* (pp. 13–103). New York: Macmillan.

Messick, S. (1995). Validity of psychological assessment. *American Psychologist, 50*(9), 741–749.

Norris, S. P. (1983). The inconsistencies at the foundation of construct validation theory. In E. R. House (Ed.), *Philosophy of Evaluation. New Directions for Program Evaluation, no 19* (pp. 53–74). San Francisco: Josey-Bass.

Wittgenstein, L. (1968). *Philosophical Investigations.* Oxford: Blackwell.

Author Index

Gamoran, A., 236, 253
Garbin, M. G., 42, 47
Gardner, H., 151, 165
Gardner, R. W., 45, 47, 127, 130, 144
Getzels, J. W., 300, 302, 317
Gigliotti, R. J., 287, 296
Gillmore, G. M., 284, 290, 292, 296–297
Gillmore, J. M., 293, 297
Glaser, R., 179–180, 186, 189, 191
Gleser, G. C., 132, 144
Goetz, E. T., 134, 146
Goff, M., 121, 124, 137, 144
Goffman, E., 156, 164
Goldberg, I., 194, 204
Goldberg, L. R., 9, 16, 41, 47, 97, 101–102, 106–108, 111, 124–125
Goodenough, D. R., 45, 48
Gorsuch, R. L., 100, 124
Gould, S. J., 76, 93
Gough, H. C., 54, 66
Green, B. F., 233, 253
Greene, R. L., 59, 67
Greenwald, A. G., 284, 287, 290, 292–293, 295–297
Gregory, R. P. F., 186, 191
Greig, J., 183, 186, 191
Gross, A., 148, 164
Guilford, J. P., 77, 93, 102, 124, 171, 178
Gulliksen, H., 76, 93, 170, 178
Gur, R. C., 52, 54–55, 57, 62, 64, 66, 69
Gustafsson, J.-E., 73–74, 75, 78–81, 83, 85, 87, 89, 91, 93–95, 110, 124

H

Haertel, E. H., 210, 214–215, 217, 223, 226–227, 247, 249, 253
Hall, C. S., 62, 68
Hamilton, L. H., 158, 164
Hamilton, W. G., 158, 164
Harman, H. H., 81, 93
Harmik, R. C., 173, 178
Harrison, C., 186, 191
Hartshorne, H., 52, 66
Hathaway, S. R., 52, 54, 66,

Heggestad, E. D., 105, 121–122
Heiman, J. R., 58, 67
Helson, R., 159, 164
Hendriks, A. A. J., 20, 23, 27, 29, 33–34
Hess, R. D., 173, 178
Hilts, V. L., 129, 144
Hofstee, W. K. B., 20, 23–24, 26–27, 29, 31, 34
Hogan, J., 99, 102, 105, 120, 124
Hogan, R., 56, 62, 66–68
Holden, R. R., 51, 65, 67
Holmes, D. S., 277, 287, 297
Holtzman, W. H., 37, 43, 47
Holzinger, K. J., 79–81, 87, 93
Holzman, P. S., 45, 47, 130, 144
Hoorens, V., 57, 67
Horn, J. L., 77, 93
Horvath, J. A., 31, 35
Howard, G. S., 282, 286–287, 297
Hull, C. L., 171, 178
Humphreys, L. G., 76–77, 85, 94, 111–112, 125
Hundleby, J., 43, 48
Hunt, E., 128, 131, 144

I

Innerst, 233, 253
Inouye, J., 97, 110–111, 119, 124
Ippel, M. J., 138, 145

J

Jackson, D. N., 4, 7–11, 13–17, 41, 48, 49–52, 54, 60, 67–68, 73, 94, 104, 124, 127, 136, 144–145
Jackson, P. W., 300, 302, 317
Jacobson, L. I., 53, 67
Jenkins, J. G., 169–170, 178
John, O. P., 25, 34, 53, 59–60, 63, 65, 67–68
Johnson, E. A., 59, 67
Johnson, J. A., 99, 105, 120, 124
Jones, L. R., 200–201, 204
Jöreskog, K. G., 83, 94, 112–113, 124

Subject Index

A

Ability tests, 171
Accuracy constructs, 53
Achievement tests, 171
Adjusted Goodness of Fit Index (AG-FI), 112
Adventurousness, 157
Alpha, 119
Antisocial personalities, 108
Assessment, 221, 244
Assessment scores, 221

B

Balanced Inventory of Desirable Responding (BIDR), 57-58
Beck Depression Inventory, 42
Beta, 119
Big Five Personality Traits, 57, 61, 98

C

California Psychological Inventory (CPI), 9
Childhood activity checklist, 159
Clinical assessment, 39
Clinical depression, 13
Cognitive
    ability, 103
    construct, 140
    research, 179
    style, 44, 127, 133
Cognition, 134
Coherent, 31
Cohort differences, 193
Competence, 181
Computer base testing, 202
Conative construct, 140
Consequential, 174, 255, 311
Consistency, 188
Construct differences, 193
Construct validity, 57, 171-172, 175, 190, 195, 282, 299, 301, 303
Constructs, 3-4, 212, 307, 311, 312

Content, 173
    lean-process constrained, 184
    open, 185
    process space, 183
    relevance, 257
    rich-process open, 183
    rich-processed constrained, 186
    standards, 216, 238, 240
    validity, 234
CRESST validity criteria, 257

D

Desirability factor, 104
Diagnostic and Statistical Manual of Mental Disorders (DSM), 40, 98

E

Educational achievement, 179, 208
Educational experiment, 302
Ego-resiliency, 53
Elaborate constructs, 52
Emotional stability, 33
Emotionality, 157
Essentialist thinking, 129
External, 174
Extraversion, 118
Extroversion-introversion, 157

F

Face-validity, 266
Fair test design, 198
Fairness, 193
Five-Factor Model, 101, 121
Five-Factor Personality Inventory (FFPI), 27, 33
Five-Factor Personality Model, 97, 99
Flexibility of closure, 74

G

GCE Exam, 200
GPA, 199
GRE, 257
GRE Mathematical Reasoning Test, 261
Gender differences, 201